To the Fairest Cape

Also by Malcolm Jack

The Social and Political Thought of Bernard Mandeville
Corruption & Progress: The Eighteenth-Century Debate
William Beckford: An English Fidalgo
Sintra: A Glorious Eden
Lisbon: City of the Sea
The Turkish Embassy Letters of Lady Mary Wortley Montagu (editor)
Vathek and Other Stories: A William Beckford Reader (editor)
The Episodes of Vathek (editor)
Erskine May: Parliamentary Practice (24th edition)

To the Fairest Cape

*European Encounters in the
Cape of Good Hope*

M ALCOLM J ACK

LEWISBURG, PENNSYLVANIA

Library of Congress in Publication Control Number: 2018025930

978-1-68448-000-5 (cloth)

A British Cataloging-in-Publication record for this book is available from the British Library.

♾ The paper used in this publication meets the requirements of the American National Standard for Information Sciences—Permanence of Paper for Printed Library Materials, ANSI Z39.48-1992.

www.bucknell.edu/UniversityPress

Manufactured in the United States of America

*To Randolph Vigne, a fighter for freedom
and a champion of learning.*

Contents

Illustrations

Preface

Crossing the remote southern tip of Africa has fired the imagination of
European travellers from the time Bartolomeu Dias opened up the passage to the East by rounding the Cape of Good Hope in 1488. Dutch, British, French, Danes, and Swedes formed an endless stream of seafarers who
made the long journey southward in pursuit of wealth, adventure, science,
and missionary, as well as outright national, interest. The Cape lands they
passed were sparsely inhabited by the nomadic Khoi and San tribes (the
"Khoisan"), hunter-gatherers and pastoral peoples who represented savage "otherness" to the European travellers. The rugged terrain, stormy seas,
and uncertain climate did not present an alluring prospect for European
seafarers, who put into land mainly for the purpose of restocking supplies
and making repairs to their battered vessels.

It would be more than a century and a half after Dias's voyage before Jan
van Riebeeck, a captain in the Dutch East India Company (VOC), setting
foot ashore in Table Bay in 1652, declared the land to be owned by the Honourable Company. In this way the first permanent European settlement in
Southern Africa was established, beginning a new phase in the history of
the subcontinent. Cape Town itself began to grow from the small settlement around van Riebeeck's fort, placed strategically in the foreground
near the water's edge. The importation of slaves from other parts of Africa
and the East soon became the principal source of labour in the town.

In this book my intention is to chart the experiences of a small but select group of European travellers—their encounters with the local inhabitants (including the slave population) and their impression of the exotic region of the southern tip of Africa—from the thousands of visitors who called in at the Cape over a period of three centuries or more from Dias's voyage until the 1830s. I begin by considering who the indigenous people, the Khoisan, were and their origins and what contribution their beliefs made to the mythology of the Cape. Then I turn to the continuous record of European literature and iconography, the latter dominated as it has been by the image of Table Mountain and the bay below, around which Cape Town itself developed.

I consider the travel literature itself under three broad themes—the first of which is the Adamastor myth invented by the Portuguese epic poet Luís Vaz de Camões; the second is that of paradise lost and the noble (and ignoble) savage, a preoccupation of French visitors; and the third is the Arcadian image of British colonial diarists and liberals who were enthused by the sublime beauty of the Cape and its diverse fauna and flora and saw great potential for progress in a harmonious blending of the indigenous and settler communities in the growing town and expanding colony.

While the focus of my book is on the encounter of Europeans with the Khoisan who inhabited what is now the Western Cape, given that many travellers journeyed inland, both northward and eastward from Cape Town itself, many with scientific interests, I will consider their accounts in the round, dealing with natural phenomena as well as human communities. In some cases this will lead to a description of the Xhosa, Zulu, and other indigenous inhabitants, but it is beyond the scope of my study to deal with these encounters in detail or with the prolonged wars on the eastern front that began late in the VOC period and continued during the British colonisation.

Although I follow a broadly chronological pattern, cross-references and ahistorical symmetries inevitably arise in a work outlining cultural exchanges. In his early nineteenth-century diary, Henry Lichtenstein observed that every traveller to the Cape took a slightly different view of things depending on his "peculiar turn of thinking," and some were highly critical of their predecessors' accounts. Whether their descriptions were as strictly based on direct observation as many of them claimed or were enriched by comparisons and conjectures, together they form a significant record of emerging Cape society as well as of scientific aspects of Cape landscape, fauna, and flora.

Acknowledgments

A number of people have helped or inspired me over the years in the writing of this book, including Morné Abrahams, Ian Balchin, Brian and Margaret Baird, Robert Borsje, Guy Carter, Pamelia Dailey, Robert Dolby, Antenie Carstens, Sadeck Casoojee, Andrew Cumine, Boris Gorelik, Jonathan Gray, Melanie Guestyn, Ian Hamilton, Okkie Huiser, David Johnson, Annette Keaney, Barbara and Peter Knox-Shaw, Lila Komninck, Stanley Kwong, Jeremy Lawrence, David McClennan, Will Maswan, Marina Nel, Fundile Phaqa, Richard Reid, Christopher Saunders, Sandy Shell, Sinethemba Twani, Yas Ueda, Randolph Vigne and Joanne Wiehahn.

The staff of the Archival Service at the Parliament of the Republic of South Africa and the staff of the National Library and National Archives of South Africa, Cape Town, have been most helpful.

I am grateful for permission to reproduce images from the archive of the Parliament of the Republic of South Africa and from the National Library of South Africa.

My thanks too to the community of book dealers on Long Street, whose shops are always a pleasure to visit.

I would also like to record my particular thanks to Greg Clingham of the Bucknell University Press, for his support and suggestions in the final stages of this book. The team of copyeditors and publicity personnel at Bucknell University Press, Rutgers University Press, and Westchester Publishing Services has been most helpful.

Chronology

To the Fairest Cape

CHAPTER 1

Ancient and Mythical Place

ANCIENT ORIGINS

The grand range of the Cape Mountains and its hinterland has been a place of human habitation from earliest times. The first hominid skull was discovered in 1924 by the paleoanthropologist Raymond Dart, who named it *Australopithecus*, claiming it was the long sought after "missing link" between men and apes.[1] The oldest evidence of hominids, the first creatures to stand erect, in South Africa has been found at the Sterkfontein caves in Gauteng, where hominid remains date back to between two and three million years ago. The likely provenance of these early ancestors of man is East Africa (modern Kenya and Tanzania), where their existence has been dated to between six and eight million years ago. The evidence suggests that hominids migrated across the continent at a very early stage. It is now thought that a number of different species of man evolved simultaneously rather than descending in a single line from *Australopithecus*, although the cultural evolution of anatomical man is still the subject of considerable speculation and dispute. One theory is that identifiable humans emerged only between 40,000 and 50,000 years ago; another is that modern people evolved in the Middle Stone Age, about 250,000 years ago. At any rate, the newcomers included *Homo habilis*, *Homo erectus*, and Neanderthal man.[2]

Homo habilis (handy man) spread across Africa, hunting animals for food and, wherever possible, living in caves or rock shelters. *Homo habilis's* ability to make stone tools marked the beginning of the Stone Age. *Homo erectus*, a more advanced hominid with a larger brain, pushed forward tool-making technology and showed some signs of being the first "social" human with organising powers.[3] Neanderthal man was another species, distinguished by a large brain size (although little of it was used). The remains of primitive tools that Neanderthal man was able to make suggest that he was a formidable hunter, already inhabiting the region of the Cape before the appearance of *Homo sapiens sapiens* from about 200,000 to 300,000 years ago. The latest, local discovery is of *Homo naledi*, also from this period, bones of which were found north of Johannesburg in 2015. Meanwhile, other remains have recently been discovered in North Africa. These species coexisted for some time. DNA studies and physical remains suggest an extended time scale of this period of coexistence, with a slow and gradual evolution of the human species over the millennia. Hominid migration out of Africa to Eurasia had already taken place by this time, although recent discoveries in Bulgaria and Greece of remains from a period substantially earlier may suggest that Europe was already populated with hominids by the time of this migration.[4]

Some indication of human occupation in the Cape area dates back to the Early Stone Age and has been labelled as "Stellenbosch culture"; at the Klasies River site, between Plettenburg Bay and St. Francis, fossil fragments of 120,000 years of age have been discovered. However, most firm evidence of human life in the region dates to about 75,000 years ago. The best remains from that phase have been found in caves, sheltered from sun and rain. Material exposed aboveground has tended to be destroyed by the fierce climatic conditions, which include violent summer winds. The caves were the chosen dwelling places of the Cape inhabitants because, in addition to sheltering them from the elements, they offered some protection from predators.

Artefacts, including rare ochre pieces, bones, and scrapers, of about 77,000 years of age have been excavated at Blombos Cave on the Southern Cape coast. At Hopefield, north of Cape Town, skulls 75,000 years old have been found. Flake stone remnants have been uncovered in the area around Elands Bay Cave further north, indicating habitation in the Late Stone Age. A good example of a sheltered cave used by Stone Age man was discovered at Peers Cave, near Cape Town in 1927. Situated high above sea level, complete protection from the northeasterly wind is afforded by a projecting roof, rock talus, and growth. The cave is likely to have been inhabited during this early period, although the skeletal remains found there date to a much later time.[5]

Recent discoveries at the Pinnacle Point Caves in Mossel Bay suggest that the use of fire to make materials might be dated as early as 72,000 years ago, pushing back the date of heat technology from the previously understood 25,000 years ago in Europe. The technique involved using fire to convert local silcrete stone, which was not suitable for making stone tools, into a raw material from which knives and hunting weapons could be made. Kyle Brown is reported to have suggested that the experiment probably began with a "eureka" moment when someone pulled a stone out of the fire, realizing that with its flaking quality it would be easier to make tools. This process indicates complex cognition, and probably the use of language, on the part of these early technologists.[6] At the same site the oldest engraved ochre has been found, evidence of the earliest form of art, also suggesting the development of cognitive capacity and intellectual application, with symbolic meaning ascribed to various colours, particularly black, white, and red.

The use of more advanced tools, such as stone hand axes and pointed sharp ends, dates from a much more recent period (approximately 8,000 years ago). As technology advanced, better tools could be made. These advances in tool-making techniques marked an important stage in man's prowess as an effective hunter. Some of the smaller microliths of this

period were still being made when Europeans arrived at the Cape, thereby
providing evidence of lifestyles in ancient times. At the same time scrapers and other implements were used to produce art in the form of petroglyphs scraped on the walls of caves over a wide region. The discovery of
the Boskop skull, with an enlarged brain and small face, suggests that during the Middle Stone Age, the evolving aboriginal race was already of
mixed stock, even before the arrival of later tribes. Middens revealing the
existence of fish traps and fossil remains at the Rock Shelter at Keurboom-
strand provide further links to the Middle Stone Age.

The oldest of the known indigenous people are the San, or "Bushmen,"
who may have evolved from *Homo sapiens sapiens* but in any case have
been inhabitants of Southern Africa for over 150,000 years. They too are
likely to have migrated to Southern Africa from East Africa, where ancient
fossil remains indicate a hunting culture in the Early Stone Age. The
Khoikhoi, known as "Hottentots," arrived about two thousand years ago
at the dawn of the Common Era and were the principal people the first
Europeans encountered in the fifteenth century.[7] This so-called Second
Transition takes us into the Late Stone Age, a true blade and scraper phase,
typified mainly by the Smithfield and Wilton complexes.[8] The tools then
being used included bored stones and were part of a hunting, coastal culture with habitation in rock caves similar to patterns found in parts of
Europe, such as southwestern France, in the Stone Age. Hand axes and
other implements show a considerable advance in the production of tools
and weapons.

Although reconstruction of the past from scraps of archaeological evidence is an important addition to travellers' accounts gleaned from contact with indigenous peoples whose tradition was entirely oral, it can also
lead to distortions of view—for example, by concluding that man was pre-
dominantly carnivorous because of the longer survival of bone than of
perishable materials such as vegetable matter, and by stressing the importance of cave dwellings, sheltered from sun and rain, in comparison with

structures above ground that would have been destroyed by the elements. Overall, the abundance of game, together with the richness of grassland and ready supplies of fruits and other edible plants, would have made the southern Cape area hospitable enough for prehistoric man arriving from East Africa to sustain a nomadic life.

THE TERRITORY

The territory occupied by the indigenous inhabitants of western and central South Africa was a vast, solid land mass covering an area of approximately 2,370,000 square kilometres. The interior of the region consists of a high plateau, at its highest elevation 1,500 to 2,000 metres above sea level; the escarpment bounding it southward and westward consists of extensive mountain ranges that fall steeply toward the lower level of the country on the coast to the west and south. The Sneeuburg, Nieuwveld, Roggeveld, and Kamiesberg ranges provide barriers to the west and south, with the semi-arid Karoo extending southward. The Cape Fold Mountains cut off the coastal strip from the interior; the coastline itself is marked by headlands and promontories battered by the sea and stormy winds. Rivers wash down through gorges in the mountain to the sea in torrents in rainy seasons but dry up into sand beds during much of the year. In the high plateau the climate is more continental, with scorching summers and cold, even frosty, winters, while the southern coastal area is more temperate and damp—although there can be wide variations of daily temperature at all times of the year. There is a marked difference in the rainfall pattern: most of the country receives the bulk of its rain in the summer, but on the Cape coast, the rain falls in winter. As a result of this climate, the coastal plains to the south are rich in vegetation and flora, with good supplies of forest and woodland. Further north and west, stretching toward Namibia, rainfall is much less, and arid, desert conditions prevail.

Table Mountain: Geology, Landscape, and Myth

Table Mountain itself has a special geology that, in its topographical effect, has fired human imagination. When John Barrow ascended its slopes in 1797, he found a mass of white and flat-lying sandstone ("Table Mountain sandstone") supported by a base of granite and stones (the latter known as "Malmesbury beds") from the region below. These slates form the mass of Signal Hill and the lower slopes of Devil's Peak, giving rise to smooth topographical features in contrast to the rugged features of Table Mountain sandstone. The junction between slates and granites led to the formation of jagged, barren gorges, but the slopes of the mountain contain sufficient soil to support a diverse floral life. At several points the basal layer of sandstone can be seen resting horizontally on the upturned edges of the slates. The hard Table Mountain sandstone was bent by movements of the earth into great arches, forming the inspiring range of the Cape Fold Mountains. From the summit of Table Mountain, about 1,100 metres above sea level, the peninsula can be seen stretching to Cape Point, with a range of peaked mountains, the Apostles, hugging the Atlantic coast.

The Castilian explorer, António de Saldanha, employed by the Portuguese Crown, was the first European to climb Table Mountain, in 1503. It seems that Saldanha evoked the image of a table because of the flatness that he found; what is certain is that Joris van Spilbergen, arriving in 1601 with the Dutch fleet, used the term "Tafel Baay" "by reason of the high hill, flat above a square like a table, and visible for 14 to 16 kilometres to seaward, whereby the said bay is recognised."[9] Saldanha's ascent began a long tradition of climbers in the decades that followed, the markings of some of whom were found in the mid-seventeenth century by Jan van Riebeeck when he founded the Dutch settlement.[10] In the late eighteenth century, the Swedish botanist Carl Thunberg remarks upon "plants and trees that grow nowhere else in the world."[11] A succession of keen flower hunters marvelled at the rich flora found only on the mountain itself, including the red Disa known as "The Pride of Table Mountain."[12] Barrow himself discovered a curious relic—an anchor—when he climbed Table Mountain; other monuments, such as a stone marking of Simon van der Stel, have vanished. The intrepid Lady Anne Barnard insisted on having a picnic on the summit. William Hickey, visiting in the early nineteenth century, sets the whole scene in glowing terms: "The approach to Cape Town is extremely beautiful and romantic. In one direction is Table Bay, where during the summer months, which are the reverse of ours, the ships anchor. To the southward and eastward is a long range of stupendous mountains, the nearest of which is the Table Land, so called from the top of it, for many miles in extent, being quite flat and, when seen from a distance, appearing like a table"[13] (see figure 7).

The rugged and fantastical mountain range and the expanse of ocean, stretching in one direction across the Atlantic to South America and in the other to the Antarctica and the South Pole, could hardly be more inspirational for those intent on mythmaking. The Russian writer Ivan Goncharov captures the romance of the scene in his visit in 1853: "Gigantic cliffs, almost completely black from the wind, guard the southern shore of Africa like the battlements of a huge fortress. It is an everlasting clash of titans—the sea, the winds and the mountains, the endless surf, the almost endless gales."[14]

Wild and exaggerated features of the mountain and the choppy waters of Table Bay feature in many early European images of the Cape (see figure 21). Mountains have been associated with gods in all cultures and the fathomless ocean, battered by incessant waves, might be the home of all kinds of imagined creatures. Climate added to this sense of myth: the sheer unpredictability of the Cape weather, the lashing storms, and gale-force winds suggested an environment in which only supernatural beings could thrive and human life could be sustained only with their acquiescence.[15] Attacks from wild animals and from runaway fugitives hiding in the forests added to the dangerous reputation of the place.

Both European and indigenous mytho-poetic references predate the dominating myth of Adamastor, which we will consider in the next chapter. Rob Amato has drawn attention to canto 26 of the "Inferno" stanzas of Dante's *Divine Comedy*, where the earthly realm of paradise is situated at the summit of a mountain that is also predicted to arise, with a flat surface, from the sea.[16] As the mariners approach it with relief after a long journey, their ship is battered "from the new land" by a wind, very reminiscent of the infamous Cape southeaster.[17] Malvern van Wyk Smith observes that in this way "southern Africa was effectively invented before it was discovered, a circumstance of crucial importance to sub-sequent European attitudes to the sub-continent, especially when seen in the persistent notions of a southern, terrestrial paradise."[18]

On the other side of the divide, the myth of Umlindi Wemingizimu is recalled by the Zulu sage Credo Mutwa. This is an epic struggle of the great gods and goddesses on a classical scale: Nganyaba, the great dragon of the sea, like Adamastor who follows him, resents the notion that part of his domain shall be handed over to the gods, who wish to create land. His adversary in this battle is Qamata, the creator of the world who was born from the union of the sun god Tixo and the earth goddess Djobela. Djobela helps Qamata to achieve his objective by creating four gigantic beings who will guard the extremities—north, west, east, and south—of land. After many fierce battles, the mother goddess is asked to turn the guardians into mountains so that the land will be forever protected. One of these, the largest is in the south, Umlindi Wemingizimu (Watcher of the South) becomes Table Mountain.[19]

Earliest Inhabitants

The racial and cultural mix of the Holocene period in Southern Africa was complex. Although communities or groups might not have day-to-day contact—separated in some cases by physical barriers—there was a good deal of genetic mixing, and boundaries between them "were never imper-meable."[20] The two main aboriginal groups were the San and the Khoi-khoi. Both groups were a particular development of the Negro race with

possible links to Hamitic or semi-Caucasian genes. According to R. R. Inskeep, they should be regarded "simply as African negroids with a long
history of differentiation in the southern part of the continent."[21] This differentiation makes them "ultra African," since they were cut off from the
Negros, with their genetic mix, to the north.[22] At a later date, probably
between 750 BCE and 750 CE, the Negro races of Bergdama and Bantu (the
latter, strictly speaking, being a set of languages) were spreading into the
Eastern Cape. The Bergdama were racially a true Negro people different in
appearance from the San and Khoikhoi. The Bantu speakers, essentially
Negro, had various Hamitic strains and so were different in appearance
from the Bergdama. The intermingling of different races influenced language, so that Khoisan words crept into Bantu languages and vice versa.
While conflicts arose over territory, the intermingling of tribes was also a
feature of the increasingly complex racial mix.

The San (Bushmen)

There were striking differences between the Khoikhoi and San, both
physically and in lifestyle, despite the fact that they were of the same
genetic lineage, sharing a similar language and cultural traits. The San
(the oldest inhabitants, whose skeletal remains date to the Middle Stone
Age) were shorter, a yellow-skinned race of nomads whose provenance was
probably modern Kenya or Tanzania. Some attempt has been made in the
past to link them to the pygmy races of central Africa (the Congo), but
despite a shared shortness of height, their physiognomy and bodily shape
suggest different variations of a common Negro stock. The southward
migration of the San from East Africa probably came about because of
pressures from other Negro peoples invading their territories from further north. Over a large area of Southern Africa, the San replaced the
aboriginal Boskopoids, choosing caves or sheltered ledges for their habitations. Later they themselves were driven out from these traditional
territories to remote regions, such as the Kalahari, by the arrival of the
Khoikhoi.

Different San tribes, distinguished by different dialects, spread over a very wide region, often in isolated pockets away from the invaders. The physical characteristics of members of these tribes also differed—height and colouring varied, in some cases suggesting intermingling with other races. The northern San were taller than the southerners, with darker skin, but there was a continuous gradation of physical type among tribes. One common feature was dry, lean skin that formed into deep wrinkles, giving the San a very distinct facial appearance; some Hamitic influence in the face (aquiline nose) is also evident in some groups.

Their nomadic, hunting existence meant that there were no permanent social structures but rather loose hunting groups, brought together into tribal life by common language. Although there was little social solidarity or what might be recognised as political organisation, groups did claim exclusive hunting rights in specified territories. These areas would not be marked by any boundary other than natural ones—such as river beds, dunes, and trees—but the San recognised their limits and kept out of their neighbours' territory. There was a close identification with particular places, which sometimes became enshrined in San mythology.[23] Nevertheless, villages were always movable. Although huts might be arranged in some order of importance (those of chiefs separated from the others) the family unit occupied each particular hut and was the basis for all social organisation. Isaac Schapera describes how the move of a whole encampment might occur: "When it becomes necessary to move camp, for example after a death has taken place, the whole community takes up all its goods and chattels, and, led by the *gei-khoib* (chief) sets off in search of a new site to be selected by the latter. Having found a suitable one he places his belongings on a spot on which his own hut is to be erected. His followers, passing on his left, take up suitable places for their huts in like manner."[24]

Recognition of some persons of authority—usually older men with hunting skills—provided a degree of communal regulation in larger groups, even in some cases taking the form of a hereditary chiefdom. Even in these communities the chiefs tended to remain leaders rather than rulers with absolute command over subjects. Nevertheless, certain moral precepts were understood and enforced communally, agreement on action being reached by consensus rather than being imposed from above. Murder and adultery were punishable by death; other less serious offences such as stealing would be dealt with by ostracising offenders. The economic life of San tribes was also limited since most of their needs were met directly from the environment. Some making of tools—in particular, arrows from reeds or utensils for cooking—and the use of animal hides for *karosses* (traditional clothing made from skins) and other garments were the main manufactures. It was only later, with the arrival of the Europeans when expectations for tobacco and alcohol arose, that the San started to barter and trade.

According to various travellers the San were "more active and lively"[25] than the Khoikhoi, with a vibrant tradition of music, dancing, and visual art, as well as a strong tradition of storytelling (*kukummi*). Most travellers remarked upon their diminutive height (four feet was average) and a "Chinese" touch to their appearance.[26] They led a nomadic life as hunter-gatherers, reflected in the subject of their art where game, particularly the eland, figure repeatedly. Agile in movement and swift runners, they were also expert trackers who could cover great distances in search of game, which they shot with bow and poisoned arrow. Sometimes they disguised themselves with animal hides and feathers so as not to alert their prey to their presence. Carrying charms for luck, they were accompanied by packs of dogs, half-wild and starved that would attack almost any creature being hunted by their masters. Certain conventions about which parts of animals could be eaten by whom indicated a recognition of hierarchy and discrimination against women. Game was not the only part of their diet. Ostrich, partridge, and other birds were also eaten. If settlements were near water, fish provided another source of food; all forms of insects, including locusts and ants, were also part of San fare.

The San were gradually driven out of their homelands by different invaders, including the Khoikhoi. In some cases they intermingled and became absorbed in other cultures, but numbers of them resisted

integration, preferring to migrate to less hospitable areas such as the
Kalahari. These were harsher environments than the ones from which
they had come, but the Bushmen adapted to them with their survival
skills intact. Remarkably they also continued to paint the walls of the
caves and ledges where they lived in these remote areas.[27]

The Khoikhoi (Hottentots)

The Khoikhoi were taller in stature than the San, also of yellow or red-
dish skin, leading to the sobriquet of the "red people" (a term also used
about Xhosa warriors daubed with red ochre). Their likely provenance was
also East Africa; once in their new, southern territories, there was considerable intermingling with the San. When later European settlers arrived,
the Khoikhoi were forced to move into more scattered communities away
from their original coastal territories around the Cape of Good Hope. As
with the San there were distinct groups—Schapera identifies four: Cape
Hottentots, Eastern Hottentots, Korana, and Naman. Although the border-
line between these tribes was not always clear, the tribes were independent of one another even if regional chiefs gained some recognition from
different groups. Within the Naman (possibly the name of a remote ancestor) various different tribes, sharing a similar language, evolved. As with
the San, the tribe was headed by the *gao-aob* or chief. The tribes themselves were divided into clans, descended through a male line. Each clan
also named itself after an ancestor; a loose confederation of family groups
made up the clan. Such social fragmentation suggests that tribal leaders,
although accorded respect, had no real control over members of different
clans who could be engaged in warfare over the ownership of cattle or the
use of pasturing lands. Encampments were as often as possible made near
good grassland and water supplies in the form of streams or pools.

The eighteenth-century botanist William Paterson made drawings of
the Khoikhoi. They are shown as being as tall as Europeans but more slender, with small hands (sometimes with mutilations) and feet; their faces
contain ceremonial markings.[28] Later portraits of faces done by Samuel

and William Daniell and Lady Anne Barnard show "Chinese" features (see figures 3, 23, 24, and 25). Their habit of rubbing themselves with animal grease—a practice that offended most European visitors on account of the rancid smell it gave off—meant that they could wander about almost naked but for some sheepskin covering even in the coldest weather. Their habitations were beehive-like, family huts of reed matting that provided good shelter from the wind but could easily be taken down and rebuilt. The encampment in which the huts were placed in a circle—each facing inward toward the centre—would be protected by a fence of thorns. The huts of the chief and his family would stand slightly apart placed to catch the morning sun first; the huts of clan families would be huddled together. While the immediate family circle would be of parents and children, extended kinship was important in the social and moral fabric of Khoikhoi communities. As we have seen with the San, certain kinds of behaviour—murder, incest, and adultery—were proscribed, and offenders were punished by the community. Khoikhoi society exhibited a greater degree of regulation of public life than was the case with the San, but when natural resources dwindled, groups tended to break away to fend for themselves.

The Khoikhoi of the interior, unlike the San, were keepers of livestock—sheep, cattle, and goats—probably already their preferred pattern of subsistence before their migration southward from East Africa. While each family would have its own animals, families living together would pasture their animals in common. In some cases animals would be marked so as to indicate ownership; herding would have to take place around known water holes. The cattle, sheep, and goats they kept provided an important source of food, both in the form of milk and meat—although there was a reluctance to kill domestic animals for consumption except in extreme cases. Nevertheless, having them available in such cases was important when there was a shortage of hunted food, rather than having to rely solely on plants and other fare that could be gathered in the veld. Animals would be brought into the kraal or centre of the enclosure at night to protect them from predators and the inclement climate. Men would be in charge of livestock (cattle were regarded as their exclusive responsibility); women laboured in gathering food including edible plants, carrying water, and tending to domestic chores. Great care was taken to prevent pollution of cattle in the kraal; if purification ceremonies took place, animals would be included. Sheep, for example, would be forced to jump through a fire in a special ceremony, the belief being that the smoky smell left on their fleece would distract predators.

There appeared to be no clear sense of private ownership of land even where, in the case of water holes, a communal resource might be regulated by an individual. The nomadic existence of the Khoikhoi, in constant search for new pastures, suggested the lack of any frontier or defined territory; their movement was directed primarily by seasonal rainfall and following game that they, like the San, hunted with considerable skill. Ostrich, zebra, and antelope were among the animals they preferred. The Khoikhoi did not cultivate the land except for the occasional planting of *dagga* (cannabis). As pastoralists, with larger and larger herds of cattle, they were spread across the entire southwestern part of the region; the Cape tribe frequenting the area of Table Bay was the Goringhaicona or "Peninsulars," known to the Dutch as the Strandlopers or "beachcombers" (see figure 2, *Le Pays de Hottentots* map).[29] The coastal dwellers were not cattle keepers like their neighbours in the interior; rather, they lived in the caves around coastal bays and collected plants and mussels for food. After the arrival of the Europeans in the seventeenth century these indigenes sought the protection of the newcomers, eventually becoming subservient to them. A mixed race of Khoikhoi and Europeans soon became a feature of Cape society.

LANGUAGES

Much has been written about the language of the San and Khoikhoi. The earliest European travellers remarked upon the peculiar click sounds given to consonants. Schapera says that although there were a variety of dialects among the Bushmen, "these languages are so clearly related that they must be regarded as belonging to the same language family."[30] Pioneering work in the San language was begun in the nineteenth century by Dr. Wilhelm Bleek, a philologist who (with the encouragement of the Cape Governor, Sir George Grey) began to compile a dictionary. Bleek was unable to complete the dictionary in his lifetime, but the work was taken forward by his sister-in-law, Lucy Lloyd, and eventually by his daughter, Dorothea Bleek. After a lifetime's research on many aspects of folklore and rock art, Dorothea completed the dictionary, which was published just before her death in 1948. According to her classification there were three main groups divided geographically into Southern, Northern, and Central languages. Schapera adds a fourth group—the Khoikhoi tongue—as he says that it is clear that this language is more closely related to the Bushmen family than to the Hamitic languages of East Africa with which it had been previously associated.[31]

The Southern dialect of the /Xam group of the Cape San has been one of the best studied. While vowel sounds in this dialect are muted, the reversed or imploded consonants come over as "clicks," a phenomenon remarked upon by almost all European visitors to the Cape from earliest times. At least four different positions of the tongue produce variations on the "clicks"; a further complication is that, as in Chinese, tone or pitch gives different meanings to words that have the same phonetic pronunciation. Five significant tones have been identified. These refinements of pronunciation made the language difficult for foreigners to learn—except, as Barrow observed, by Dutch farmers brought up by native servants.[32] The vocabulary of all the Khoisan languages tends to be restricted to terms relating to daily life and the environment; words for animals, plants, and trees being abundant, while those for abstract ideas are rarer. Noel Mostert eulogises the sound of the language, saying that in it one could hear the "cadences of the wild, of water and earth, rock and grass roll onomatopoeically along the tongue."[33]

THE BANTU SPEAKERS

A more sophisticated culture of Bantu-speaking tribes interrupted what might be regarded as the "near ideal existence"[34] of the San and Khoikhoi in the Helocene period. These Negro tribes were of complex genetic stock, including Hamitic elements. Schapera warns that "the elasticity of its [Bantu] forms make it impossible to give rigid classification,"[35] especially as integration with local races would have taken place as their colonisation advanced. Nevertheless, very marked features of these cosmopolitan newcomers, who had connections with the Arab trade of East Africa (and possibly even with Chinese traders of the Han dynasty), stand out in comparison with the aboriginal Khoisan. The invaders were agriculturalists who grew sorghum and millet; lived in settled, rather than in nomadic, communities; and had the use of metals such as iron and copper. They produced ceramics and iron pottery and were barterers, evolving an economic system of communal life based on monarchical principles. Ownership of cattle in their societies indicated wealth and social status. An aristocratic class consented to rule in chiefdoms, although allegiances could change as particular leaders attracted new followers. The main Bantu occupation was on the east coast, between Delagoa Bay and the Great Fish River, but further north, the Bechuanas settled near the Orange River and the Ovampo to the west coast.[36] In the eastern part of modern South Africa outside the Cape colony, the Zulus and Xhosa were the chief peoples. A vast variety of languages are cloaked within the Bantu label.

MYTHICAL PLACE: KHOIKHOI LEGENDS

The Khoikhoi settlers of the Cape brought their own sense of myth and magic to the Cape setting of the jagged mountains and the stormy sea. In their vivid images, flying elephants traversed the ether of the Cape ranges; like many ancient people, the importance of the moon (T'Kaam) was a prominent feature of their belief. One of the abiding lunar myths was about the sending of a message of immortality to man from the T'Kaam. The generous message of hope, conveyed by a louse, was changed by a hare, bringing the unwelcome news that man was doomed to an allotted and not limitless, life span. T'Kaam was infuriated by the hare's interference; as a punishment he inflicted a cleft lip, which the hare bore ever after. In this way, the hare came to represent evil and deceit, and the meat of this animal could on no account be eaten. If a Khoikhoi hunter encountered a hare on his path, he would turn home at once; if the hare ran in the same direction as him, that might presage good fortune.[37]

By contrast, the mantis is revered as the harbinger of good fortune. In his re-creation of Khoikhoi mythology, André Brink tells us that the Afrikaans name for the mantis, *hotsnotsgot*, means "Hottentot gold."[38] Although the Khoikhoi did not formally worship the mantis, they believed in its supernatural powers and influence, often wearing images of it carved on amulets to bring themselves good luck. In Brink's novel *Praying Mantis*, the birth of the hero Cupido is marked by the appearance of a mantis, an omen that someone of unusual destiny has been born. The mantis's appearance is brief: it disappears as suddenly as it had appeared, startling the gathering of onlookers, who nevertheless understand the significance of its presence at the birth.[39]

While not written down as metaphysics or theology, good and evil are represented in Khoikhoi eschatology in the form of Tsui-Goab, the great father and giver, the source of all good fortune, and Gaunab, the quintessentially evil spirit whose whole existence is given to creating mischief and harm. Tsui-Goab was the creator of mankind as well as of all animal life, but his first act was to make a stone that, symbolically, would remain on the earth long after the disappearance of all living creatures. He lived in a radiant heaven, while Gaunab inhabited gloomier, shady regions. Tsui-Goab (meaning "wounded knee") gained his name as a result of an injury sustained in a heroic fight with Gaunab. Gaunab's evil ways are many and

subtle—sometimes appearing in the dead of night to steal children or
haunting the living through the ghosts of those who have died "bad
deaths," perhaps abandoned by their own people and their carcasses
devoured by wild animals. These spirits or ghosts—*sobo khoin* (people of
the shadows)—stalk the living and bring with them a nightmarish sense
of dread and destruction, aiding and abetting Gaunab in kidnapping
children and causing other havoc in earthly communities. Brink vividly
portrays the evil perpetrated by Gaunab:

> Night-walkers came into our temporary huts to suck the men dry and
> ride the women and terrify the children. *Sobo khoin*, Shadow people.
> The dun-coloured ones. As if all the graves in that vast land had opened
> to vomit up their dead. Trees suddenly bursting into flames at night.
> Rocks breaking open to let out liquid fire. Snakes crossing our tracks
> and sprouting wings to fly off through the dead-wood trees and dis-
> appear into the searing white light of the sun. Never before had we
> lived through times like those.[40]

One of the most prominent rituals among the Khoikhoi was connected
with the mythical hero, Heitsi-Eibib, a hunter who also had the character
of both a prophet and a magician. The rite involved recognising burial
mounds as those of Heitsi-Eibib by throwing stones or branches at them
while passing. As Heitsi-Eibib was said to have died many times and been
reincarnated many times, he had numerous graves that were scattered over
vast areas of Southern Africa. The godlike figure was regarded as the
ancestor of all the Naman Khoikhoi. He was thought to have lived in the
east and been a chief of some wealth and status, owning many cattle. His
birth and early life were remarkable—immaculately conceived and committing incest with his mother, as a young boy he was already fighting and
killing monsters. His ability to change his form made him a formidable
opponent in any fight. While respected as a protector of his people, some
of his wayward behaviour made him less than godlike. In throwing stones
on his grave, a hunter would mutter the following prayer:

O Heitsi-Eibib,
Thou, our grandfather,
Let me be lucky,
Give me game,
Let me find honey and roots,
That I may bless thee again,
Art thou not our Great-grandfather?
Thou Heitsi-Eibib.[41]

Like the Bantu tribes of the Eastern Cape, the Khoikhoi did not believe that bad things happened by accident; rather, they were always visited upon people by evil forces that could, nevertheless, be countered by magic. Particular care was taken over death and burial. Gaunab lurked and waited for every opportunity to strike at the living by exploiting any irregularities in the burial of the dead. A "bad" death was where a person was abandoned in death, with his or her body left unattended and perhaps devoured by predators. Burial of the dead was done speedily, either on the day of death or the next day. The hut of the dead person was left alone with individual possessions still in it; any disturbance of burial ceremonies could lead to the haunting of the living by the dispossessed souls of the dead. One important ritual to fend off bad luck was to wash hands in cold water at the scene of the death. Magicians (shamans), endowed with special powers would be available to give guidance on the proper treatment of the dead as well as in other ceremonies. Sometimes they too were corrupted by Gaunab and turned their arts to sinister ends.

Nevertheless, when evil did strike, the only recourse was to the shamans, since they alone had an understanding of how things worked in the dark world of evil. If a person was bewitched, the magician knew how to bring them out of the spell; they could also interpret omens, thereby suggesting ways of preventing evil falling upon individuals. Prayers to the god of rain, always an important feature of Khoikhoi culture, were more efficacious if directed through magicians or prophets who were endowed with extrasensory perception.

SAN MYTHOLOGY

The San shared with the Khoikhoi the general attitude toward evil and the dangers of upsetting the spirits of the dead. The fate of humans was set by the moon and in the stars, the latter believed to be animals or peoples of the past. While there is an undercurrent of determinism in the *kukummi*, or orally transmitted stories, some indicate an ability of humans to affect the course of events. J. D. Lewis-Williams transcribes the touching story of one hunter who was inadvertently killed by his fellows in the cloud of dust that surrounds the hunted springbok. A chorus chants that the man should have avoided the arrow, and he himself says, "I should have avoided the arrow. I should have avoided it nicely."[42] In another story a man is eaten by a lion because he recklessly insists that it is a dog, when all those round him have warned him it is not. In that way he has sealed his own fate.[43]

The most efficacious way in which men could act to avert evil was by careful performance of ritual. This was, as with the Khoikhoi, especially important in matters of death and burial, the latter also performed as soon as possible after the decease of the person. Although due respect and lamentation were shown to the dead person, once the perfumed body was buried with a few private possessions and a final farewell made, no one ever returned to the grave, fearing the ghosts that might lurk there. If unexpectedly passing a grave, small stones were thrown to appease the spirits of the departed in a similar manner as in the Khoikhoi practice.

A rich mythology of the moon, stars, and animals suited the striking Cape landscape that the San roamed across. The moon was appealed to in the hunt:

Ho, Moon lying there,
Let me kill a springbok

Tomorrow,

Let me eat a springbok

With this arrow;

Let me shoot a springbok,

With this arrow;

Let me eat a springbok,

Let me eat filling my body

In the night which is here,

Let me fill my body.

Ho Moon lying there,

I dig out ants' food

Tomorrow,

Let me eat it.

Ho Moon lying there,

I kill an ostrich tomorrow

With this arrow.

Ho Moon lying there,

Thou must look at this arrow,

That I may shoot a springbok with it tomorrow.[44]

The creation of the universe by !Khwe is described in a myth that begins with the dark void of nothingness: "Then the First Being of the Early Race who we call !Khwe took the sun under his armpit and threw it up. Everything began. His breath made nine Early Race People who were low stars and six ants and three beetles who were people too."[45]

As in the Khoikhoi legends, the mantis was an object of great reverence for the San, even though its ways could be whimsical and wayward at times. The mantis, having witnessed the creation of the universe, then presided over the entire mythical world and had the power, through dreams, to prophesy the future and even to resurrect the dead. The moon, also the provenance of rain, could be seen as the slipper of the mantis. The mantis's wife was Dassie, the rock rabbit, whose son was killed by baboons while a porcupine was adopted as her daughter. These animals were thought to be reincarnations of earlier humans—the ancestors of the San—and many of them, including frogs, tortoises, and snakes, were represented in Bushman art. A good spirit, Huwe, wards off disease and protects men, while Thora represents evil and threatens men with illness and misfortune.

As with the Khoikhoi, magicians or shamans were influential figures. Their most important duty, especially as the San moved to drier areas, was to predict rainfall. No doubt these diviners were good meteorologists who could tell when the clouds, over which they claimed power, were about to burst and provide much needed rainfall. They claimed to be able to discern, in the spiritual world, various forms of animals associated with different kinds of rainfall. They blessed hunting expeditions to ensure success and officiated at ceremonies connected with puberty. Their powers extended beyond their own mortality; even in death their powers could affect the course of life. These rites continued to be practised as the San were driven further north into inhospitable areas as the settlers advanced the boundaries of the Cape colony.

Rock Art of the San

The most significant cultural expression of San mythology is to be found in rock paintings, which have been found mostly in caves but also on rock surfaces over a wide area of Southern Africa. While much of the San rock art to be found extant is likely to be of more recent times, there is evidence that its origins can be traced back to the Stone Age. Examination of deposits of ash, bone, and shells around painted stones can be reliably dated by modern archaeological methods, offering an indication of the age of the paintings themselves. Partial though that evidence may be, it is more reliable than trying to interpret styles of rock art to determine age and sequence. In some cases the subject matter is a good guide to dating: where fat-tailed sheep or cattle are represented, the images must have been made at least after the time of the arrival of the Khoikhoi, who first brought sheep into the area and later cattle. Similarly representations of European figures and sailing ships would have to have been made after the arrival of the newcomers. Nevertheless, it has not been possible to establish a reliable chronology overall: Peter Slingsby says exact dating is precarious but suggests the possibility of rock drawings in parts of the Cape area being 6,500 years old, while those in the Cederberg could be 8,000 years old.[46] Others have suggested even greater ages, dating the art to a possible 27,000 years ago.[47]

The two distinct art forms are the paintings to be found on the cave walls and the peckings, or engravings, on the rocks—the petroglyphs executed with sharp stone tools. The pigment for the paintings would come from the earth (iron oxides, kaolin, manganese, etc.), while the petroglyphs were more prominent in dry, barren areas. It now appears that the earliest paintings were fine-line ones, executed with an implement or a brush (perhaps a feather). Occasionally handprints are found, or cruder finger drawings. These appear to have been superimposed on fine-line paintings, suggesting that they are more recent. It seems that the fine-line technique was lost at about the time the Khoikhoi introduced cattle into the area, as the earlier images of sheep were in fine-line drawings, whereas those of cattle were finger drawings.[48]

Game, particularly the eland, are prominent figures in San artistic representation, underlying the search for meat to supplement a diet of berries and plant food found growing in the wild. Hunting scenes, in this case showing elephants in chase, lions, and rhinoceros, are all represented, as they are in European cave paintings of the same period.[49] There appears to be no symmetry in the composition of the pieces; animals are often represented in distorted, elongated forms, as are human figures up to one and a half metres in height, suggesting trance-like states.[50] There are mysterious monstrous animals while some species, such as buck and giraffe in the petroglyphs, show the influence of a particular locale on the artist. In one particular cave in Bushman's Kloof (Fallen Rock) there are unusual

drawings, some in deep ochre red, of semihuman figures in a state of
trance expressing movement out of the body. Along the walls are what
appear to be earlier paintings; lichen grows on some of the surface, dis-
torting and eventually destroying the images.[51] In other cases the natural
structure of the rock face was used by the artist to dramatize situations:
snakes would be painted entering or exiting cracks in the rock. Sometimes snakes would be depicted bleeding from their noses, a trance
metaphor.[52] The aesthetic quality of these works is now widely recognised,
although perceptive early visitors, like Barrow, had already appreciated and
remarked upon their excellence.[53]

Specimens of petroglyphs in the Albany Museum in Grahamstown
show the depiction of a wide variety of animals—antelope and rhinoceros
appear alongside the ubiquitous eland on flat, smoothed-out surfaces of
rock. The drawings stand out on grey surfaces; sometimes there is colour
(usually reds and browns), which adds considerable interest to the mono-
tone images. White pigment, used for colouring faces and sometimes limbs
of animals, has faded away with time, leaving curiously hook-shaped out-
lines of human heads.[54] A large collection of different instruments are
on display in the museum; some such as rounded stones were used for
smoothing surfaces but sharper instruments, developed for better definition, are also to be seen.

In the absence of any written records, interpreting rock art in terms of
the spiritual beliefs of the San is difficult. While some of the scenes depicted
clearly relate to episodes in daily life—for example, hunting scenes or
dancing groups—in other cases mysterious and grotesque figures suggest
a greater licence on the part of the artist and an expression of other, less
worldly, preoccupations. Such images lend themselves to interpretation on
shamanic lines—that is, they relate to rituals observed and connected to
states of trance. As in other art forms, symbolism may not easily be understood by outsiders, but it is remarkable that prehistoric man, concerned
as he had to be with securing food on a daily basis, should have given time
and energy to these aesthetic pursuits.

A State of Nature

The physical environment of the Cape and its landscape immensely influenced the life and culture of the Khoisan aboriginal inhabitants. The
green pasturelands fed by a good rainfall and plentiful rivers and streams
provided not only abundant fruit and plant food but also fuel in the form
of wood. The rich, fertile land also supported a variety of animal life—
buffalo, giraffe, zebra, quagga, and kudu—important to hunters, as well
as to fierce predators such as lions, leopards, wild dogs and hyenas, vul-
tures, and various species of reptiles. The plentiful grasslands later
enabled the Khoikhoi to keep large herds of animals, an insurance against
times of drought and other hardships. There was therefore no shortage of
food, and the hunting skills of the Khoisan—especially the San—were
based on a close knowledge of animal habitats and behaviour. The plentiful rain and abundance of game also gave little incentive to cultivation,
encouraging a nomadic life with, in the case of the Khoikhoi, some
pastoralism.

Schapera makes the point that southern Africa is "an ethnological cul
de sac" since it is surrounded by sea on three sides, preventing any further movement of people within its boundaries. The most direct link with
other regions and migration routes extend northward, and invasions have
come from that direction. Being enclosed by the sea has meant that "invading peoples must either wipe out their predecessors completely or live
side by side with them, the latter condition likely to result in intermingling and the formation of hybrid races and cultures."[55]

This pattern can be recognised in the migration southward, first of the
San and then the Khoikhoi. As the San had wiped out the original Boskopoids, so the Khoikhoi fought the San as they in turn pushed down from the
north. However, as one observer puts it, "while the Hottentots drove the
Bushmen into kloofs and caves, they did not bother to exterminate them."[56]
The San were pushed into less and less hospitable territory and, every so
often, would raid Khoikhoi holdings to steal cattle or sheep. When the

Khoikhoi retaliated, they would sometimes seize a woman or child as hostage. Their adoption into the tribe led to the intermingling of different peoples referred to by Schapera. In time further invasions—of Bantu tribes—led to renewed territorial struggles but, once more, to an intermingling of racial groups. One legacy of that miscegenation was the incorporation of click sounds from Khoikhoi into the Xhosa and Zulu languages.[57]

However, the Khoisan pattern of life that had existed for thousands of years was only decisively interrupted at the end of the fifteenth century by the arrival of newcomers from Europe. Their demands would change the traditional way of Cape life, especially once a permanent physical settlement was established in Table Bay a hundred and fifty years later. Travellers to the Cape, as we shall see in subsequent chapters, formed various views about the condition of the indigenous peoples they encountered, many of which were highly negative. However, there were exceptions. Anders Sparrman, the Swedish botanist, recognised both their successful adaptation to their environment as well as a form of order in their social arrangements. Eighteenth-century Frenchmen, influenced by the myth of the noble savage, began to see the Khoisan in a new light. While no citizen of polite Europe was seriously suggesting a return to the uncomfortable state of nature, some advantage was seen in the freedom that "savages" enjoyed from the constraints of life in civilised society. Nor did it appear that men in that state were unhappy or dispirited. Whatever ideological slant began to appear at that time, it is a fact that before the advent of the Europeans, a nomadic style of life had been sustainable in the Edenic garden of the Cape; a rich mythology, art, and music (see figure 5) were also evident in the culture of its early inhabitants.

CHAPTER 2

Adamastor's Reign

Rounding the Cape: Bartolomeu Dias

The first recorded European travellers to the most southern tip of Africa, the Portuguese, were not seeking to establish colonial territories; rather, they were on a quest to find the fabled Christian kingdom of Prester John, vaguely thought to be near Ethiopia, and on a worldlier note, to open up a sea passage, if it existed, to the East.[1] Both ventures were keenly supported by the Portuguese Crown, whose Avis dynasty monarchs were determined to be the most glittering princes in Christendom. Nevertheless, they and their naval commanders knew that rounding the Cape would prove to be a great challenge, if indeed it was possible at all. A voyage to the extremity of Africa would test all the known navigational science of the time and involve sailing in an area of wild, tempestuous weather. On board the sleek caravels that made up most of the Portuguese fleet, rates of mortality were high; the testing climatic conditions of the Southern Atlantic added a further challenge. On land things did not prove to be much better: when first contact was made with indigenous people, it proved disastrous, giving rise to the view that the locals were dangerous, wild savages from whom no help could be sought.

Speculation about early voyages around the Cape has been made since ancient times. Herodotus in his *History* raises the possibility that

Phoenician ships sent by the Pharaoh Necho II sailed down the East African coast, rounded the Cape Peninsula, and then sailed up the west coast, returning home via the Mediterranean. Ptolemy, the geographer, discounted this story, saying that rounding the Cape was an impossibility. He postulated that the Indian Ocean was landlocked, and his opinion remained influential throughout the Middle Ages. It encouraged the Portuguese to search for ways of crossing Africa from west to east by river systems in their search for Prester John's kingdom.[2]

Pliny the Elder, without entering the argument, nevertheless warns that the unexpected should always be expected from Africa. In 1291 certain Genoese brothers, the Vivaldi, set off in search of a route southward down the west coast of Africa. They vanished without a trace.[3] Recent claims have been made for Chinese circumnavigation of the world, including rounding the Cape in 1421 on their way westward, although this is a matter of considerable controversy.[4] Behind all these accounts there lurks the idea of a mysterious, faraway place that, if accessible at all, would not be hospitable.

At any rate, what is certain is that the Cape was rounded in 1488 by Bartolomeu Dias de Novaes (1450–1500), paradoxically without realising what he had done. King João II's dispatch of Dias was the culmination of decades of Portuguese exploration, first to the Atlantic islands and then gradually down the coast of West Africa. The spur to this new venture was the capture of Ceuta in Morocco in 1415, an event that appeared to open up a new world to this marginalised country on the westward edge of Europe, hemmed in by its powerful Spanish neighbour, Castile. From the 1420s this effort was directed from Sagres in the Algarve by Prince Henry the Navigator, who had founded an academy dedicated to navigational science. Prince Henry's programme was ambitious and the pace he set relentless. By his death in 1460, Madeira, the Azores, and the Cape Verde islands had been taken and the West African coast explored by Gil Eanes.

Two significant events spurred on Portuguese ambitions. The first was the commissioning of the Fra Mauro map in Venice by Prince Pedro,

Henry's brother and regent during the minority of Afonso V. The map, produced around the late 1440s, showed Africa surrounded to the west, east, and north by ocean, suggesting the so-called Plan of India—the opening up of a sea route to India—might be a distinct possibility. The other was the arrival of an embassy in Lisbon from Prester John in 1452.[5] These two events encouraged several generations of Portuguese monarchs to believe that a sea route could be found to India around the African continent. In 1481 the ambitious new monarch King João II succeeded to the throne, determined to press ahead with the Plan of India and taking care to keep secret its details lest they were taken up by rival seafaring nations. European explorers from other countries became increasingly suspicious of the official Portuguese representation of the Cape as a dangerous and inhospitable place, among them Sir Francis Drake.

The king looked among his courtiers to find a suitable captain who might lead an expedition. He decided to appoint Dias, superintendent of the royal warehouses, as the man who could undertake what would be an epic voyage. Little is known about Dias except that he was trained in navigational skills and could himself design ships. Leaving Lisbon in October 1487 from the Tower of Belém, the traditional place of departure on the Tagus, the fleet he captained consisted of two vessels (the *São Cristóvão* and the *João Infante*), supported by a square-rigged supply ship commanded by Pêro Dias, Bartolomeu's brother.[6] Another Pêro, Alenquer, acted as pilot.

The first part of the journey was relatively plain sailing. From the time of Prince Henry the Navigator's sponsorship in the 1440s, the Portuguese had taken great care in charting the West African coast as they extended their reach further south. By 1446 they had reached the Guinean coast, where they established a settlement that would provide a base for those further southward explorations. In 1482 Diogo Cão reached the tributary of the Zaire, and contact was made with the kingdom of the Congo— whose court thereafter became fashioned in the European style, with dukedoms and knighthoods conferred on the tribal chiefs.

In December 1487 Dias's ships arrived in Walvis Bay in modern Namibia, which was the furthest point south that Cão had reached, carrying among the crew Negro interpreters his predecessor had captured. From there the stormy southeast winds blew the ships right out into the Atlantic for several weeks; when land was sighted again, it was at Mossel Bay (São Bras), east of Cape Point. Dias called it the Bay of the Herdsmen (Bahia dos Vaqueiros), since the indigenes were found to be cattle herders. Without knowing it, Dias and his crews had rounded the Cape. However, landing to forage for food and supplies proved impossible: the Khoikhoi pelted the Portuguese ships from the shoreline with stones and arrows, and in the return fire, one of the tribesmen was killed.

The small fleet continued its eastward course, reaching Kwaaihoek, near the mouth of Bushmen's River in the present Eastern Cape. There Dias planted the traditional stone cross (*padrão*), which was only discovered in the twentieth century by the antiquarian scholar Eric Axelson. By this time the mutinous crew had had enough and forced the reluctant Dias to turn back. The chronicler João de Barros, recollecting the incident in the next century, says: "When [Dias] departed from the pillar which he had erected there, he was overcome by a great sadness and deep emotion, as if he was saying goodbye to a son banished forever; he remembered the great danger faced by him and all his men, how long they had journeyed only to come to this point, then that God had not granted him the main prize."[7] It was only on his return to what he called the "Cabo das tormentas" (the cape of storms) that Dias realised he had actually rounded the Cape. He arrived back in Lisbon after more than a year's sailing, having opened up over 1,600 kilometres of thitherto unknown seaboard.

The most significant result of Dias's voyage was that it had established the existence of a sea route to India. Such a discovery meant that the Portuguese could trade independently there without needing to deal with middlemen on the overland routes through the Middle East. It was a development that would bring great wealth to Portugal and to the Portuguese Crown. Ironically, a dozen or so years later, on another voyage, Dias himself perished at the Cape, his ship wrecked in the place that by then had been renamed the Cape of Good Hope.

Dias's experiences at the Cape began a negative feeling about the land and its inhabitants that was never entirely dispelled in the Portuguese imagination. While the wildness of the weather was legendary, the hostility of the indigenes contrasted to the fairly friendly relations that had been established with the local population in West Africa—for example, in Guinea, where Dias chose to live in between voyages. No doubt mutual fear and suspicion played its part in creating hostility between the locals and the newcomers, the latter usually concerned with bargaining for provisions but often not trading fairly.

The local view of the foreigners is imaginatively described by André Brink in his re-creation of these first encounters, albeit in a fictional form. Spying the arrival of the Portuguese ships and thinking them birdlike creatures, the Khoikhoi observer sees men coming out of them:

> But people like the ones that were hatched from those eggs we'd never even set eyes on before. Like birds you might say, all colours under the sun. We first thought it was feathers but then we made out it was a kind of clothing. And strutting about stiff-legged like ostriches and their heads so overgrown with beards and moustaches you could hardly see their faces. Just as well, for they didn't seem to have much in the line of skin, all pale and white like grass that had grown under a rock for too long.[8]

After their initial reaction of fear, the Khoikhoi gained confidence, at least partly on discovering that the newcomers also worshipped a god who might be their own Great Hunter. But the period of peaceful coexistence did not last—suspicion of treachery turns to open hostility and violence as the story unfolds.

The incident between Dias and Khoikhoi inhabitants of Mossel Bay confirmed the unease with which the Portuguese viewed the territory of southern Africa. Nevertheless, although momentous events took place

in the two decades after Dias's voyage, including Christopher Colum-
bus's voyage westward and the discovery of Brazil by Pedro Álvares
Cabral in 1500, Portuguese efforts remained focused on the route to
India, opened up by Dias's epic journey.

VASCO DA GAMA, 1497–1498

At the head of this renewed effort was now the Captain-Major (*capitão-
mor*) Vasco da Gama (1460–1524). Da Gama came from the town of Sines,
where his father had been the civil governor. Sines, on the Atlantic coast
south of Lisbon, was the home of a largely seafaring community. Da Gama,
chosen to head the Indian voyage, was about thirty-six years of age and
an expert navigator. He was a strict disciplinarian of a somewhat austere
nature; an achiever himself, he believed in promotion by merit rather than
by social connections. In the difficult conditions of the voyages it was particularly important to have men who knew their business; da Gama was
an able commander, but he needed the support of a good team.

The fleet sailed from Lisbon in 1497, with da Gama as captain of the
São Gabriel and his brother Paulo captain of the *São Raphael*, accompanied by a caravel and a supply ship. The two main vessels had been designed
by Dias himself. Drawing on his experience of rounding the Cape, he made
them of a heavier model than the traditional caravels so as to withstand
rougher seas and keep to a steadier course. They were tiny on modern
standards, being about 90 to 100 tonnes.

Much preparation had taken place, and no expense had been spared—
the Captain-Major had studied all the available charts and other documents, including the log books kept by Dias on his epic voyage. There
were men of experience and skill in his flotilla, including Pêro Alenquer,
the pilot, who had been on the Dias expedition and was therefore a
veteran of rounding the Cape. The crew had been encouraged to learn as
many useful crafts as they could, and the supplies brought with the ships
were calculated to sustain a voyage of several years. Crew members were

paid more than the customary wage, and advances were paid to their families.[9]

A vast concourse gathered at the Tower of Belém to see the four ships, their sails decorated with the red cross of the Order of Christ, sail out to sea from the Tagus estuary.

Learning from Dias's experience, da Gama decided to steer a wide compass through the South Atlantic so that he might be able to avoid the area of the worst weather that his predecessor had experienced by hugging the coast. In this case the *roteiro*, or log book (kept up by an unidentified member of the crew), gives some description of the voyage along the African coast with sights of whales, seals, and various birds resembling herons.[10] Axelson has warned about the authenticity of the "Diary" (as he prefers to call the log book), since the extant version is based on a sixteenth-century copy rather than being the original.[11]

The great arc that da Gama made took the ships toward the coast of South America before turning back toward Africa and eventually arriving in St. Helena Bay. The ships had been three months at sea and had covered a distance of 7242 kilometres. On arriving, da Gama went ashore to get accurate bearings from his primitive astrolabe and to effect repairs to the vessels, which had suffered considerable damage after their prolonged period in the stormy Atlantic. While the crew foraged for wood and fresh water, they came upon a tawny Strandloper[12] clad in a skin *kaross* who led them, after having some food aboard the ship, to the kraal where the Khoikhoi had established themselves. At first the encounter proved reasonably amicable, but soon trouble arose when one of the Portuguese foraging crew members was attacked. In an ensuing skirmish on shore, da Gama himself was wounded in the leg.

The seafarers took again to their ships and continued their journey, rounding the Cape and arriving, as Dias had done, at Mossel Bay. Here contact with the locals went off better—da Gama was surprised to be made welcome and soon started trading with the Khoikhoi, who arrived with much welcomed livestock and other supplies. Both sides proceeded to entertain each other—the locals playing flutes, the Portuguese their trumpets. They even danced merrily together. However, another quarrel seems to have arisen. Soon the Portuguese were firing warning shots in the air, and the Khoikhoi fled. Having gotten fresh supplies, da Gama decided to continue on the voyage.

The flotilla soon passed the furthest point Dias had reached before he had turned back. Da Gama's ships sailed further east along the coast, which they named Natal (Christmas) to mark the day when they passed by. The encounter with the Xhosa of the eastern coast was more cordial than the reception with the Khoikhoi had been. A crowd had assembled on the shore, and Martim Affonso, a member of da Gama's crew who had learnt some Bantu dialects in West Africa, was sent ashore as interpreter. He and the landing group were hospitably received, enabling the traditional exchange of presents to be made. The copper ornaments worn by the Xhosa caused da Gama to name the Limpopo River the Rio de Cobre (Copper River); the positive reception the Portuguese had received made him call Natal the "Terra da Boa Gente" (Land of the Good People).

From there the fleet sailed again northward to the Muslim-controlled East African coast, where the Arabs ran the ivory and gold trade. Da Gama was wary of how they would be received, but at Malindi the visitors were welcomed by the Muslim ruler. According to Luís Camões, da Gama was soon confident enough to be explaining the geography and history of Europe to the attentive sultan. He sketched out the geographical position of the peninsula of Iberia—at the far end of which, facing the expanse of the ocean, was Portugal, the crown of the continent. No doubt da Gama passed lightly over the period of Moorish occupation of Portugal.

A pilot was provided by the sultan to help his guest, and with that man's knowledge of the seas and after some weeks of sailing, the flotilla reached the port of Calicut on the Indian coast. At last King Manuel, known as "the Fortunate," had gained the prize of establishing a trade route directly to India, something that had been so much sought after by his predecessors. Within five years the first European factory was operational on the coast of the subcontinent. The direct sea route to India had opened up a lucrative trade (from which the Crown benefitted by a direct tax) that turned Lisbon into the foremost European commercial city.

After da Gama

The next Portuguese contact with the Cape came in 1503, when two ships were dispatched on the new sea route to bring back much-prized Indian spices to Europe. One of them was commanded by António de Saldanha, a Castilian courtier of King Manuel and brother of the comptroller of the queen's household. At least part of the purpose of this expedition was to wrench control of the East African trade from the Arabs—not only traditional enemies of Portugal from the time of the Moorish occupation but serious commercial rivals for the valuable Indian supply of pepper and other spices to Europe. The ships of the small convoy parted from each other at São Tomé, Saldanha proceeding south and reaching Table Bay (at first called Saldanha Bay), where he went ashore to get new provisions. Energetic and thinking the area was uninhabited, Saldanha climbed the mountain looming over the bay and was thus the first European to ascend to its summit.[13] However, it soon became apparent that there were people living in the area. In his account of their meeting with the Portuguese, the chronicler Barros claims that these indigenous inhabitants showed themselves to be thoroughly traitorous, for while ostensibly bartering with the newcomers over animals, they laid an ambush, attacking the Portuguese and wounding their commander.[14] Fernão Lopes de Castanheda, in his chronicle of the discoveries, gives a slightly less dramatic account. He portrays Saldanha and his men hunting penguins in Table Bay (probably near Robben Island) and recounts more peaceful intercourse with the Khoikhoi. It appears that Saldanha returned to São Tomé before rounding the Cape on a later expedition, this time making successful contact with rulers on the East African coast. The rest of his illustrious career was spent in India, where he commanded the spice fleet.

The battle to control the sea routes and contain piracy led to the establishment of a new office, that of the viceroyalty of India. In 1505, D. Fran-
cisco de Almeida, an experienced soldier, was appointed first viceroy, with
sweeping powers "to wage war, conclude treaties and regulate commerce."[15]
Although this move was a step in the direction of colonisation, Almeida
was wary of too great a commitment of Portuguese manpower and continued to rely on the building of strategic fortresses along the important trading route, rather than attempting to occupy the hinterlands. Maintaining
good relations with local chiefs, wherever possible, remained the central
feature of what was still a commercial, rather than imperial, policy based
primarily on maintaining safe passage for the ships of the line. The somewhat fanciful belief that Hindus were some sort of Christians became a
convenient excuse for putting aside the missionary and crusading pur-
poses urged by the Church on the Portuguese Crown in favour of con-
centrating on commerce.

Almeida's time in the East was turbulent. Both the Egyptians and Otto-
mans fought the Portuguese in an effort to keep control of the lucrative
trade with India, which was now threatened by the opening of the route
through the Cape. Almeida was a hardened soldier, losing his own son,
D. Lourenço, in one of the battles with the enemy. In 1509 he routed a
combined Egyptian and Gujarati fleet off the coast at Diu, in a stroke
consolidating Portuguese control of the Far East. At the end of his term as
viceroy on the way home to Lisbon, his ship put in at Table Bay to gain
fresh supplies. The foraging party that went ashore was attacked by the
Khoikhoi and had to withdraw. On board, at a council of war, the Portuguese decided that they would need to meet the local hostility with force.

Almeida, although with some premonition that things would not go
well, led the expedition ashore himself. He and his men were ambushed
by the Khoikhoi, using their effective spears (*assegai*) and cutting off their
enemy's retreat by blocking the shoreline with cattle. Sixty-five Portuguese
were killed, including the viceroy himself. This incident, added to the
series of earlier ones, sealed the idea for the Portuguese that the Cape was

a highly dangerous place—in Barros's words "a very famous name among us, because of the many noblemen who died there at the hands of the people of this land."[16]

THE CREATION OF ADAMASTOR

The most brilliant evocation of that unease was to be expressed by the epic poet, Luís Vaz de Camões (1524–1580) in his monumental *Lusíads*, published in 1572 with the approval of the censor of the Holy Office as "containing nothing scandalous or contrary to faith and morals."[17] In a stroke of genius, the poet incorporated the accumulated experience of threat and disaster at the Cape into the neoclassical mould of his epic in a form that would be immediately familiar to European readers steeped in Renaissance literature.

Camões's own background was highly colourful. He was born into a stratum of the lower aristocracy, though of a family with good connections—his uncle being the prior of the Santa Cruz monastery and the probable sponsor of his education. This took place in the hands of the Jesuits at Coimbra, where the Court occasionally assembled, adding much glitter to the distinguished academic community there. It is likely that Camões became fluent in classical Latin and Greek at the university, although he is not registered as a student. Eventually he left the idyllic surroundings of the scholarly town for the bustling capital, Lisbon.

In a recurring pattern of his life, he seems to have got into various scrapes in Lisbon. Like other young noblemen or *fidalgos*, he was sent off to fight the enemy, the Moors, in North Africa. He served in the army and was blinded in his right eye in action at Ceuta in 1549. His bust usually shows him in triumphal Roman laurels with the right eye closed (figure 6). In 1551 he was back in Portugal, where he resumed a bohemian life in the demimonde. He was imprisoned for fighting a duel with a member of the king's entourage, whom he had wounded. Interventions by his family—especially by his mother—earned him a reprieve but involved a sentence of three years service in the Orient. His louche lifestyle did not change in Goa: he was imprisoned for debts and only reprieved by taking up a post in Macau where, it is claimed, he began writing his epic poem in a grotto. Further legendary accounts attach to the manuscript of what became the *Lusíads*; one was that he carried it above his head when swimming from a shipwreck in the Mekong River. Camões gathered much geographical knowledge from his travels and adventures in the East, and it is displayed in many detailed descriptions and references in his verse.

In the *Lusíads*, Camões uses his classical knowledge in an ambitious new poem whose object would be to lionise the achievements of the Portuguese explorers. The epic, starting in Virgilian mode, would take the form of a poem of ten stanzas; Vasco da Gama would be its hero. Camões realized that the image of the navigator rounding the Cape presented a graphic centrepiece for his epic but needed a mythical figure to consolidate its symbolism: he rose to the artistic challenge by his dramatic creation of Adamastor, the great monster of the deep who had been banished to the chilly waters of the Cape by Jupiter for his impertinent desire for the nymph Tethys, the daughter of the sea gods Nereus and Doris, favoured by the father of the gods himself. Long after da Gama and his men had passed the Tropic of Capricorn and continued southward, they entered "that least known region of the world" where Adamastor dwells.[18] He is described as a creature of:

> Grotesque and enormous stature,
> With heavy jowls, and an unkempt beard,
> Scowling from sunken, hollow eyes,
> In complexion earthy and pale,
> Its hair grizzled and matted with clay,
> Its mouth coal black, teeth yellow with decay.[19]

The exact location of the Cape was of course known to Camões as it had not been to the ancients such as Ptolemy, who speculated about a great peninsula somewhere in the south. In his poem Camões merges these hazy ideas with the reality of the Cape's existence so that the discoveries of Dias and da Gama could be set in the context of the myths of the ancient world. Direct classical references are used to align his style to classical epics. The nymph Tethys explains to da Gama in the tenth canto of the poem the Ptolemaic system of extended spheres, the standard scientific orthodoxy until the time of Copernicus and Kepler. Best of all the spheres is the first, the Empyrean, from which a dazzling light emits. In this radiant circle live the gods and one all-powerful god who manifests himself in the world only through his agents, the prophets.

Meanwhile, Adamastor himself does not welcome the intrusion of the Portuguese seafarers into his distant and stormy domain. He calls the seafarers "reckless" although "bolder than the world has even known" for daring to enter his remote kingdom.[20] Then he delivers his chilling threat:

No matter how many vessels attempt
The audacious passage you are plotting
My Cape will be implacably hostile
With gales beyond any you have encountered;
On the next fleet which broaches
These turbulent waters I shall impose
Such retribution and exact such debts
The destruction will be far worse than my threats.[21]

Even while Adamastor is raging in the stormy seas of the Cape, the gods on Olympus are debating the merits of da Gama's voyage of discovery. Jupiter is sympathetic to the Portuguese, but Bacchus argues that they are challenging Jupiter's sway over vast territories and oceans. They had to be checked for their impertinence. It is Venus, at her most seductive, who persuades Jupiter to protect her people, the Portuguese, employing every wile and even tears to get her way. Jupiter is unable to resist her charms and casts aside Bacchus' counsel, determined that da Gama shall succeed.

Threatened with shipwreck and drowning, the intrepid da Gama, having offered prayers to Venus and relying on her protection, is not daunted

by the monster's dark mutterings and demands to know who or what
he is.

Adamastor gives his sonorous answer:

> I am that vast, secret promontory
> You Portuguese call the Cape of Storms,
> Which neither Ptolemy, Pompey, Strabo,
> Pliny, nor any authors knew of.
> Here Africa ends. Here its coast
> Concludes in this, my vast inviolate
> Plateau, extending southwards to the Pole
> And, by your daring, struck to my very soul
> I was one of the Titans
> With Enceladus, Aegeon and Briareus,
> I am called Adamastor.[22]

Adamastor then recites his place in the pantheon of Titans, the fabulous
creatures of Greek mythology who fought against the gods but who
were eventually defeated by Zeus, aided with thunderbolts provided by
Cyclops.

But before long there is a distinct change in tone. The threatening sound
disappears. Adamastor is painted in a more sympathetic light, pouring out
his longing for Tethys in a poignant lament:

> Tethys approached, with her glorious
> Face and her naked, matchless body;
> Like a madman I ran, with arms
> Outstretched, to her who was my
> Soul's life, heart's joy, body's prayer
> Kissing her lovely eyes, her cheeks, her hair.

This did not placate the father of the gods. Jupiter has an unpleasant shock
in store for the fallen Adamastor—as he tries to embrace her naked form,
he finds that he is only grasping a rock. His shock is palpable:

I was cheek to cheek with a boulder

I had seized as her angelic face,

Unmanned utterly, dumb and numb with shock,

A rock on an escarpment, kissing rock.[23]

The once proud Titan has himself been reduced to a rock even though it is the most prominent feature of the Cape coast, Table Mountain.

Camões's fantastical handling of the Adamastor myth inextricably links the Cape and Cape Town itself to European classical mythology. It is, of course, a mythology subverted to Camões's political purpose of lauding the achievements of the Portuguese explorers. The pagan classical gods (pre-eminently Bacchus, who wishes to destroy the Portuguese, and Venus, who is their protector) are suborned to the poet's purpose of glorification of his seafaring nation. Camões writes back da Gama's odyssey into the classical mythological background, structuring his poem as an epic in the ancient style. In the expanse of his ten cantos, da Gama is able to relate the history and geography of Portugal to a Muslim (the friendly sultan of Malindi, who provided a pilot to guide the Portuguese across the Indian Ocean) and to a Hindu (the *samorin* of Malabar). And it is from another Muslim, Monsayeed of Morocco, that da Gama learns about the culture and history of India.

Nevertheless, despite these cosmopolitan exchanges, the *Lusíads* can be read as a statement of European culture against the long-standing dominance of Islam, and in that way it is in the tradition of Dante's *Divine Comedy* and Cervantes's *Don Quijote*. Moreover, whatever baroque elements may creep into the telling of his tale, the poet has brought the Cape firmly into the European, neoclassical heritage, albeit in an entirely new setting—that of Africa and its threatening physical demands.

THE LEGACY OF ADAMASTOR

Camões's image of Adamastor, dormant for some time, had a considerable revival among South African poets writing in English during the nineteenth century, as on the one hand a symbol of triumph over dark forces, and on the other a doubt as to whether victory had actually been achieved or was indeed achievable at all.

Two significant translations of the *Lusíads* had been made into English by the time these writers were versifying. The first was that done by Richard Fanshawe in 1655, reproducing the octavo form of the original but not allowing it to block the flow of the sentences leading up to the final couplet. While not necessarily obsessed with strict accuracy, Fanshawe's version, according to Landeg White, the latest translator of the epic into English, "reads throughout like a thinking man's version, conveying the intellectual excitement of opening up the world that remains central to the poem's meaning."[24] The same scholar expresses less enthusiasm for William Mickle's widely read version, in heroic couplets, of 1776. Not only does Mickle include material that is not in Camões, but he "obscure[s] the architecture of the *Lusíads*, its shaping and pacing, substituting rhythms wholly alien to the original."[25] Furthermore, his covert intention is to steal the epic from the Portuguese and instead hand it to his own fellow countrymen, dressed anew as a paean to British commercial prowess.

Whatever its limitations, it was probably Mickle's version that was most used by South African writers who, living in the shadow of the Cape, were enthused with the myth of Adamastor. The early treatment of the myth tended to emphasise the daunting challenges faced by da Gama and the early explorers, whether on account of the wildness of the seas or the hostility of the indigenes on land.

There is a buoyant tone to the opening lines of George Marshall's poem of 1812:

> From Afric's point the goddess bids me sing
> Elysian Fields, an ever-blooming spring!

This highly optimistic note is soon qualified by the introduction of a sinister undertone, hinting at dark forces lurking in the terrestrial paradise of the Cape:

> Forth from their dens, impatient of delay,
> The savage monsters prowl in search of prey.[26]

The tone of the poem becomes even more disillusioned when the poet considers the indigenous inhabitants: they are described as squalid savages, hostile to any idea of progress, scarcely belonging to the human race.[27]

That sinister undertone never entirely disappears from the writing of this period, although in some writers it is more ascribed to the harshness of nature than to failings in man. One of these voices is that of Thomas Pringle, who has been hailed as the father of South African poetry. His view of the Khoikhoi was remarkably progressive. At the Moravian missionary outpost in Bethelsdorp, Pringle was struck by the attentive and devout congregation lost in harmonious singing. He speculates on their pristine freedom, probably remembered by the older surviving generation among them.

Despite these sympathetic utterances, in his *African Sketches* (1834), Pringle issues an ominous warning about the physical dangers of the Cape.

> O Cape of Storms although thy front be dark,
> And bleak thy naked cliffs and cheerless vales,
> And perilous thy fierce and faithless gales
> To staunchest mariner and stoutest bark.[28]

In Pringle's hands, the myth of Adamastor becomes a distinctly discomforting one. While glad that the land where he feels affinity even to rocks and trees has been saved from the monster, there is a sense that a curse has been laid upon those who must live there and endure its physical turbulence. There is something unresolved in the poet's mind, something that cannot entirely make up for his joy in the love of his adopted land and its inhabitants. The poem presages the continuous theme of a tension between a European identity in an African setting that is disquieting and unsettling.

By the middle of the century, mid-Victorian confidence temporarily takes over. John Wheatley, writing in the 1830s, creates a biblical setting with da Gama's ship riding the heavy billows like the ark. Da Gama's voyage is seen as a crusade against the evil forces personified in Adamastor.

In William Roger Thompson's poem of 1868, a crescendo of national pride is linked to the glories of conquest.

> Land of 'Good Hope' thy future lies
> Bright 'fore my vision as the skies!
> O Africa! Long lost in night,
> Upon the horizon gleams the light
> Of breaking dawn.[29]

Adamastor's fierceness is gradually diminished: by the late nineteenth century the monster is reduced to the status of a quiet caretaker. D. C. F. Moodie writes:

> And here the patriarch in his old Cape home—
> A paradise of creeper, heath, and wood—
> Rules in benignant way; nor more to roam
> From ancient halls where lares stand and stood.[30]

Much of the old threat posed by the monster has gone, although in his poem of 1892, W. C. Scully returns to the theme of a demonic force. He sets the scene clearly in Table Bay, set between Devil's Peak and Lion's Head:

> On my right a demon stands,
> On my left a lion couches
> Year by year he, watching crouches;
> Where the foam lipped sea expands.[31]

In Scully's poem, having successfully battled through the perils of the Cape,

> [Da Gama] homeward passed, and told wild tales
> Of guardian giants—horrid gates—
> Perils to him who southward sails.[32]

In the new century, despite celebrating da Gama's achievement, the earlier, dormant disquiet reappears in the canon. Lance Fallaw tells his readers (1909):

> The Spirit of the Stormy Cape,
> That frown'd on Vasco's ships,
> Still wears at times that dreadful shape
> And speaks with threatening lips.[33]

However, the most powerful evocation of the Adamastor myth in the twentieth century was Roy Campbell's *Rounding the Cape* (1930). Campbell, a prodigy and rebel, was by this time an acknowledged poet of standing. After earlier journalistic writing aimed to *épater le bourgeois*, he achieved literary recognition with his poem *The Flaming Terrapin* (1924). Taking the form of an allegory about the great flood and how Noah survives it on the ark, *The Flaming Terrapin* was seen as an assertion of heroic survival in a postwar period of gloom and pessimism in Europe. Moreover, despite its biblical, universal setting, African aspects appear in the poem, which celebrates the grandeur and majesty of life in the wild. The narrative of Noah being guided by the terrapin alludes to a triumph in conquering the sea—more particularly, the sea around the Cape of Storms. The mythological status of the Cape is once more asserted.

In *Adamastor*, the poet engages directly with this dilemma of identity. The scene is set majestically:

> The low sun whitens on the flying squalls
> Against the cliffs the long grey surge is rolled
> Where Adamastor from his marble halls
> Threatens the sons of Lusus as of old.[34]

Adamastor's appearance is sinister, and although mariners have managed to round the Cape despite his presence, they are not confident that his reign is entirely over.

Campbell expresses that sentiment in this way:

Farewell, terrific shade! Though I go free
Still of the powers of darkness art thou Lord:
I watch the phantoms sinking in the sea
Of all that I have hated or adored.[35]

Campbell's poem, appearing in 1930, provided succeeding generations of
South African poets with a new lifeline to the Adamastor myth but one
that is disturbing in its ambivalence rather than triumphalist. Campbell
used Mickle's late eighteenth-century translation of the *Lusíads* (Campbell's own command of Portuguese was never as assured as his command
of Castilian, as many of his own Portuguese translations show). Campbell emphasises the paradoxical, twisted nature of the myth. The epic is a
confrontation between the known and the unknown, and it is not clear
which in the end triumphs.

Arnold Bennett, reviewing Campbell's work, says "Mr Campbell is
quite outrageously a poet. He has plenary inspiration. Emotions, crude and
primeval, surge out of him in terrific waves."[36] The "emotions, crude
and primeval" may have provided inspiration for the poet but it is an
inspiration of inner darkness rather than light.

Campbell's *Adamastor* was immediately hailed as a great work by the
critics. Desmond McCarthy proclaimed the birth of a book "destined to
be famous."[37] T. S. Eliot snatched it up for Faber, while Jonathan Cape,
Campbell's previous publisher, gnashed his teeth at having turned it
down. Campbell's own reputation was consolidated with the poem
(which soon became a best seller), but he does not fail to pay tribute to
Camões as a hero who "shouldered high his voluntary Cross."[38]

An important revival of the Adamastor myth was to come from a Portuguese poet whom Campbell had translated and who himself had
connections with Natal, where he was brought up—namely, Fernando
Pessoa. Pessoa's tone in *O Mensagem* (*The Message*) is elegiac, reviving
the dark side of the myth with its threatening undertone:

The monster who is at the end of the sea
In pitch black night went flying upwards;
Around the ship it flew three times,
Three times did it fly and screech
And said, "Who then dared enter
My inmost caverns, unrevealed,
My black roofs at the end of the world?
And the man at the helm said, trembling:
King John the Second!"[39]

It is this darkness "at the end of the world" that troubled Guy Butler, when
he produced a new translation of the Adamastor stanzas of the *Lusíads* in
1988. In his *Elegy*, Butler returns to the theme of the torn identity of a European exiled to the "Dark Continent," still threatened by the shadow of
Adamastor. So he says:

In all of us two continents contend:
Two skies of stars confuse us, on our maps
The long and latitudes contort and rend
Our universe to twenty-acre scraps.[40]

This confusion of identity continues into modern times. In the 1960s it is
linked in the poem of Roy Macnab once again with the very topography
of Table Bay:

Spill to a town that on its knees
Goes crawling backwards from the seas
To where in mist and myth far up
The Devil and the Dutchman sup.[41]

Musings about Adamastor and the image of "an old Titan moaning older
threats"[42] continued to haunt South African verse in the last decades of
the twentieth century. Many of the poets who alluded to it made direct

reference to Camões, but even when they did not, the shadow of doubt about identity either lost, stolen, or unacquired lurks in their thinking and stirs up seeds of doubt and disturbance. Others, of a more directly anti-colonialist stance, seem to wish to evoke the malediction promised by the monster—a revenge on Europeans who have entered and upset the equilibrium of a sustainable lifestyle in Africa, in Noel Mostert's words "that uneasy questioning of the dark side of universal involvement."[43] On whichever side of the divide—whether seeing the European arrival in Africa as an advance in the civilising of a "dark" continent or an intrusion into an idyll of noble savagery—the idea of a monster with evil intention has never disappeared from the imagination of South African writers.

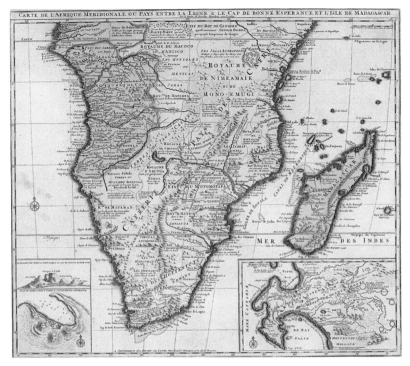

Figure 1. *Carte de L'Afrique,* by Nicolas Visscher, c. 1749 (copyright Parliament of the Republic of South Africa).

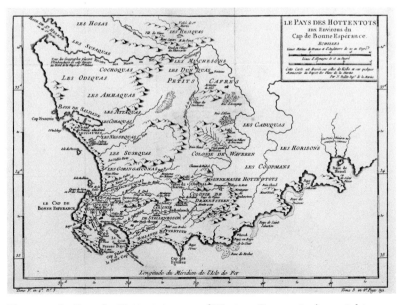

Figure 2. *Le Pays des Hottentots,* map of Western Cape, 1760 (copyright Parliament of the Republic of South Africa).

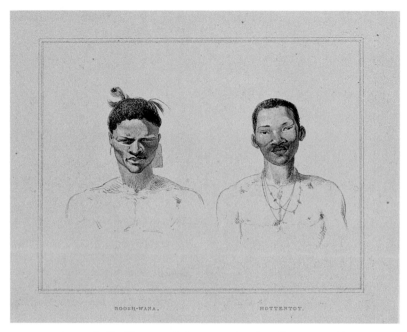

Figure 3. *San and Khoikhoi Heads*, by Samuel and William Daniell, 1801–1802 (copyright Parliament of the Republic of South Africa).

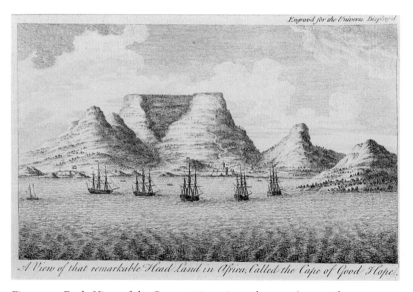

Engravd for the Universe Display'd

A View of that remarkable Head Land in Africa, Called the Cape of Good Hope.

Figure 4. *Early View of the Cape*, 1668, artist unknown (copyright Parliament of the Republic of South Africa).

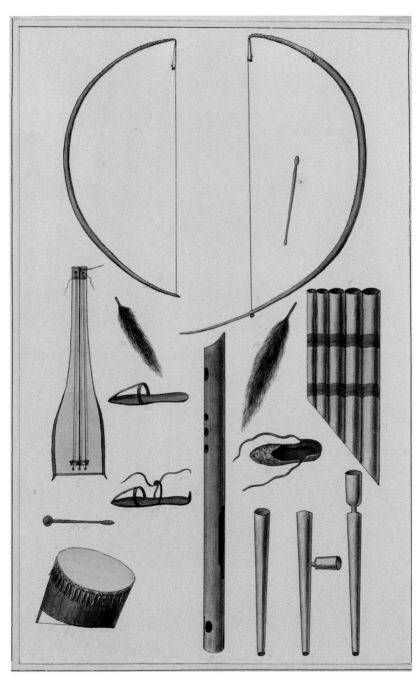

Figure 5. *Khoikhoi Musical Instruments,* by Samuel and William Daniell, 1820 (copyright Parliament of the Republic of South Africa).

Figure 6. Bust of Luís Vaz de Camões, Mozambique, 1920s (copyright Malcolm Jack, author).

Figure 7. *View of Table Bay*, 1790s, artist unknown (copyright Malcolm Jack, author).

Figure 8. *View of Table Mountain*, by François Le Vaillant, 1811 (copyright Parliament of the Republic of South Africa).

Figure 9. *Kodoo,* by François Le Vaillant, 1811 (copyright Parliament of the Republic of South Africa).

Figure 10. *Rhinoceros,* by François Le Vaillant, 1811 (copyright Parliament of the Republic of South Africa).

Figure 11. *Cape Gemsbok,* by François Le Vaillant, 1811 (copyright Parliament of the Republic of South Africa).

Figure 12. *Hottentot Square,* by Samuel Daniell, 1805 (copyright Parliament of the Republic of South Africa).

Figure 13. *Aloe dichotoma,* by François Le Vaillant, 1811 (copyright Parliament of the Republic of South Africa).

CHAPTER 3

Paradise Lost

BEFORE VAN RIEBEECK

In Rowland Raven-Hart's monumental collection of entries on travellers to the Cape, over 130 names are listed between 1572, the date of Camões's *Lusíads*, and 1652, the year when Jan van Riebeeck laid claim to an area of Table Bay for the Dutch East India Company (VOC). In some cases the travellers made more than one stop—typically the second being on the return journey from the East. There were considerable differences in their lengths of stay, sometimes prolonged by inclement weather forcing their ships to remain moored up in the harbour. The usual purpose of stopping at the Cape was to refresh supplies—particularly of water and meat—after voyages that took some months from Europe. The mix of nationalities of the visitors is marked: the Portuguese, English, Dutch, and French were the most frequent, but others in the employ of the VOC included Germans and Scandinavians. Their accounts, sometimes merely recording details of the voyages and ships, often also included observations on the locale and on the indigenous population that they met and with whom they attempted to barter or trade.

We have noted an elegiac tone in Camões's epic, reflecting the political reality that by the time it was published, Portuguese influence was beginning to decline. The English and Dutch were proving to be rivals on the profitable trade route to the East; Lisbon itself was losing its status as the only European port handling goods from India and further east. In 1578 the Portuguese suffered a severe setback in the campaign against the Moors that King Sebastião led in person to Morocco. At the battle of Alcácer Quibir, the king and the cream of the Portuguese aristocracy were killed in a disastrous battle with the enemy. Two years later, in 1580, Portugal was annexed by Spain, and the "Spanish domination" (as it has been labelled by some Portuguese historians) lasted until 1640. At first it seemed that Lisbon's pre-eminence might not be lost as Filipe I (II of Spain) considered locating the court there, but in the event the decision was made to stay in Madrid. The result was an exodus of talent from Portugal and a decline in maritime interest at the very time when rival ports in the north of Europe and in England were beginning to take significant volumes of trade away from what was once a near Portuguese monopoly.

As part of this political shift, English and Dutch explorers began to pay more attention to the Cape and the sea route to the East. The newcomers challenged what was seen as a deliberately off-putting picture of the area given out by the Portuguese, who had been extremely secretive about their knowledge (acquired over a long period) of the sea currents and best routes to navigate. A famous account ascribed to Sir Francis Drake in 1580, but possibly made by a member of his crew, highlighted the suspicion that the Portuguese had exaggerated difficulties so as to discourage their rivals: "From Iaua Maior we sailed for the Cape of Good Hope . . . we ran hard aboord the Cape, finding the report of the Portugals to be most false who affirme, that it is the most dangerous Cape of the world, never without intolerable stormes and present dangers to trauailers, which come neare the same. The Cape is the most stately thing, and the fairest Cape we saw in the whole circumference of the earth."[1]

A decade later a fuller account is given by Sir James Lancaster, whose party spent three weeks on shore searching for food and water after having experienced considerable difficulty in landing due to winds blowing them offshore. Once on land, the sailors managed to find some fowl and collect mussels on the beach; the Khoikhoi or Strandlopers (beachcombers) whom they had at first encountered disappeared and were not seen for some days. It was only when the sailors mounted an expedition inland that they found signs of habitation; the Khoikhoi then reappeared with bullocks and oxen, as well as sheep, which they traded for knives, copper, and other trinkets to wear as ornaments. Lancaster's men also went to Robben Island, where they hunted penguins and seals, while further inland they discovered red and fallow deer, as well as, more exotically, monkeys.[2]

From this and other early accounts a clearer image of the Khoikhoi begins to emerge, largely negative in tone. They are universally described as "savages," often considered to be barely human and sometimes accused of cannibalism. Johan von Mandelslo gives a typical summary in 1639: "The people found here are black, more resembling beasts than men; they give off a nasty smell because they smear their bodies with fish-oil, so that they shine from it. The hair of their heads, their noses and lips are not like those of the Moors. Their hair is stiff, wild and matted; their faces are full of wrinkles and ugly to see."[3] Mandelslo then goes on to describe the two main tribes—of "Watermen," who live near the shore scratching out a living on fish and roots, and the "Solthanimen" ("Saldanhians"), who keep cattle and goats but also do not cultivate the land, despite the fact that it is fertile enough to support all kinds of crops and fruit. Their animals, however, are well fed and look inviting to the hungry visitors. Mandelslo notices the peculiarities of the local sheep, which are "large, and strange in shape, with long hanging ears and a thick, fat tail weighing fifteen or twenty pounds; they have no curly wool like our sheep, but only hair."[4]

Although the Saldanhians lead a better life than the shore dwellers, there is still not much about them to report with favour. When the cattle they had sold to foreigners were killed on the shore, they would ask for the entrails, which they would eat raw and warm, without cleaning them, only shaking out the largest of the dung from the intestines of the animals with which they proceeded to smear their faces.

The smell given off by the Khoikhoi habit of rubbing their bodies in oil—as a protection against insects and inclement weather—is remarked upon over and over again by early visitors. Cornelis de Houtman (1595) says bluntly that they "always stank greatly,"[5] while Cornelis van Purmerendt a decade later, in 1609, observes: "The inhabitants of these lands are yellowish, like the Javanese, smearing themselves with some grease which makes them very ugly, indeed horrible, with around their necks the guts of beasts plaited two or three times together, with the skin of a beast around their upper bodies but otherwise naked except that their male organs are covered with a little scrap of skin about a hand wide and a span long."[6] The eating of the raw entrails of animals horrified most travellers even in an era when hygiene in Europe was not exemplary. Added to the unfounded slander that the Khoikhoi were cannibals, the Cape inhabitants are portrayed as a nasty species of highly dangerous savages. Here and there a redeeming physical feature is noted. Cornelis Matelief (1608) says:

> They are a large folk, not quite black, with curly hair, well made both of face and body, and very swift runners so that they can overtake a bull and catch him by the horns or the hind feet and so bring him to a standstill. Because of their greasing they can be smelt fully a rood downwind, and they look as if they have never washed in their lives. Around their body they have a leather thong, to which the tail of a fox or wildcat is fastened just in front of their privities.[7]

Another feature of the Khoikhoi that attracted a negative reaction was their language. Europeans claimed that the click sounds suggested an "inarticulate noise rather than a language"[8]; in another account, their mouths are described as sounding like a rattle.[9] Doubtless the tonal range of the click sounds, which we have already considered,[10] did nothing to ease the difficulty Europeans had in understanding the language, which was only mastered later by Dutch farmers who had been brought up by Khoisan servants.

Despite the existence of a rich Khoisan mythology, which we have also considered,[11] most Europeans ascribed no spiritual values to the locals and certainly not any intelligible religion. The lack of a written language meant that their customs and traditions were not recorded and could only be discovered by close observation of their rituals and practices. Most of the early visitors were not inclined to study that behaviour. A typical conclusion is that of Seyger van Rechteren (1629), an interpreter, who says "that no laws, policies, religions or ordinances can be discovered to exist among them."[12]

Aspersions were also cast upon their moral character. Willem ten Rhyne accuses them of being vicious and says: "In faithlessness, inconstancy, lying, cheating, treachery and infamous concern with every kind of lust they exercise their villainy. They are so bloody in their inclinations as to practice their cruelties even upon their vanquished enemies after their death, by striking their arrows and weapons into their dead carcasses."[13]

While the great majority of early travellers recorded these negative opinions, there were some exceptions. Even while condemning the locals for idleness and lack of foresight, a number of Europeans remarked upon their physical prowess and, to that extent, were acknowledging their adaptation to the environment in which they lived. The first slightly less hostile portrait of the locals is given by the Dane Jón Ólaffson, who arrived on board the *Christianahaven* in 1623. Although he and his party were wary of people reputed to be cannibals, he observes: "They are black, smiling, mild-eyed, with curly hair somewhat like the wool of young lambs. Their lower lip drops somewhat, and they have snow white teeth."[14] Moreover, they could be jolly, especially when engaged in dancing: "Their dance was after this fashion; on uttering the word 'Hottentot' they snapped two of their fingers and clicked their tongue and feet, all in tune."[15] In 1624 William Minors, an Englishman, is even more positive: "You may please to take notice that we had good quarter with the Saldanians, more than was expected, so much never as before, shewing themselves very affable and tractable unto us, and not so base and beastlike disposition, and voyde of all reason as commonly it hath been reported of them."[16]

However, the most comprehensive and favourable account is given in a report to the directors of the VOC by Leendert Janszen and Matthijs Poort in 1649. The authors admit that the Khoikhoi are without laws and government, but they ascribe their hostility to Europeans as arising from something never mentioned—namely, that their cattle are often seized and taken from them, often without payment, something that would provoke the same response if it happened in Europe among the peasantry. The authors of the report believe that, if treated properly, the locals will behave well, and they record the Khoikhoi coming "with all friendliness to barter" with their cattle and sheep[17] to the great benefit of the crew of the passing ship, *Princesse Roijael*. A policy of fair treatment and good relations would lead to a highly beneficial regime for both Europeans and locals, but it would require wise leadership by a commander who would be respected for fair dealing.

A generation later, Olfert Dapper, whose account was based on various written sources, points out to the Khoikhoi generosity in sharing whatever they have among themselves and their intolerance of offences such as theft,[18] but he still refers to the barbaric habit of eating the entrails and guts of animals raw.[19]

These latter accounts, somewhat more balanced and just, mitigate something of the negative tone of many travellers in their assessment of the "other," but they do not influence the view of the majority of visitors and, even less, the settlers. Over the generations, the Khoikhoi were generally regarded as savages, degraded and barely human, who had the good fortune to live in an earthly paradise.[20]

1652 AND ALL THAT

The sixth of April 1652 is a date of considerable significance in South African history, for it is the day when Jan Anthonissen van Riebeeck, originally an assistant surgeon in the employ of the VOC, made a claim to land in Table Bay and thereby started the first permanent European settlement.

Van Riebeeck hailed from a middle-class family from Culemburg and had joined the VOC for adventure and to make his fortune after completing his apprenticeship as a surgeon. Before coming to the Cape, he had switched from medical support to administration of commerce, having worked in Batavia and also acted as head of the trading post in Tonkin, Vietnam. He had also visited Japan, where the Dutch had ousted the Portuguese (who had held a monopoly of the valuable silk trade) and set themselves up on the island of Dejima, near Nagasaki. These experiences gave him a very solid grounding in the way the VOC was run and what the commercial interests of the Dutch were in the East. They also greatly influenced his policy at the Cape, since he would have readily understood its importance in supplying ships on their way to and back from the company's widespread Eastern trading posts.

In 1647, following the shipwreck of the VOC ship *Haerlem*, a group of the company's seamen remained behind in Table Bay for a year before returning to Europe. Serendipitously their stay turned out to be a test of the possibility of establishing a permanent post at the Cape. Salvaging cargo from the wreck, they survived by bartering some of its contents with the Khoikhoi in exchange for food and other supplies. Van Riebeeck was on one of the ships returning from Batavia that collected the men a year later, giving him a chance to question them firsthand about local conditions. The decision of the directors of the VOC (the "Herren XVII") was greatly influenced by the report of Janszen and Poort, two of the VOC group who had spent the year in the Cape. As well as putting aside criticism of the locals as we have seen, the authors say: "The soil in the said [Table] valley is very good and fruitful and in the dry season all the water one could wish for could be led through the gardens with little toil. Everything will grow there as well as anywhere in the world, especially pumpkins, water-melons, cabbages, carrots, radishes, turnips, onions, garlic and all sorts of vegetable (as those of the shipwrecked ship *Haerlem* found to be the case, and can testify to it)."[21]

Turning to the subject of governance, the reporters say:

If the proposed fort is provided with a good commander, treating the natives with kindness, and gratefully paying for everything bartered from them, and entertaining some of them with stomach-fulls of peas or beans (which they are greatly partial to) then nothing whatever would need to be feared, but in time they would learn the Dutch language, and through them the inhabitants of Soldania bay and of the interior might well be brought to trade, of whom however nothing definite can be said.[22]

Such a commander the directors deemed was van Riebeeck. He was despatched with clear instructions not to colonise the Cape (in the sense of seizing tracts of land) but rather to secure a limited base, treat with the indigenous peoples, and set up a station that would be able to provide VOC ships headed for the East, and returning from there, with all the provisions that they needed. Cape affairs would be managed by the Council of India in Batavia as well as from the directors in Holland. While a governor-general presided in the East, van Riebeeck was given the rank of a mere commander at the Cape.[23] VOC policy was strictly commercial: as much profit as possible with as little expenditure as possible was its central feature. Given hostilities with England, it was essential to set up some defensive system at Table Bay in case of attack from the sea. By the time of van Riebeeck's return journey to the Cape a few years later, a Council of Policy or coordinating body had been set up to manage the new settlement. The council met on board his ship, the *Dromederis*, as it sailed south. The minutes of these meetings began a long and detailed record of the Dutch period at the Cape, first as a refuelling base and later as a colony that lasted for almost a century and a half, until the first British occupation of 1795.

Van Riebeeck followed VOC policy to the letter. He first began by building a fort on the foreshore, as well as establishing a system from Signal Hill to warn of ships coming toward Table Bay, indicating whether they were flying friendly or hostile flags. The system worked well. To provide the necessary vegetables and fruit, he began planting an extended garden—the beginning of the Company Gardens in the middle of Cape Town—but the first crop produced was washed away by torrential rain. The greatest problem remained securing a supply of meat, which had to be done by bargaining not with the "Peninsulars" (Strandlopers) living nearby (because they had no cattle or sheep, subsisting as they did on fish, mussels, and wild vegetables) but with the Cochoqua and Guriqua ("Saldanhians"), who lived further up the coast and a little inland and who had vast herds of cattle and flocks of sheep. These nomadic Khoikhoi were very reluctant to trade animals even for the coveted copper that the Dutch could give them in exchange; they themselves rarely killed their livestock except on special occasions, otherwise only eating animals that had died. When the bargaining became too strident for their tastes, to the extreme frustration of the commander, the herders simply vanished with their herds and flocks inland. Van Riebeeck expresses his surprise at this behaviour: "They are an extraordinary people: they suddenly withdraw and drive away their cattle as if they were terrified of something, although we do all in our power to satisfy them in every way. The result was that today we did not secure more than 1 cow, 1 calf and 11 sheep, for more copper and tobacco than we had ever given."[24] Food supplies dwindled, and conditions at the settlement became grim. Another difficult problem facing van Riebeeck was a severe shortage of manpower. The original group of settlers numbered little more than a hundred people. It was impossible to get all the work done on the fort, in the gardens, and on military duty from such a limited number of people, often further depleted by illness. Work on the fortifications came to a standstill for months. Moreover, it proved impossible to recruit the local Strandlopers, who were "jealous of their freedom"[25] and unwilling to engage in hard labour for any length of time. VOC policy prevented van Riebeeck from conscripting them, and he began to think of importing labour.

Van Riebeeck's service in the Far East had also made him familiar with the VOC slave trade, which followed the Portuguese monopoly of the trade that had existed before.[26] Slaves were shipped from Bengal and Aracan to the headquarters in Batavia. The conditions on the slave ships were extreme, with many deaths en route. In Batavia itself, the slave population outnumbered the European by five to one. Chinese slaves were particularly valued for their skills, as were the Malays who later came to the Cape. The first slave to reach the Cape appears to have been one Abraham van Batavia, who arrived in 1653. In 1654 a small number of slaves were brought to the Cape from Madagascar, but in the years that followed, Angola and Guinea on the West African coast became the principal sources of supply. Before long the numbers of slaves being imported increased, with arrivals housed in the Slave Lodge in the centre of the growing town. At first the expense of ownership confined slave owners to the higher-level VOC officials who resided in Cape Town. Few slaves were found in the farms outside, where labour came from Khoisan conscripts. The slaves were regarded as valuable commodities to be looked after carefully. An entry in van Riebeeck's journal for 17 April 1658 makes that clear:

> Arrangements were started for establishing a school for the Company's male and female slaves brought here from Angola by the *Amersfoort*, which had taken them off a prize Portuguese slaver. . . . To encourage the slaves to attend and hear or learn the Christian prayers, it is ordered that after school everyone is to receive a small glass of brandy and two inches of tobacco. All their names are to be written down and those who have none, are to be given names, paired or unpaired, young or old. All this is to be done in the presence of the Commander, who will attend for a few days to put everything in proper order and subject these people to proper discipline, signs of which are already apparent. All slaves are also being properly clothed to protect them against the daily increasing cold.[27]

Despite that care over their welfare, insubordination or desertion on the part of slaves was harshly treated, as it was among Company employees.

As well as running away, slaves sought revenge on their masters by committing arson, with particularly serious consequences in dry seasons.[28]

Relations with the Khoikhoi were also difficult on account of language. Van Riebeeck had to rely on the services of Autshumato (a local leader known as "Harry" or "Herry") as an interpreter, mentioned as one "who speaks a little English."[29] Harry had had much to do with visiting English fleets and had sailed to Java in English service. There is a tone of lingering suspicion in van Riebeeck's journal, which suggests that he may have thought that Harry's loyalty lay more with the English than with the VOC. However, in the earliest days, Harry guides an expedition over the mountain to a "beautifully closed bay with many fine forests" and protection from the wind.[30] This was Hout Bay, which, with its sheltered harbour, for a while seemed a more attractive option for basing the new settlement than Table Bay.

Throughout the diary Harry is frequently mentioned, usually as a go-between in negotiations with the cattle-owning Saldanhians and other interior tribes, though at times van Riebeeck's suspicions were fuelled by requests from some of those tribes to deal directly with him rather than through Harry. When negotiations did take place, Harry spent hours in long discussions with the chiefs, without giving the commander a clear idea of what was being agreed. Moreover, Harry proved elusive, sometimes disappearing for months on end and then reappearing with a deal he had clinched with the tribes of the interior. The main bartering commodity was copper, highly prized by the Khoikhoi and used by the Dutch in exchange for cattle. With limited numbers of men, van Riebeeck could not send out too many expeditions to track down and barter with the ceaselessly moving nomadic cattle owners of the interior. He therefore had to rely on Harry and another interpreter, one Doman, to do business for him.

Van Riebeeck found it increasingly difficult to maintain the VOC policy of friendliness toward the locals, although he was later described by François Le Vaillant as "an able peacemaker."[31] He considered that the

Khoikhoi responded insolently to his courteous and generous overtures. A tone of deep frustration enters the *Journal*:

> Although our men nevertheless adopted a friendly and amicable attitude and invited them [the Khoikhoi] to trade, they, on the contrary, insulted our men the more, giving the sick-comforter a hard thump on the chest and the bookkeeper Verburgh a lusty clout on the head, so that if they had not been a little forbearing, a new rupture in the alliance could easily have been caused. But as our instructions are rather to suffer somewhat than to come to blows, our men thereupon, to avoid further contention, returned without giving to any of them a bit of tobacco or anything else.[32]

Incidents between the newcomers and the indigenous inhabitants occurred regularly but, as the *Journal* entries show, his men had to be restrained from taking revenge on what they perceived as ill behaviour and treachery on the part of the locals. Van Riebeeck remarks on the lack of discipline among the Khoikhoi and their inexplicable changes of mood and unwillingness to co-operate. In an attempt to corral them into the system, van Riebeeck designated various leaders as "captains," who were entitled to carry a baton of authority given to them in the name of the Honourable Company.

By 1654 progress had been made on defences. Bricks known as Leiden bricks—partially mud—were made locally and used to strengthen the walls of the fort. The signalling system that had been set up on Signal Hill was working effectively. As Anglo-Dutch hostilities ceased, one of the most dangerous enemies, the English, no longer had to be contained; indeed, when passing the Cape they could actually be entertained at the fort, as they were on a number of occasions. The fort soon became a symbol of the strength and authority of the newcomers—when hostilities from other tribes threatened the Strandlopers, they would seek protection by camping outside its walls, which their enemies would not dare to approach lest they themselves were fired on by the Dutch cannons within.

The problem of food supplies continued to be serious. Although in most seasons there was a good supply of water streaming down from the mountain, the weather was unpredictable, and several times violent winds and searing heat destroyed the crops that were being grown in the Company Gardens. Six months after arriving, in his journal entry, van Riebeeck attempts to put a brave face on an increasingly difficult situation:

> Meanwhile we are at present provided with only 89 cattle and 284 sheep, young and old, from which we have to feed the men on land every day, as the Dutch victuals are finished and for a long time no fish have been caught. If no more cattle are obtained—and for this we see little hope as the Saldanhians would already appear to have been glutted with copper—a rather modest supply of fresh meat will be left for the ships. We shall live in good hope, however, until such time as it may please the Almighty to send us a better supply.[33]

A further threat to livestock came from wild animals. Lions still roamed the Cape, as well as hyena. A typical *Journal* entry records that: "Last night a sheep in the kraal was almost totally devoured by a wild beast, notwithstanding the fact that throughout the night a man was walking through and round the kraal with a musket and burning linstock, and every now and again answering the call of the patrol guard on the ramparts of the fort."[34] In an attempt to improve the situation, exploration of the area around Table Bay, and particularly of Robben Island, began. Members of the early expedition to Robben Island found not only the seals after which the place was named but also good grazing land for sheep. Rabbits too abounded (as they did on Dassen Island), and soon a community was set up on Robben Island, with strict regulatory instructions, to supply the main base in Table Bay. Van Riebeeck himself later visited both islands "to investigate the local conditions more closely."[35] The Company Gardens continued to be cultivated, with a variety of vegetables and fruit better suited to the local conditions being grown there.

As time went on, the besieged commander began to realise that to improve the supply situation effectively so that the growing demand for food supplies could be met, there would have to be a change of policy that would allow settlers from Europe to own land and, as farmers, to supply food for the garrison and for passing ships. These settlers were given tracts of sometimes extensive land and soon began to produce butter and milk and crops of a more realistic amount needed for the growing Cape Town community and the passing ships. Although tied to conditions of contract with the VOC administration, the giving of land to individuals was a significant step that changed the nature of the settlement from a staging post to a colony, though one where there was no clear embargo on sexual fraternisation between the different communities.[36] Under Harry's leadership, the Khoikhoi tried, unsuccessfully, to resist the continuous invasion of their hunting grounds.

The piecemeal nature of the extension of the colony was a result of individuals who pushed beyond the barriers of the frontier. Karel Schoeman gives examples such as that of the Coetzee family, whose first member gave up his profession as a tailor to farm land and whose family moved further out toward Stellenbosch as land around Cape Town itself was taken up.[37] He explains that expansion was "a matter of independent and isolated movements by individual hunters, traders and cattle farmers, largely pragmatic and opportunistic by nature, in the case of farmers sometimes merely on a temporary basis in search of grazing."[38] In that latter respect the newcomers were imitating the nomadic habits of their Khoikhoi predecessors on the land.

The redoubtable commander was still beset with problems of all sorts. Khoikhoi groups would make night raids to steal cattle; shortages of food led to thefts by his own men. In the latter cases punishment was very severe, as the *Journal* entry of 17 January 1656 records: "To set an example to the others, Gerrit Carstensen of Swol, arquebusier, and Severijn Abrahamsen of The Hague, soldier, were today sentenced for stealing from the gardens. They have to perform menial labour in chains for half a year, to receive corporal punishment of 50 lashes administered by the provost-marshal, and, in addition, to forfeit one month's pay. This sentence was executed today."[39]

An early visitor, Johan Jakob Saar, remarks upon van Riebeeck's tough leadership: "The Commander here had treated the poor soldiers of the garrison set there as harshly and as miserably as if they had been less than serfs and slaves. In the day they had to cut wood in the forests, and by night continually stand their watches."[40] By enforcing this strict regime, van Riebeeck was able to maintain personal authority, but he was known also for fairness and respected by the Khoikhoi for his interest in their affairs (not always shared by his successors) and for keeping his word on promises. However, as George Theal says, the "one object ever present in his mind [was] the gain of the Honourable Company."[41] His own small house was located within the fort, and early on mention is made of the adoption into the household of a young girl called Krotoa or Eva, niece of Harry, the interpreter. Schoeman wonders about the mutual relations that must have existed within the crowded family home, for the van Riebeecks had several children and a staff of slaves to perform domestic chores.[42]

Eva soon learned Dutch, became a Christian, and dressed in a European style. She appears to have learned Portuguese as well—the lingua franca of the slaves—and soon began to assume the role of an interpreter, unusual for a woman. She had particularly good relations with the Saldanhians and other cattle-owning tribes and was therefore an important go-between. When she left the fort to negotiate trade with them, she reverted to dressing with traditional skin cloths and seemed to be entirely accepted despite her new life in the VOC fold. In time she married a Dutchman, Pieter Van Mierhoff, living with him on Robben Island. There she stayed after his death, as her alcohol-fuelled behaviour no longer made her welcome in Cape Town.

Less is known about another Khoikhoi interpreter, Doman (Khaikana), whose "gifts as an interpreter were highly regarded by Van Riebeeck."[43] Doman took on the job when relations with the immediate inhabitants of

Table Bay were deteriorating, as the demands on both sides could no longer be made matters of compromise. For their part the Khoikhoi raided settlers' livestock by night, while the settlers became ever greedier to possess more land. In a move of defiance, the Khoikhoi encamped on the edge of the moat surrounding the fort, declaring that in their own land they could set up their tents wherever they liked. Van Riebeeck's granting of land to settlers in the Liesbeek Valley (from about 1657) was bound to exacerbate the already difficult relationship, since that was a traditional area used by the Khoikhoi for grazing their cattle.

Doman himself was of humbler stock than Harry and Eva, but clearly he was a bright character. In the traditional VOC way, he was sent to Batavia to improve his Dutch and learn more about the commercial business of the Company. However, that was not all he learned, for the trip made him realize the vulnerability of the Company ships if they were not adequately supplied. On returning to the Cape, after serving as interpreter for a while, Doman disappeared, only to reappear in 1659 as leader of Khoikhoi raiders on the settlers' farms, aimed at interrupting the supply chain both to the fort and to ships refuelling in Table Bay. Doman's force managed to capture most of the farms, but they could not storm the well-protected fort, to which the Dutch farmers retreated with their remaining livestock. In one of the attacks, Doman himself was injured. His failure in leading the rebellion lost him the support of his followers; he died in relative obscurity in 1663.[44]

THE SETTLEMENT BECOMES A COLONY

In 1673, after van Riebeeck had left, there was a major Khoikhoi attack on the settlers. A Dutch hunting group had been robbed the year before, but on this occasion seven members of a hippopotamus hunting group were killed. The leader of the Chocoqua was Gonnema (a captain), who during van Riebeeck's time had been received at the fort when he had accompanied Oudasoa, the chief of the tribe, on an official visit. At the time the command of the Cape forces was in the hands of Isjbrand Goske, a military man who had seen service in the East. He planned a vigorous response, sending off an expedition of heavily armed soldiers supported by some of the other Khoikhoi tribes who had always been enemies of the Chocoqua, whom they resented. Despite the rainy conditions, the campaign was a success, particularly as the Dutch forces had the support of Dorha, or Claas, who brought a group of men to help in the garrison. Claas was a petty captain of the Chainouqua who also acted as an important trader in the endless demand for cattle and sheep by the Dutch. He organised many expeditions to the interior. His privileged status included invitations to the castle (as the fort had become), but later as he himself became financially independent, he became less keen on serving the VOC. At one point he was seized and imprisoned on Robben Island, but he was later released.

The success of these campaigns against the Khoikhoi and the gradual expansion of the area in which Dutch farmers were settling, including the fertile lands east of the Liesbeek River, amounted to a change in the nature of the VOC Cape from settlement to colony. Ironically this change took place under the commander (and symbolically later governor) Simon van der Stel, who was himself of mixed race since his mother was the daughter of a freed Indian slave woman. Born in Mauritian waters where his father was the commander, van der Stel spent a considerable part of his childhood in Batavia. Through influential connections in the Netherlands he was appointed commander of the Cape in 1679.

Van der Stel approached his duties with great energy—tackling the important matter of completing the castle, starting a market in the town, and extending the range of crops grown in the Company Gardens. Foreseeing the expansion of the settlements outside the town, he encouraged partnerships whereby the farmers, in exchange for land rights, were contracted to supply specified numbers of cattle and sheep to the Company, as well as foodstuffs (wheat, rye, and barley) on a regular basis and at fixed prices. He also encouraged the planting of vines and fruit orchards, realising that Stellenbosch was an important centre of supply for Cape Town. Not only did he found the village itself, but he also set up a system of local administration to run the community of settlers once they were already set up there. In Cape Town itself, he took steps to improve sanitation, medical care, and schooling. By 1684 the colony was self-sufficient in foodstuffs.[45]

The reputation of the Company Gardens spread far and wide. A decade later, in 1695, Sir William Temple in his book on gardening records:

> The picture I have met with in some relations of a garden made by a Dutch governor of their colony, upon the Cape de Bonne Esperance, is admirable, and described to be of an oblong figure, of very large extent, and divided into four quarters, by long and cross walks, ranged with all sorts of orange trees, lemons, limes and citrons; each of these four quarters is planted with the trees, fruits, flowers, and plants that are native and proper to each of the four parts of the world; so as in this one enclosure are to be found the several gardens of Europe, Asia, Africa and America.[46]

So enthusiastic is Temple that he labels the gardens as the contemporary gardens of Hesperides, wherever the original garden may have been.[47]

One of the most interesting visitors to Cape Town during this period was a Jesuit priest, Father Guy Tachard, who arrived in 1685. He was part of a mission that the French King Louis XIV sent to Siam to develop relations with that country, including sharing with them the latest advances in astronomical sciences. The expedition was well equipped with telescopes, microscopes, and thermometers. Tachard set up an observatory in Cape Town and began to study the southern skies. As Jesuits, the priests might have fallen under suspicion, so Tachard decided to make a direct approach to Governor van der Stel on arrival to explain exactly what they were doing. He was cordially received, as he tells us: "We were greatly surprised to find such refinement at the Cape of Good Hope, and very much more so by the attentions and marks of friendship which we received at this first interview."[48] To foster this good relationship, Tachard makes sure that the authorities are kept informed of what he is doing, and officials are even invited to the observatory to take part in examining the skies through his telescope. On one occasion the officials stayed until ten o'clock in the evening, watching Tachard taking his measurements and using the equinoctial quadrant. As well as founding the study of the southern skies by identifying thitherto unknown constellations, Tachard's work provided new means of adjusting longitudinal readings of the Cape and thereby of correcting previous, less accurate charts.

However, Tachard's account of his time at the Cape covers many aspects other than his scientific breakthroughs. He is interested in the flora of the Cape, admiring both the indigenous and foreign plantings in the Company Gardens. He has sketches of insects—lizards particularly seemed to appeal to him—and exotic animals such as the quagga added to his book as illustrations. He records with some amusement that "large monkeys"[49] (presumably baboons) descend from Table Mountain to steal fruit from the Company Gardens.

As to the Khoikhoi, his initial opinion of them was rather orthodox and negative—their lack of hygiene, their habit of smearing themselves in foul-smelling oils, and their use of entrails of animals as bodily decorations are all remarked upon with distaste. But unlike many travellers of the time, he does not see these habits as ruling out their having a moral character. Indeed he sees virtue in their behaviour: they are loyal and good-natured; the Khoikhoi "are neither cruel nor fierce, and do not lack docility and wit. Every day this is becoming clearer."[50]

He notes that their good nature is shown by their generosity in sharing everything with their fellows, even when there is little to go round. What they seem most reluctant to do is to lose their pristine liberty and be bound to the constraints that inevitably come by living in a settled society. However, even more worrying for the devout priest is their lack of knowledge of Christianity. On that matter he says, "but their great misfortune, which cannot sufficiently be deplored, is that so many and so populous tribes have no knowledge of the true God, and that no one tries to instruct them."[51] Given what seems to be a lack of understanding of religion in a formal sense and a reluctance to be tied down to the obligations of social life, progress toward integration of the Khoikhoi into colonial life will be slow, but if the effort were made to win them over, it could be successful. Moreover, given the abundance and fertility of the land, the integration of the local community would turn the Cape Colony into a highly attractive place.

Despite the economic progress during this period and the efforts of van der Stel, there was widespread unrest among the settler community. The free burghers in the town resented the restrictions on their trading activities imposed by the Company, which they considered was impeding economic progress. The farmers, for their part, resented the fact that they could not charge prices that they considered appropriate for their products but were bound by the Company's fixed pricing system. The ban on bartering with the Khoikhoi added to their annoyance. Furthermore, there was a direct conflict of interest between the VOC's policy of wanting to keep costs to a minimum and the colonists' attempts to inflate the price of their produce to make the more comfortable living to which they felt entitled.

During van der Stel's tenure of command a significant group of immigrants, the French Huguenots, arrived in the Cape in 1688. Although some French Protestants had joined the VOC and come to the Colony at an earlier period, their emigration came about as a result of Louis XIV's revocation of the Edict of Nantes, which had guaranteed religious freedom to Protestants. In 1685 a small number—less than 200—of the 5,000 Huguenots who fled from France to Holland, fearing persecution, arrived in the Cape.

Van der Stel was keen to absorb these impoverished, but skilled, refugees into the dwindling European population of the Cape, while at the same time he was concerned that the newcomers should be loyal to the Dutch regime. Accordingly, although they were granted land in the

Franschoek area, establishing a French-speaking community with its own pastor, van der Stel dispersed some of them among the various Dutch landowners so that integration would take place more easily. Among the skills brought by the Huguenots was that of wine production, something appreciated by van der Stel—who had planted his own vines at his estate in Constantia, his place of retirement, in 1699.

The policy of assimilation worked. For a while the Huguenots tried to maintain an entirely distinct French-speaking community, even teaching the Khoikhoi who worked for them the language. Church services were held in French, as were the names given to their homes and school. However, the Huguenots realised that they had to deal with the Cape Town authorities in Dutch. Within a generation or two, they had entirely integrated into the Dutch community, and the use of French disappeared among a younger generation. Eighteenth-century French visitors, including Abbé Nicolas Louis de La Caille and Le Vaillant, note the almost total disappearance of the language.[52]

For their part the Khoikhoi, from the 1690s onward, were increasingly assimilated into the colonial society as labourers or servants, having already been the providers of livestock. Richard Elphick says that by this time "both Khoikhoi men and women milked the farmers' cows, there being no taboo in Khoikhoi culture against female contact with cattle. In addition, they knew how to slaughter; to treat skins and hides; to render animal fat; and manufacture skin bags, *veldschoenen,* whips and thongs. These skills enable their employers to capitalise on the by-products, not only of pastoralism, but also of the hunt."[53] They would soon be trained to make butter and soap, important sources of revenue for the Boer farmers, and to act in various domestic roles in the household. As guides and interpreters, the Khoikhoi also played an important part in the settlers' dealings with the Xhosa inhabiting the areas to the east of the expanding colony.

This assimilation was not welcomed by all. There were periodic frontier clashes and uprisings within the settled areas. A series of so-called

Bushmen's Wars took place in 1739, 1754, and again in the 1770s. While at first the VOC attempted to settle disputes by mediation, maintaining the policy of co-operating with the locals whenever possible, it gradually lost control of the situation. The attempt to draw boundaries to the colony had to be constantly revised, as expansion took place de facto. It was often after the event that details of disturbances and how they had been dealt with were reported to the governor in distant Cape Town, with its organised governance and clearly defined social hierarchy.

The frontier battles were fought by self-organised commando units formed by the farmers and largely outside the VOC's control. As the Boer settlers moved into areas such as the Nieuwveld and Sneuberg, occupied by the San as well as the Khoikhoi, they met with resistance and reprisal raids on their cattle stocks. The fighting became more ruthless as the extension of the colony moved further north and east. Elphick records:

> The "Bushman War" of 1739 was a turning point in the evolution of the commando. Freeburghers in threatened areas were for the first time made subject to compulsory commando service, though they were free to bring their Khoisan dependents along. The commandos of 1739 were almost certainly more violent than their predecessors. They attacked all the Khoisan communities they could find, sequestering livestock and weapons and killing or wounding their members.[54]

The Bushmen had taken up European technology, so that stolen firearms were used in the place of the traditional bows and arrows and *assegai*. Their attacks on settler farms were also violent—slaves were kidnapped, and such crops as they could not carry away were destroyed. At a later date the Cape authorities themselves reconstituted the commando system, recruiting mixed-race Bastaards as well as Khoisan in their ranks. The commandos raided areas of San territory indiscriminately, meting out death and destruction to anyone who crossed their path. There was little regard to the framework of law as laid down by the VOC.

The emergence of the Bastaards indicated the extent of miscegenation that had taken place in the colony. Typically offspring of a European male and a Khoisan female, the Bastaards, with their Dutch surnames, regarded themselves as superior to the Khoisan and were accorded a different status in the colonial hierarchy. Brought into the Dutch Reformed Church by being baptised, they were registered as free burghers and were permitted to own property, such as farms leased by the Company. They gradually became an economic force and figured prominently in the expansion into the northern zone of the colony.

Khoikhoi men and women who had been captured were taken into the service of the advancing settlers, since at first there was little slave labour in the interior, away from Cape Town and its environs. During the eighteenth century the price of slaves became more affordable, and the slave population throughout the colony increased exponentially and was less confined to Cape Town itself. By the end of the century the slave population marginally outnumbered both the white free burghers and the Khoisan.[55] Some of the slaves freed by manumission formed a social group of their own, still speaking the Portuguese and Malay patois of their ancestors. By 1834 there were 36,000 slaves in the colony, approximately six times the number of the white population.[56] Meanwhile, several smallpox epidemics, the worst in 1755, had greatly reduced the Khoikhoi population.

Meanwhile a significant Muslim community had been established in Cape Town. A series of learned religious leaders—some of whom, like Sheik Yusuf (1626–1699), were political prisoners, banished from Batavia for opposing Dutch rule—began to preach in the Cape. For a long period mosques were not allowed to be built, so worship had to take place in private places. Sheik Yusuf is regarded as the founder of the Cape Muslim community. In 1770 the sage Tuan Guru wrote various significant pamphlets while a prisoner on Robben Island. These teachers encouraged conversion among the slave population. The Muslim community soon showed the wide mixture of ethnicities, including Javanese, Arabic, Indian, Ceylonese, European, and African, that made up the population of Cape Town. The language of this community became Arabic Afrikaans: the first book written in Afrikaans was in that script. Eventually, a circle of *kramats*, or sites of holy tombs, surrounded the city.[57]

Cape Town itself continued to grow and be embellished with new architectural features. Grander houses, with great descending staircase balconies (*stoeps*) leading down to the street, appeared in the grid system of the Strand and Long Street, with the Buitenkant as the eastern border of the town. Some of these houses were of considerable proportions, with public rooms at the front and extended servants' quarters and storehouses at the rear. The merchants who owned them commissioned furniture for the interiors, often made of local wood such as stinkwood but reflecting Dutch style. However, two of the most significant of the architectural refinements were made to public buildings. They were the work of Anton Anreith, the sculptor who had come to the Cape in 1777. The first was at the castle, where—together with the architect L. M. Thibault—he redesigned the so-called Kat Gate. The architect G. E. Pearse comments on this work: "It is singularly graceful and the elevation is well proportioned in all its detail. Flanked by curved steps leading to a landing, it is paved with Robben Island slate, greenish in colour. The steps are also of slate. The central balustrade, in wrought iron, is a splendid example of craftsmanship."[58] The second of Anreith's works, his masterpiece (namely, the pulpit of the Lutheran Church in Strand Street), was also done in the same period. During the long VOC period, the Dutch Reformed Church had been the only church allowed to hold religious services in the colony. As the Lutheran community at Cape Town steadily increased, the directors in Holland were petitioned to allow its followers to hold services in their own church. Finally permission was given in 1780, and a barn was converted into the first Lutheran Church. Five years later Anreith was commissioned to rework the facade of the church and design the wooden pulpit in high rococo style. Herculean figures hold up the pulpit; a swan,

Martin Luther's symbol, is an additional adornment. The facade of the church itself became a great landmark of the town, sketched by numerous artists, including Lady Anne Barnard (figure 22).[59]

The End of the VOC Period

Tensions between VOC officials and the colonists continued to simmer throughout the period. During the governorship of Willem Adriaan van der Stel the free burghers petitioned the directors of the VOC, complaining of the restrictions put upon them by the officials who, in the meantime, enjoyed a high standard of living themselves. Among the most egregious cases was the governor himself, who "had been granted the 400 morgen estate of Vergelegen in the Hottentots Holland (subsequently enlarged by a further 117 morgen) which he set to transform into a productive giant. Using company slaves and servants as if they were his own, van der Stel constructed extensive farm buildings, planted some 500,000 vine stocks and tended over 18,000 sheep and 1,000 cattle."[60] The two chief grievances of the farmers were the fixed-term contracts (already imposed in van Riebeeck's time) and the ban on the settlers' rights to barter with the indigenes for cattle. The farmers were obliged to sell their produce to the Company at a price that the Company determined and could not sell to anyone else. The market for all their produce was controlled through various complicated mechanisms known as the *pacht*, or contract of supply, which was sold to leaseholders at auction.[61] The settlers argued that the restrictions had a dampening effect on the local economy and on their ability to supply the required agricultural produce for the Company's passing ships, undermining the whole purpose of the VOC settlement at the Cape.

Van der Stel, for his part, claimed that the petitioners were dangerous anarchists who refused to comply with what was essentially VOC policy, which was being enforced by him in the Company's name. Apparently his dictatorial manner alienated the directors, who eventually discharged him from the governorship but made little change to the monopoly restrictions enjoyed by the Company. Some of the governor's closest officials were also replaced, and there was a slight easing up of trading conditions.

In the following decades the expansion of the Colony to some extent mitigated some of this underlying tension: wealthier cattle-owning farmers bought the leases of those less well off, installing their *knechts*, or overseers, to run them. In some cases these managers were Bastaards, like Adam de Kock, and had the advantage of speaking Dutch. They were accused of ruthlessness even greater than that of their masters. As in all frontier situations, the settlers also broke the Company rules with reasonable impunity by extending into Khoikhoi areas and trading without much control from Cape Town. When the VOC took measures to try to curb these practices in an effort to preserve the policy of maintaining good relations with the locals, trouble broke out anew. In 1739 an ineffective rebellion was led by one Etienne Barbier (a soldier of French origin), protesting against the policy that prohibited bartering for cattle. While his view was widely shared by the settlers, the uprising was badly organised and was soon suppressed by the authorities. After some time on the loose, Barbier was caught and executed for treason in the customary gruesome manner.

In 1778 a more serious challenge to the VOC officials arose from the Cape Patriot movement. A first approach through the governor was rebuffed, so the settlers drew up a petition and travelled to Holland to put their points to the directors directly, thereby bypassing the Cape officials. Their complaints, as had been the case with previous petitioners, were that the local officials were doing nothing to promote the economy of the colony, instead merely enriching themselves. They demanded the right to have a direct channel of communication with the directors and clearer laws about what the respective boundaries between them and the officials were. The VOC called for a response from Cape Town. Like earlier complainants, the patriots were portrayed as extremists, trying to upset the entire existing order and acting against the Company's interests. Failing to make an impact on the Herren XVII, the settlers regrouped a few years later and petitioned the States General directly. They may have made the fatal mistake of allying themselves with a movement in Holland, that of the Dutch patriots, against the House of Orange. For whatever reasons, they too failed in their demands.

In the meantime, exploration of the interior continued apace. One of the important explorers of the period was a Dutch officer, Robert Jacob Gordon. He made his first visit to the Cape in 1773, returning to settle in 1777. He had catholic tastes, with an interest in botany, anthropology, cartography, and geography. Gordon became a well-known figure in the colony, eventually being made the colonel-in-charge of the garrison. We shall see that in the company of Carl Thunberg and William Paterson, Gordon made a number of expeditions to the interior that took him as far as the Orange River and are recorded in detail in his journals. However, it appears he fell out of favour with the Dutch officials on account of his alleged collusion with the British. He took his own life in 1795.[62]

Meanwhile the VOC itself was beginning to implode. Financial problems were pushing it to insolvency. The fourth Dutch War of 1780–1784 opened up trade to French and also to British ships. The Company's grip on affairs in the interior of the colony, always tenuous, was collapsing. Serious rebellions broke out in Graaff-Reinet and in Swellendam in 1795, when the burghers declared their loyalty to the States General instead of the VOC. The complaints against the officials in Cape Town echoed previous grievances. In the same year, when there were also Khoikhoi disturbances, the British took control of the Cape with the agreement of the House of Orange. Although the colony was returned to the Netherlands in 1803 under the Treaty of Amiens, it was seized by force in 1806 by Sir David Baird after a British victory at the battle of Blaauwberg. The long reign of the VOC was at an end.

CHAPTER 4

Enlightenment Visitors

Introduction

During the long VOC tenure at the Cape through the eighteenth century, among the adventurers and soldiers of fortune, a succession of scientists and naturalists also arrived in Cape Town, intent on exploring the interior of the gradually expanding colony. The naturalists were attracted by the exotic fauna and flora, and the scientists by the possibility of studying the southern skies if they were astronomers, or the structure of the land and its animal and bird species if they were geologists or biologists. Many of these visitors were in fact sponsored by the VOC through contacts that they had in the Netherlands, both in the academic institutions (of which Leiden was the most important) or in the Company itself. They were of mixed nationalities, including Germans, Frenchmen, Swedes, and Englishmen, some of whom travelled to other parts of the world after their sojourns or had already visited distant lands by the time they came to the Cape. While the Cape was regarded mainly as a staging post for the lucrative trade to the East by the commercially minded VOC, for these visitors it proved to be a rich source of new discovery that could enhance their reputations and careers in Europe. In the primitive conditions of the times, they had to find ways of preserving the specimens of animals, plants, and insects that they collected and wanted to take back to Europe. Many specimens were lost or damaged on the journey north, but some of the earliest examples of exotic species did reach Europe as a result of their efforts.

Most of them did not confine themselves to purely scientific matters when they published their accounts of their travels at home. Their commentaries contain graphic descriptions of the landscape and terrain of Southern Africa, the climatic conditions, and details of the abundant fauna and flora of the Cape. In addition to describing the organisation of the European colony and the way of life of its inhabitants, these visitors also recorded detailed descriptions of the life and habits of the indigenous population, thereby providing a primary source of information on the early European encounters with the "other." Although there was a great deal of borrowing of information from their predecessors, there were also disputes among them about the veracity of earlier accounts. All of them felt the need to prove the authenticity of their own commentaries, usually by pleading firsthand experience. While lip service was paid to their readers' expectation of encountering the exotic, something of the negative attitudes of previous travellers to the Cape in respect to its inhabitants was dispelled, or at least modified, by these Enlightenment writers.

In his comprehensive account of travel writing in this period, Siegfried Huigen claims that the "eighteenth century epistemology" of the scientists, based on empirical methods, resulted in the production of more valuable records than those made by VOC officials who explored interior parts of the colony, since in these latter cases the reports concentrated on commercial considerations.[1] On the other hand, Robert Boyle's dictum about "not writing as a philosopher to broach a paradox or serve an hypothesis"[2] meant that in some respects the commercial accounts were more straightforward because they were not involved in special pleading. As we have noted, the scientists too tended to take account of whatever records were available from their predecessors (whether of a scientific nature or not) and, if necessary, to question their veracity. The interconnections of the commentaries of scientists and writers with other focuses therefore form a complicated tapestry of information and comment. In some cases the emphasis is on the commercial, and later the territorial, potential of areas described; in other cases the concentration is on natural phenomena, with the idea of bringing into European science the exotic and unknown species of fauna and flora to be found in Southern Africa. There were obvious benefits to the careers of those who introduced them.

One tool that became of increasing importance was that of the use of better maps of the colony, the borders of which had always been unclear. The very earliest European maps were the colourful charts of the Portuguese, whose princes, as we have seen, were inspired by the Fra Mauro map of 1450. That map, oriented with the South at the top in the manner of Eastern practice, clearly showed Africa as a continent surrounded by sea and the East accessible from it by ships sailing around its most southerly cape. In 1513, a map showing details of the southern coastline of the continent was produced by the German cartographer Martin Waldseemüller. Although the map defined the shape of Africa in greater detail, it had little navigational value, as there remained difficult problems in measuring longitude until much later, when a clock measuring natural phenomena would tell the reader exactly where he was.[3]

Mapping of the interior began in earnest in 1659, when Pieter Potter, an untrained surveyor, was instructed to produce a map of the area between Table Bay and Saldanha Bay. Further VOC expeditions—mainly those of Olof Bergh in 1682 and, three years later, of Simon van der Stel, led to the production of more detailed maps.[4] While the mapping out of territory was an advance in geography, it also served the interests of defining greater areas of colonial territory from which the indigenous population would be excluded. This was the case both eastward towards Xhosa country and northward into Namaqualand. Robert Jacob Gordon, whose contribution we shall consider later in this chapter, was seized with the importance of making better maps for that purpose, although by then other maps of the interior had been produced by Anders Sparrman and François Le Vaillant. In the early British period, Sir John Barrow drew up new maps of the interior, which were later used when the Cape once again came under British control to define new borders of the Colony eastward. It became de rigueur for travellers to include maps showing the routes they took by lines or dotted lines on maps, adding authority to their claims of firsthand reporting (see figures 1 and 2).

PIETER KOLB AT THE CAPE (1705–1713)

The most notable of the early eighteenth-century scientific visitors was Pieter Kolb (1675–1726), an astronomer and mathematician who had studied the usual mix of theology and philosophy with scientific studies (in this case, physics and mathematics) at Halle University. His thesis on comets, describing them purely as natural phenomena, was an early indication of his naturalistic proclivities. Kolb served in the Prussian court but at the same time seems to have formed links with the Dutch authorities dealing with the Cape. In 1705, with a letter of introduction from the mayor of Amsterdam, he arrived in Cape Town to be received by Adriaan van der Stel, the governor who was embroiled, as we have seen, in a protracted, personal confrontation with the settlers. Astronomical studies were to be part of Kolb's mission, building upon the work of Father Guy Tachard, the Jesuit priest who, as we have seen in the previous chapter, came to the Cape in 1685 and established an observatory near the castle, making the first telescopic observations of the southern stars. Although Kolb set up his own observatory to chart the stars, it seems that he made little progress in his work. A terse report from the governor is set out in a resolution of the council:

> The astronomer, Pieter Colbe, who arrived here in the year 1705, in the
> ship called the *Unie* from Holland, and who has for a considerable time
> been idling about without prosecuting his astronomical observations
> or rendering any burgher service . . . it was thought advisable to demand
> from him whether he intends to remain here much longer, in which case

he will be considered as a burgher, and thus become liable to taxes and burgher-duty; otherwise we shall give him his discharge so that he may return to Europe.[5]

In the local dispute between Adriaan van der Stel and the settlers, Kolb appears to have sided with the colonists against the governor, thus placing himself beyond the official pale. Together with his failure to advance the astronomical work he was supposed to undertake, it began to look as if he might be forced to leave. However, his fortunes changed: in 1711 under Louis van Assenburg, the new governor, he was rehabilitated and given an administrative post as a VOC secretary at Stellenbosch. He finally returned to Europe in 1713, apart from any other reason, to seek treatment for failing eyesight.

Kolb's account of the Cape was contained in his vast work the *Caput Bonae Spei Hodiernum* (*Present State of the Cape of Good Hope*), published in Nuremburg in 1719, in which he gives graphic details of Khoikhoi life and culture as well as an account of the settler colony and voluminous descriptions of animals, birds, snakes, and insects. This magnum opus had been preceded by two other books—on the Cape southeaster and on Cape water, respectively. Some controversy has surrounded his account, made more difficult to unravel by poor translations of the original German into Dutch, French, and English. Various subsequent travellers—including Sparrman, Le Vaillant, and Otto Mentzel—cast doubts on the accuracy of Kolb's descriptions, questioning whether he had direct knowledge of the subjects he was writing about. The French astronomer Abbé Nicolas Louis de La Caille was scathing about his astronomical work; Mentzel accused him of superficiality and pandering to the European taste for the exotic. Later scholars have tended to rehabilitate Kolb—Theophilus Hahn, a nineteenth-century Nama linguist, who calls him the "worthy German Magister,"[6] points out that many details in his description of the "Hottentots" that had been upheld as fictitious were in fact well-founded. There remain curiosities—for example, his theory that the Khoikhoi were descended from the Jews and comparisons he makes between their customs and those of cave dwellers in the Nile Valley.

While there can be no doubt that Kolb's comments on the Khoikhoi are sometimes taken from others—in particular, from Olfert Dapper and Tachard—there are descriptions of so detailed a type as to suggest that he must have had firsthand information on which to base them.

One of these detailed matters is his investigation of the Khoi practice of partial castration, which seems to have become an obsession of his and which he linked to the somewhat fanciful idea that the Khoikhoi may have been descendants of Jews who had immigrated to Africa. Kolb was following a long European interest in the subject of partial castration, or monorchy.[7] Accounts differed as to whether the right or the left testicle was normally removed, and there was no agreement as to the purpose of carrying out the operation. To find answers to these questions, Kolb examined a large number of men, observing that it was the left testicle that was usually removed. While the operation was taking place—without any anaesthetic—the ritual slaughter of a sheep took place. Kolb also discovered that until the circumcision had been made, no man was allowed to sleep with a woman. In essence the practice was a rite of passage from boyhood to manhood, something that provided the link he was looking for to Jewish practice.

In another example, he considers in detail the various rituals connected with childbirth. He relates that as soon as a Khoikhoi woman went into labour, men were banished from the precincts (including the father of the child about to be born) and risked punishment if they broke the rule excluding them from the scene of the birth. Instead, the woman would be assisted by a midwife and comforted by female relatives. In the meantime the men would prepare a sacrificial animal to celebrate the new birth. When the child was born, rather than cleaning it with water, the indigenous habit was to smear its body with cow dung and then animal fat, hardly likely to appeal to European observers.

Passages of that sort might suggest that Kolb was indeed pandering to the prejudices of his readers. Nevertheless, like all foreign observers, although he takes a moral tone condemning the idleness of the locals and their unwillingness to give up a nomadic existence, he refutes the suggestion that they are without religion or a spiritual sensibility. He describes a ceremony practised at dawn (which Hahn says he also witnessed) in which the Khoikhoi "assemble and take each other's hand and dance calling out toward the heavens."[8] Kolb says that this evidence that the Khoikhoi believe in a god was noticed by Tachard, even though it is not the Christian God of creation.[9] He concludes, "It is obvious that all Hottentots believe in a God, they know him and confess it; to him they ascribe the work of creation, and they maintain that he still rules over everything and that he gives life to everything."[10] Kolb's general tone toward the Khoikhoi is more sympathetic than that of most previous commentators, "on account of his admiration for their simple and unvarnished manners"[11]—for which he was attacked by La Caille, among others.[12] Huigen has a very high opinion of Kolb's contribution, saying his work was of the utmost significance. According to Huigen, Kolb "transformed the Khoikhoi from a stereotyped subject in a travel account that mentioned South Africa merely in passing to a complex subject of scholarly research in a book that dealt exclusively with the Cape."[13] The seminal importance of *Caput Bonae Spei Hodiernum* is attested to by continuous references to it for the next hundred years in the accounts of writers such as Le Vaillant, Barrow, and Henry Lichtenstein. Much later on, ethnographers and anthropologists like the highly influential Isaac Schapera rely on English translations of Kolb's work in their studies of the indigenous peoples. Unfortunately those translations were very much abridgements of the original and therefore, in some ways, misleading. Kolb's intention was to present as systematic an account of the Cape environment as possible, including an examination of animal and plant life, although he does not claim to be an expert in these areas. For his detailed examination of the appearance, customs, and material culture of the Khoikhoi, he relies on detailed notes that he made at first hand.[14] Finally he tackles the organisation and life of the colonial society of Cape Town itself.

On that subject, Kolb paints a rosy picture of an emerging, prosperous Cape Town with its impressive civic planning:

> Several beautiful country seats, vineyards and gardens are to be seen on almost every side of the Table Hill. The Company has here two very spacious, rich and beautiful gardens. In one of them stands, erected at the Company's expense, a noble pleasure house for the Governor, and near it a beautiful grove of oaks, called the Roud-Bush from which this garden (Rondebosch) takes its Name, being called the Round Bush Garden. The other garden which is at some distance from this is called Newland because but lately planted. Both these gardens are finely watered by the springs on Table Hill and the Company draws from them a very considerable revenue.[15]

The most graphic legacy of Kolb's account of the Khoikhoi was the use by Jean-Jacques Rousseau of a plate from his work depicting a servant taking off his European clothes to return to his own people in traditional dress, which appears as a frontispiece for the *Discours sur l'orgine et les fondements de l'inégalité parmi lest hommes* (A Discourse on the Origin and Foundation of the Inequality of Mankind, 1755).

OTTO FREDRIK MENTZEL AT THE CAPE (1732–1741)

Two decades after Kolb left the Cape, Otto Fredrik Mentzel (1709–1801) arrived in 1732, as a soldier in the service of the VOC. His stay lasted almost ten years, during which time he gained employment as a tutor and a minor official, trading as most of them did on the side. Like Kolb he also had connections with the Prussian court but hailed from an impoverished Junker family, having little formal education beyond basic schooling. Like many others he applied for a job in the Cape, hoping to make his fortune, but soon found that service for the VOC could be a hard calling. He experienced the life of a *knecht*—that is, a soldier or sailor who became an indentured servant to a farmer—eventually being released entirely from military service. Some *knechts* succeeded in making a better life for themselves, but their lot was not an easy one, nor was it always a path to riches as they hoped.[16]

However, Mentzel's fortunes changed when, after arriving at the Cape, he was befriended and employed by another Prussian, Rudolph Alleman (a captain in the military command), as tutor to his son. From that connection he was introduced into Cape society, and his circumstances and standard of living improved considerably. It seems that he was regarded as a sociable and eligible young newcomer, enjoying the renowned hospitality of Cape families, imbibing the local wine, and being pampered by the attentive service of domestic slaves.[17] He delighted in the moderate climate of the Cape, which he considered as restorative of health as any medical treatment.

His account of his times at the Cape, the *Beschreibung des Vorgebirges der Gulen* (*A Geographical and Topographical Description of the Cape of Good Hope*), was not actually published until 1787, when the author had reached the ripe old age of seventy-eight. A few years before, he had published a biography of his mentor, Alleman.[18] The preface to the *Description* indicates that it will be a wide-ranging work: "Wherein is described clearly and accurately the rural parts according to their division into districts, mountains and rivers; the Christian inhabitants and their customs; the agronomy and viticulture, stock farming, the ordinary expeditions, and finally also the aborigines, namely the Hottentots, besides many other lately discovered curiosities."[19] At the centre of what was becoming a vastly expanded land area, Table Valley was still to be "regarded as the heart and centre of the entire country, where everything produced, harvested, bartered, gathered, delivered and contributed in this country is accumulated and thence redistributed in all directions."[20] Africa is, nevertheless, a "land of contradictions."[21] The diversity of climate and terrain make it difficult to describe coherently, but some features of the "contradiction" are the result of lack of enterprise rather than physical difficulties. Like other overseas observers, Mentzel notes the dependency of the colony on European imports and questions it. Despite an abundance of local wood, the colonists rely on expensive imports from Holland and Scandinavia. It is only by manufacturing products locally that this trend will be reversed to the benefit of the colony. Occasionally a new discovery—such as the medicinal use of aloe—had already had that effect, but it was an exception.[22] Sometimes he is coy about writing on certain subjects, claiming that he is "neither zoologist nor naturalist" and therefore unqualified to give detailed descriptions of animals.[23] In fact, this does not stop him meeting his readers' expectation of such descriptions, though in some cases he relies on Sparrman's work. The reader meets springbok, tigers, zebras, and other exotic creatures in his pages.

However, Mentzel's most notable comments are about the Khoikhoi. His chapter on the subject begins with a bold pronouncement that although the "Hottentots are counted among the uncivilized races by all writers of travels who have visited the Cape of Good Hope," they are, in fact, in comparison to many other African peoples "far more human, just, honest and faithful," although he excludes the "wild Hottentots" (the San) from that eulogy.[24] Moreover, he denies La Caille's assertion that the "tame Hottentots" conspire with the San in their raids on European settlements, for they are "too honest, too timid and faithful for that."[25] His strongest criticisms are directed at Kolb, who he says invents the causes of disputes between Khoikhoi tribes as arising from claims to ownership of cattle. He finds that unlikely because the tribal kraals (or enclosures where cattle were kept) were always far apart from one another, thereby minimising the chance of mistake over ownership. Despite these assertions, Mentzel's defence of the Khoikhoi is mainly based on negative rather than positive qualities. The reason for their submission to Europeans is the result of a combination of stupidity and idleness. They are perfectly content with their situation of subsistence, however precarious, and their pleasure is to avoid any thought or effort.[26] Moreover, he adds: "They are incapable of improving on any-thing and all things which they make for themselves, are so impractical and clumsy that nothing cruder can be imagined."[27] Like other travellers, he remarks on the lack of religion and the impossibility of understanding their language, as well as the unpleasant habit of smearing themselves with dung and then animal fat. He claims to have asked the Khoikhoi the reason for this habit, which they tell him is because they believe that by smearing their bodies in that way they will keep them slender and fit. Whether that is true or not, Mentzel praises their physical qualities highly, saying that their limbs must be reckoned to be "beautiful."[28]

After some equivocation Mentzel comes to the conclusion that the indi-genes can be lifted out of their pitiful condition if educated and led by far-sighted Europeans. That would require a spirit of enlightened gener-osity and good sense on the part of the newcomers, something lacking in the overtly rapacious behaviour of the settlers, who instead encourage the Khoikhoi to become addicted to alcohol and tobacco to trap them into a life of endless and unfair servitude.

The timing of the publication of his own work, over fifty years after his visit, gives Mentzel the opportunity to consider the accounts written in the decades between by other travellers to the Cape. It enables him to indulge in some justification of his own original observations with revi-sions where he claims to learn from others. There is a slight note of para-noia in his defensiveness. One of the commentators he enlists to support him is Sparrman (particularly on such subjects as fauna and flora), who is "truthful and reliable"[29] and is often quoted favourably. On the other hand, Mentzel takes the chance to criticise both Kolb and La Caille. So far as Kolb is concerned, he believes him to be careless of facts and descriptions to such a degree that one wonders about his direct contact with the things and people he describes, a point made earlier by La Caille. However, Mentzel adds that La Caille himself, lacking Dutch, was cut off from much direct contact with both the settlers and the indigenes and for that reason is also unreliable.[30] Mentzel's insistence on the rights of the Khoikhoi as the original inhabitants of the Cape and his comments on slavery are in the high Enlightenment mode.

ABBÉ NICOLAS LOUIS DE LA CAILLE AT THE CAPE (1750–1752)

Although the Abbé de La Caille (1713–1762) stayed in the Cape for a fairly short period, his visit was significant for its impact on the progress of knowledge of the southern skies, which he studied assiduously during that time. La Caille, as a young astronomer, had been involved in important projects with the Italian Cassini dynasty, proving to be a brilliant and sound disciple. His reputation gained him admittance to the French Academy of Sciences, and he was appointed professor of mathematics at the prestigious Mazarin College, where an observatory was set up for his use. La Caille published works on mathematics, astronomy, and cartography; when a mission to the Cape to study the southern skies was being set up with the object of aiding navigation, he became an obvious candidate to join it. When he did arrive in Cape Town, La Caille, bearing a recommendation from the prince of Orange, was received by Governor Ryk Tulbagh enthusiastically. The governor promised "not to fail to render him such assistance as may be in my power towards bringing that work [astronomical observations] to a desirable conclusion."[31] La Caille set himself up in Strand Street in the middle of the town and erected a small observatory in the courtyard, facing the sea.[32] During the following two years he charted the position of thousands of stars, grading them according to their brightness, and discovered new constellations that he named after scientific instruments, such as Apparatus Sculptoris (the sculptor's tool), Fornax Chemica (the chemical furnace), Horologium (the clock), etc. Although subsequently corrections have had to be made to his measurements (for example, by George Everest in 1820),[33] it has been said that he "laid the foundations of Southern hemisphere astronomy."[34] His extensive notebooks detail his observations, including measurements of the radius of the earth in the southern hemisphere.

In his *Journal historique*, La Caille does not confine himself to scientific subjects but gives detailed descriptions of the landscape, fauna, and flora, as well as describing the customs and practices of the indigenous inhabitants of the Cape. It is set out as a diary in which he visits sights in and around Cape Town (noting that French is still spoken at Franschoek[35]), as well as recording the trip he made inland. Much is to be admired: the gardens at Newlands impress him, and local vegetables are as good as in Europe. His description of the unusual climatic conditions of the Cape—with the mass cloud formations clinging onto the mountains and the southeast wind battering the town—give an authentically local flavour to his work. On the other hand, his sketches of wild animals in the interior, including rhinoceros, hippopotamus, and elephant, seem more to be written to meet his reader's expectations of an exotic and wild Africa.[36]

However, one of the most marked features of his diary is his sustained attack on Kolb, particularly on Kolb's portrayal of the Khoikhoi. While La Caille is conscious of the mistreatment of the locals by the settlers, he dispels any notion that the Khoikhoi are anything but savages. They are a superstitious and backward people who have no real religion; rather than worshipping the mantis as Kolb claims, they merely regard it as a sign that ill fortune will befall them.[37] Although he can see that they are adapted to their environment, the only hope for their improvement rests with the development that the European settlers will be able to bring about by the application of industry and technology.

The Swedes from Uppsala University

Throughout the eighteenth century the University of Uppsala had a high reputation as a centre of learning, particularly in the areas of botany and zoology. Two of its famous sons, Anders Sparrman and Carl Thunberg, came to the Cape and left substantial accounts of their visits.

The reputation of Uppsala derived in great part from Carl Linnaeus (1707–1778), botanist, physician, and zoologist. Educated at the university himself, Linnaeus was committed to empirical science based on the collecting of specimens from all over the world. He travelled to Lapland to study birdlife as well as plants and rocks, finally being appointed professor of botany and medicine at his alma mater in 1741. Identifying hundreds of new species of plants and flowers, Linnaeus began a classificatory system that included, along with taxonomic notes, geographical details of the location of the new species he had found. He also spent time at the learned centres of science in the Netherlands, taking with him the manuscript of the classificatory system that he was developing to work on and refine. He met and impressed the great Herman Boerhaave among others, with the result that his magnum opus, the *Systema Naturae*, was eventually published in the Netherlands in 1735. While Linnaeus had built upon the work of earlier botanists, his exposition was the first to use the binomial nomenclature (composed of the generic name, followed by a specific epithet) consistently throughout his work, thereby creating a standard new system for succeeding generations. One of Linnaeus's methods of gathering knowledge was to rely upon a number of "apostles" or favoured students (said to have been seventeen in number) who would be sent on missions across the world to collect new species and report back to him at Uppsala. Sparrman and Thunberg, almost exact contemporaries, were both "apostles" who travelled to the Cape, still an exotic locale in the eyes of Europeans, to collect specimens of fauna and flora.

ANDERS SPARRMAN AT THE CAPE (1772–1776)

Like many eighteenth-century naturalists, Anders Sparrman (1748–1820) was trained in medicine, entering Uppsala University as a precocious youth of fourteen years old. He soon attracted Linnaeus's attention as an outstanding student and became an "apostle" who would be expected, in time, to make contributions to the professor's great work on the classificatory system.

He had visited China in 1765 before coming to the Cape, acting as ship's surgeon and returning, as expected of an "apostle," with numerous new species recorded and classified according to Linnaeus's new schema. On the voyage to China, he had become a friend of Captain Carl Gustaf Ekeberg of the Swedish East India Company. Ekeberg, who was a neighbour of Sparrman's father in his country rectory at Tentsa, arranged for Sparrman to take up a post as a tutor in Cape Town, where he arrived at the beginning of 1772, a short while before Thunberg.

During his early stay in the Cape, Sparrman continued to act as a medical doctor but also took to interpreting documents for the Swedish East India Company. His stay was interrupted when he joined Captain James Cook's voyage to Australia, acting as assistant naturalist, and he returned to the Cape in the middle of 1775. By then he had achieved a certain financial independence that enabled him to embark on a journey inland to the Eastern Cape, then at the extremity of the colony. His notes became the genesis of his *Voyage to the Cape of Good Hope*, and part of its title (*The Country of the Hottentots and the Caffres*) indicates that his account would not be confined to scientific matters but would explore the customs and way of life of local peoples. When he returned to Sweden honours were bestowed on him: he became a member of the Royal Swedish Academy of Sciences in 1777 and a full professor at his alma mater, Uppsala.

Sparrman's Account of His Travels

Sparrman was something of a young adventurer, who "languished for an opportunity of seeing distant parts of the world."[38] His first impression of Cape Town, like that of other visitors, was a favourable one, finding a neat Dutch town of wide streets, canals, and merchants' houses with generous *stoeps*, or front porch-balconies with steps leading down to the street. There was plenty of greenery, avenues of impressive oak trees, and the well-laid out Company Gardens, with its grand governor's mansion, to admire right in the middle of the town. The streets were thronged with people of a large variety of races so that languages European, African, and Eastern (including the lingua franca of the slaves, a Portuguese patois) could be heard all around. In Cape Town, Sparrman was delighted to meet Thunberg, "who alone could make the Cape for me a little Sweden."[39]

Sparrman could behave eccentrically as a botanist, sometimes collecting specimens while stark naked. His collection from the Cape amounted to 360 plant species (out of over 1,000 specimens collected there as well as on the trip with Cook), which he sent back to Uppsala in a series of consignments. He seems to have been disappointed not to have matched Thunberg's output in quantity, but this he ascribed to the severe drought that plagued the colony when he made his major trips into the interior in 1776. The landscape, he tells his reader, "was horribly parched and arid"[40]; much damage had been caused to plants as well as to agriculture. Nevertheless, there were new discoveries, and hardier species, like the indigenous protea, were found flourishing in places around Caledon.

To make up for the deficiency in botanical specimens, Sparrman pays close attention to animal life, knowing that his readers will be interested in the more exotic species. First sighting leopards and tigers around Table Mountain, once in the interior he describes quagga on the plains and monkeys near Mossel Bay. The hartebeest, elephant, and gazelle are observed in their natural habitats. Some of his descriptions, as of the gazelle, contain precise measurements: "The horns ten inches and a half long, their distance from each other at the base one inch; the distance between the tips as the middlemost parts of them three inches and a half; the breadth of the forehead from eye to eye three inches and a half; the ears were half the length of the horns, or five inches. . . ."[41]

Elsewhere in his account the reader is introduced to a close-up of the rhinoceros, with its poor eyesight but highly developed sense of smell.[42] He corrects the Comte de Buffon's account of the way the animal copulates, refuting the theory that this is done rump to rump. Illustrations of rhinoceros and springbok are added to his account, with maps of his journeys inland that are similar to those of Le Vaillant (figures 9–11).

However much of a naturalist he was, Sparrman also gives a great deal of valuable information in his *Voyage* about the life of the Khoikhoi, and he makes radical criticisms of the institution of slavery. Over and again he refers to the loss of rights of the enslaved population, making the point that slavery and tyranny were common bedfellows. He cites many cases of the callous and cruel punishment of slaves by their owners, sometimes leading to death. In one tragic case, a slave who was not allowed to live with his partner stabbed her to death and then himself in a frenzy of despair. There seemed no protection in law for mistreatment of slaves by their masters. Although some owners treated their slaves humanely, Sparrman refers to slavery as a "violent outrage to the natural rights of mankind."[43] There can be no justification for it in his eyes, and unattended, it will eventually lead to a violent rising.[44]

If slavery is one object of his attack, the treatment of the Khoisan is another. Although Sparrman recognises that the condition in which the Khoisan subsist is primitive and, in some respects, barbarous, he is a stout defender of their rights as fellow human beings to fair and decent treatment. However, he does not consider, given their low expectations of comfort, that they are unhappy. He observes that their yellow-tanned skin, good eyesight, and natural agility make them well adapted to their environment. Furthermore, he believes that their animism, in place of formal religion, is simply not understood by other travellers, who have accused them of having no beliefs.

In his poetic biography of Sparrman, Per Wästberg claims an empathy on his protagonist's part with an animist view of existence. Sparrman says to Daniel Immelman, his travelling companion: "The attractive thing about our Hottentots is that they worship nearly everything: the sun, the moon, the spirits of their dead ancestors, snakes and all manner of fetishes. Near every single object has a covert meaning, incorporates a sign and is imbued with special powers. I understand that feeling. I too find corroboration where others would discern an abyss."[45] Moreover, even those habits most repugnant to Europeans—the smearing of fat on their bodies

and the addition of buchu powder—has the purpose of enabling the
Khoisan to move about at all seasons with barely any clothing but flimsy
karosses. Their homes, though simple, are adapted to their nomadic existence. The lighting of a fire in the middle of the kraal so that it can be
shared by all is a mark of their sociability. There are rules of behaviour
and decorum; a marked modesty is apparent in the deportment of women.
Nor does Sparrman accept an inherent savagery in their nature, noting
that "in their dispositions my Hottentots were, particularly in the evenings, merry and talkative, and that sometimes in a high degree."[46]

He found little evidence of violence among them, with the worst fight
he witnessed being between a husband and wife in a matrimonial spat.[47]
As for the San, regarded as the most savage of the savages by Europeans,
the main fault he finds in them is a natural indolence, especially when
given tobacco or alcohol by Europeans. Like the Khoikhoi, he does not find
them disposed to violence or revenge; rather, he ascribes their attacks on
European settlements as resulting from the confiscation of their land and
the means of any livelihood except enslavement as servants to the newcomers. Their poisoned arrows, expertly employed in hunting, are not
weapons of war but weapons of survival.

Rather than being despised, the Khoisan should be pitied and gradually educated from their "barbarous and unpolished state to a much higher
degree of civilisation."[48] The work of missionaries, particularly the Mora-
vians, showed that such an approach could achieve beneficial results as
neat Hottentot houses, with tidy gardens, replaced the more primitive
tribal huts with uncultivated spaces around them.

Sparrman comments wryly on his camp followers' puzzlement at his
activities as a naturalist: "My Hottentots, who saw I was fond of hunting
of different sorts, the chase of flies and butterflies not excepted, thought it
very strange that I should now neither shoot these animals myself, nor suf-
fer them to do it."[49] While Sparrman refers to the proverbial hospitality
of the Boer farmers—suggesting the Swedish word "Afrikaners" to apply
to the colonists born in the Cape[50]—he also alludes, as other travellers

did, to their indolence, preferring to loll on their *stoeps*, smoking their evenings away, rather than improving the comfort of their homes. They seem content with an "easy and pleasing life"[51] much dependent on the labour of slaves and servants.

Sparrman's *Voyage* is written in a language directed at his reader without circumlocution. As a scientist, his inclination is to report what he sees as accurately as possible, avoiding hyperbole or exaggeration. On the other hand, he is aware of his reader's expectation of descriptions of the majestic landscape and fauna of a distant and exotic country. When an anecdote takes him along such a path, he does not hesitate to follow it to the full. In his own words he says: "In the Swedish language I hope my style will be pleasing and flowing, a little humorous and interesting. Few medical observations. A short description of my insects."[52]

CARL THUNBERG AT THE CAPE (1772–1775)

Carl Peter Thunberg (1743–1828) was one of Linnaeus's most successful "apostles," gaining an international reputation as a botanist. He studied at Uppsala in the 1760s and, like Linnaeus, pursued further studies in the Netherlands, where he became friendly with Johannes Burman. Burman, who had been a student of Boerhaave, had been involved in Linnaeus's own reception in Holland. His son, Nicolas Burman, was later sent to Uppsala to study under Linnaeus, and the Burman family name even found its way into the Linnaean classificatory system. Thunberg benefitted from this web of connections between Swedish and Dutch scientists since Burman, whose particular interest was in Far Eastern and Cape plants, gained him a VOC commission to visit the Dutch colonies for the purpose of collecting specimens.

Thunberg's stay in the Netherlands had also enabled him to begin to learn Dutch; his journey to the Cape Colony was meant to consolidate that knowledge so that he could pass off as Dutchman when visiting the island of Dijima in Japan, where only Dutchmen were allowed admittance and where he was to collect specimens for Linnaeus. His journey began in 1772; he stayed in the Cape until 1775, from where he sailed for the VOC outpost near Nagasaki. He later published a book about his experiences in Japan.[53] Thunberg's medical background was also useful, since it enabled him to act as a ship's surgeon at sea and a medical adviser on land, with free passage and a salary. He finally returned to Europe in 1778 and met Sir Joseph Banks in London before retiring permanently to Sweden. By the time he got back to Uppsala, Linnaeus had died. Shortly after his return, Thunberg was appointed professor of medicine and natural philosophy at his alma mater in place of his mentor.

Thunberg's Account of His Travels

Like Sparrman, Thunberg's first impression of Cape Town is a favourable one. He remarks upon a town "very regularly built, street cut quarters at right angles."[54] The one- or two-story buildings look solidly made and are set out spaciously; canals run beside the main thoroughfares. Even with minimal defences, Cape Town "enjoys perfect security in a land of savages."[55] The Company Gardens, with their great variety of plants, seeds that are brought each year from Holland, and rows of chestnut trees, delight him. He notes the properly organised public service, including a hospital in Barrack Street and the fair, if harsh, jurisdictional system of the VOC to which everyone—officials, burghers, farmers, and slaves—is subject. Overall, the Colony has great promise, given its agricultural potential, but it will need proper organisation and skill to bring it up to European standards.

There is an undertone in most of his comments that suggests that he is always comparing amenities and products in Cape Town with those in European cities and finds them wanting. Although there are bountiful meadows and fruit orchards in and around the town, they are not as productive as those in Europe—the quality of the fruit is not as good, although Constantia wine is "sweet, agreeable and luscious."[56] Many other foodstuffs are still imported, at considerable expense, from Europe. Wood, which should be lumbered locally, is also imported, adding to the cost of building and fuel. At least one explanation for this state of affairs is the local lack of industry and initiative, affecting both the European settler and the local Khoikhoi.

While Thunberg observes the local Khoisan (both Khoikhoi and San) with a certain scientific detachment, acknowledging their loss of traditional lands and, with it, their pristine liberty, he is less sympathetic toward them than Sparrman or, later, Le Vaillant. His portrait of the locals is a portrait of savages. After noting, in the usual way, their habit of smearing fat on their bodies, he says: "Round the neck, arms and waist they are decorated with strings of blue, white red and motley coloured glass beads in several rows. Some of them wore rings of iron, brass or leather round their arms. A sheepskin thrown over their hips, and another over the back, constitute all their apparel."[57] Ceremonies among them confirm their primitiveness: "The ceremony is not quite laid aside of making youth, at a certain age, men from which time they are separated from women, and associate only with men. After the youth has been besprinkled, according to custom with urine, some animal is killed, and its omentum, or cawl, is tied about his neck."[58] Thunberg does describe physical attributes that have enabled the Khoisan to adapt well to a harsh environment. Most of them are as tall as Europeans and demonstrate considerable agility, especially when they are on the hunt. Their good eyesight and their skill in using bow and arrow add to their hunting prowess. He describes the bow and arrow in some detail:

> The bow is a round stick of about an inch thick, and something more than two feet long and bent by a sinew. The arrow is made by a kind of reed or cane, as thick as goose-quill, and scarcely a foot long, to the end of which is fastened, with a fine sinew, an iron point, shaped like a lancet, which is besmeared with the poison of serpents. Several of these arrows are kept in a quiver, which is the thickness of a man's arm, and about two feet in length, with a lid at the top, that turns upon hinges of leather.[59]

Thunberg has no doubt that the Khoikhoi are living in a state of nature outside the parameters of civilised society. One clear sign of that condition is their lack of written language, without which records cannot be kept or progress made in the development of civil society and its governance. Granting that they have a "proper" language, he makes the point that "In other respects, [they] are so rude and uncultivated as to have no letters, or any method of writing of delineating them, either on paper, in wood or on stone. It is in vain, therefore, to seek any kind of learning, or any antique records among them; and few nations of the world, perhaps, are less enlightened than them."[60] Although some semblance of social life exists in their kraals and villages, the houses they live in are full of vermin, and they never wash their bodies. Their moral behaviour is also dubious in the eyes of the puritanical professor: both male and females seem to have more than a single partner, which is hardly surprising as there is no trace of religion among this "most wretched of the human race."[61] Unlike Sparrman, he seems to have little sympathy with their animism and therefore with their spiritual world.

Despite these criticisms, Thunberg does acknowledge that the indigenes, instead of being educated, have been corrupted by Europeans, becoming addicted to alcohol and tobacco in addition to the traditional *dagga*, which they had always smoked. With their lands confiscated and no longer the herdsmen of cattle, the Khoikhoi's only recourse has been to become the servants of the settlers unless, like the San, they are prepared to eke out a difficult living in the hinterland, turning into night raiders to meet their needs for food. In some respects, although he does not put the San much higher up on the scale of being than the Khoikhoi, there is a hint of admiration for their toughness in Thunberg's account. These Chinese-looking men can endure great privation; with their hunting skills, they have adapted to the harsher conditions of living further north as the relentless pressure of the colonists has pushed them away from lush, coastal pastures where game are abundant.

Thunberg's attitude to slavery is also much less forthright than Sparrman's. He seems to accept it as a fact of life in the Cape, commenting that slaves are often better treated than employees. Of the forced scheme of service of their children until the age of twenty-five, he says that that at least provides them with work and a modicum of protection. He does, however, condemn unfair and unjust treatment, but there is nothing to compare with Sparrman's outburst that slavery is a denial of human rights. It may be that Thunberg, so concerned with the prospect of progress in the Cape, accommodates slavery as an economic necessity without which that cannot take place.

Throughout his stay in the Cape, Thunberg began his collection of plant and insect specimens, the former of which amounted to over 27,500 in number by the end of his career. He was immediately impressed, as we have seen, by the Company Gardens and was befriended by Johan Auge, their superintendent. While admiring the planting of European trees (oaks and chestnuts) in the town, he was also captivated by the indigenous flora, making numerous trips up Table Mountain where he found wild orchids. On Robben Island he noticed well-produced vegetables such as cauliflowers, but it was on his three trips to the interior and along the coast that he started to collect specimens in earnest, travelling with the Scottish Kew gardener, Francis Masson, and Robert Jacob Gordon. Strelitzias, proteas, and gardenias caught his eye; in time numerous species were named after him, including the *Geranium thunbergii* and the *Spiraea thunbergii*. His observations were written up in his great work, *Flora Capensis* (Cape Flora), published between 1807 and 1823.

Thunberg's writing style is terser and less discursive than Sparrman's. "Every traveller," he warns his reader, "thinks himself under obligation to turn author" and thereby becomes diverted from providing his reader with "useful matter" and "real facts."[62] Despite his own strictures, his books are not models of concision: the original Swedish version of his account runs to four volumes, large parts of which cover his experiences in Japan and

Java. Nevertheless he tries to maintain a descriptive tone, although his commentary reveals prejudices in the contemporary manner. While Thunberg's writing on the Cape is only a part of his literary output, it is a significant contribution to our knowledge of the Cape and its society of the period.

Thunberg's Travelling Companions: Robert Jacob Gordon and Francis Masson (1772–1775)

Robert Jacob Gordon (1743–1796) was born in Holland of Scottish descent, serving in the Scots brigade of the Dutch forces. He first joined the VOC army corps and came to the Cape for the first time in 1773, where he met Thunberg and joined the latter's second expedition to the interior. Gordon was very talented in a number of ways. William Hickey, who met him, describes him as a "very accomplished man, an excellent classical as well as a general scholar, spoke English well and, indeed all the languages of Europe fluently."[63] His linguistic skill extended to indigenous languages: he had the unusual advantage of being able to speak to the Khoikhoi and the Xhosa in their own languages as well as in his native Dutch. This made him extremely popular with the locals, who held him in very high regard. He was a complex, even enigmatic, character: as his biographer has pointed out, there was something erratic in his makeup that made him headstrong and vindictive when he felt he had been crossed.[64]

In 1777 he returned to the Cape as second in command of the garrison. There is some speculation that Gordon may have been a secret agent of the prince of Orange, sent to get firsthand information about conditions in the colony. His status in this capacity has been linked to the fact that he was in correspondence with Henrik Fagel, one of the prince's principal officials. This work would have been separate from his military duties for the VOC at the Cape.[65] Within months of his arrival, Gordon joined William Paterson on another journey inland from Cape Town. They were accompanied by Johannes Schumacher, an artist, who made sketches on the way—although Gordon himself was also a sketcher as well as a recorder and was interested in producing a map of the inland areas they visited eastward toward Xhosa territory. His panoramic views (perhaps worked on by Schumacher) include a remarkable dissection of Table Mountain, detailing "every geographical stratum . . . with the greatest accuracy."[66] Other sketches are scenes of strategic areas on the West Coast and views of Robben Island. In addition he made fine sketches of animals—giraffe and hippopotami—and dissected and prepared specimens (skeletons and skins) to be taken back to Europe.[67] In 1778 he made his third journey with Governor Joachim Ammena van Plettenburg, surveying the state of the colony. In all Gordon made six journeys into the interior, including reaching and naming the Orange River. The scene that took place on that occasion in 1779 is described in his usual matter-of-fact tone: "Brought the boat to the water, hoisted the Prince's flag and we drank to the health of his Highness. We bade welcome to the river to which I gave its name in 1777. Said more concerning the welfare of the Company, and all done to the accompaniment of some shots. We have still heard nothing from Pinar and his four Hottentots from Goewap. A stiff wind this evening. Sky overcast."[68] Gordon's method as a recorder was entirely empirical, gathering the facts about nature and human society by observation. His detailed drawings of the Khoisan made him very aware of the differences with the Xhosa, when he encountered the latter on the eastern borders of the colony. He seems to have been very taken with Qoba, one of the Xhosa chiefs.[69] There is no doubt that Gordon was sympathetic to the plight of the Khoisan. One of the techniques he uses in his records is to allow the Khoi to speak for themselves by reporting their speech directly. He is obviously interested in their culture and their way of life and was one of the early Europeans to inspect the San cave drawings.[70]

Francis Masson (1741–1805), who accompanied Thunberg on two of his interior journeys, was a thirty-one-year-old Scot described as "one of his Majesty's gardeners" at Kew.[71] Despite his lack of education, he left an account of those two journeys, as well as one he had undertaken in 1772, which were published in the *Transactions of the Royal Society* in 1776.

Masson had arrived in the Cape in 1772 aboard Captain Cook's ship *Resolution*, with the object of expanding the collection of plants and flowers at Kew. He had been granted the generous sum of £100 salary per annum and £200 extra for expenses by his mentor, Sir Joseph Banks.

Masson's account is terse and to the point. He describes the exact routes taken on the expeditions (remarking that La Caille's map was the only reliable one), noting in detail the flora that he sees, collecting specimens that he would classify on his return to Cape Town in between the journeys. He also remarked on geological matters (which interested Linnaeus as well as botany); the landscape; and the local inhabitants, both European settlers and the Khoisan. Some of his descriptions (such as that of the salt pans at Algoa Bay) are the first recordings of the phenomena; other details (such as the vineyards and fruit farms) are familiar from the accounts of other writers. His list of the fruits he sees cultivated is perhaps the most comprehensive and includes "apricots, peaches, plums, apples, pears, figs, mulberries, almonds, chestnuts and walnuts" as well as tropical fruits such as guava and jambo, a kind of plum from Java.[72]

Some of his description of the landscape is still familiar to the modern traveller. Ascending what was then a very rugged path (later the Sir Lowry pass), he describes the scene, largely unchanged to the present day:

> We entered a spacious plain, interspersed with an infinite number of large fragments of rocks, visibly decayed by the force of the S.E. wind, which blows here during the summer with very great force. Some of the rocks appeared like the ruins of church steeples, and were worn so thin with wind and rain, that the softer parts of them were perforated in many places. They formed the quadrum of Linnaeus . . . and abound in curious plants.[73]

He generally concurs with Thunberg's view of the civility of the settlers, and although he remarks upon friendly behaviour on the part of the Khoikhoi, he finds their condition wretched and unpromising. Most of all it is the tone of the sheer delight of the botanist from Kew at the variety and beauty of Cape flora that most strikes the reader.

WILLIAM PATERSON AT THE CAPE (1777)

Another less exalted academic traveller than the Swedish professors was William Paterson (1755–1810). He was also a young, poorly educated Scot of twenty-one years of age who nevertheless travelled to the Cape in the cause of science, being sent by the Countess of Strathmore—according to William Hickey, "a strange and eccentric woman"—to collect plants.[74] Starting life as an amateur naturalist, in due course he became a commissioned officer, serving in India and Australia and ended his career as lieutenant governor of New South Wales.

Paterson made a number of journeys into the interior, which he described in his *Narrative of Four Journeys into the Country of the Hottentots and Caffraria*, dedicated to Sir Joseph Banks and published in 1789.[75] He was lucky to be befriended by Gordon, who, as we have seen, accompanied Thunberg on his travels to the interior. Paterson describes Gordon as a "gentleman of extensive information in most branches of natural history."[76] Paterson himself proved to be an accurate observer and a good sketcher; he maintained close links with Banks and was in due course elected a fellow of the Royal Society.

Paterson begins his narrative with the bold assertion that the "reader will not be presented with a romance under the title of a book of travels."[77] He criticizes authors who produce specious publications based on "very slender materials."[78] Sparrman is not one of these writers, since he is often quoted by Paterson with approval. If his own work turns out to be less entertaining than those of writers who do provide literary flourishes, he assures his reader that it will be more authentic. Having given that warning, Paterson shows that he is not unaware of the appeal of the exotic in recounting observations, for there is "no part of the world so little known to Europeans as the regions of Africa, which lie south of the equinoctial line."[79] In his "third journey" he also adds that Caffraria—the Xhosa territory east of the Great Fish River (in the Eastern Cape)—had never actually been explored by any European before his own visit, and that subsequently no foreigner had gone there.[80]

As a botanist, Paterson is entranced by the variety and novelty of the Cape flora, but he is also captivated by the physical beauty of the landscape and the exotic animal life found roaming freely through it. His four journeys were made in the company of Jacobus van Reenan, a Cape farmer of substance, and on several occasions they were joined by Gordon. The difficulties and adventures of travel by oxen-drawn wagon are set out graphically but without a sense of exaggeration.[81] The most serious challenge was to find sources of drinkable water. Over and again Paterson and his party are forced to drink brackish water; whenever a source of good drinking water is found, it is a discovery of the Khoikhoi guides. When these resilient locals doubt the possibility of finding water in less promising terrain, they refuse to travel further. The climate itself was wildly variable—scorching sun and drought at one moment; pouring rain making the crossing of rivers almost impossible at another. Mountainous terrain added to the difficulties; animals had to be replaced due to exhaustion. Added to these problems was the danger of attack from wild animals—lions, tigers, and hippotami—and, in some areas, from hostile locals such as the dispossessed San.

One compensating factor that he, like other travellers, mentions frequently is the universal hospitality of the settler Boers. Although he too criticises them for being indolent and not making the most of their considerable advantages—of fertile soil and cheap labour—that should provide a "very comfortable manner of living,"[82] at the same time he frequently records the generous reception that he and his party are given, even in the most remote places where the farmer was not always comfortably off. It was customary throughout the Cape Colony for farmers to put up travellers in their own homes and share their meals with them, as well as

giving them vital support by providing fresh oxen to continue their journeys. Paterson enjoys the outback and seems to have less taste for Cape
Town society, in which William Hickey, visiting at the same time, "lived
a merry life, having dances, plays or concerts every evening, at which a
number of girls were always present."[83]

While Paterson is under no illusions about the condition of life of the
Khoikhoi, regarding their "mode of living . . . in the highest degree
wretched,"[84] his tone in describing them is in no way hostile. He sketches
a relationship of harmonious dependency between the traveller and the
Khoikhoi guides that is only disturbed when the former refuse to accept
the local advice about the dangers of carrying on the journey. One vital
matter on which the explorers depended was the ability of the locals to
find sources of water, without which any journey would become impossible. His general impression of the Khoikhoi, apart from the Bushmen,
was that most of them were "peaceable and well disposed."[85] Even in the
case of the San, he recognises the extreme conditions in which they live,
sometimes having nothing to eat but dead locusts. It hardly surprised him
that such privations contributed to their aggressive and hostile behaviour
toward the newcomers.

His view of the Xhosa in Caffraria (a region that he says had "never been
visited by any European before"[86]) is also benign, but his description of
them is exotic enough:

> The colour of the Caffres is a jet black, their teeth white as ivory, and
> their eyes large. The cloathing of both sexes is nearly the same, consist-
> ing entirely of the hides of oxen, which are as pliant as cloth. The men
> wear tails of different animals tied around their thighs, pieces of brass
> in their hair, and large ivory rings on their arms; they are also adorned
> with the hair of Lions, and feathers fastened on their heads, with many
> other fantastical ornaments.[87]

He observes their skill in making implements both for domestic use and
for hunting—which, together with the organisation of their permanent

settlements and social order, put them higher in the contemporary rankings of civilized or semicivilised societies than their Khoikhoi neighbours.

Paterson was of course a botanist concerned with collecting flora, and he records his delight in discovering new varieties of plants that he comes upon in the interior of the Cape. Part of his collection of specimens was given to his patroness, the Countess of Strathmore, although it appears that she cut him off financially; other parts of the collection he seems to have kept for himself. There was also a suggestion, from van Reenen, one of the travelling party, that Paterson had found gold on his northward expedition in 1778 to the Orange River. While it is possible that they came upon some gold in Namaqualand, this story may have been invented by van Reenen for his own ends after Paterson had left the Cape.[88]

Paterson had an eye for the beauties of the landscape as well as the rarity of its fauna and flora, recording that the "Country here is extremely beautiful and picturesque, very hilly and hills are shaded with impenetrable woods; the vallies well-watered and covered with grass, which affords excellent pasture for cattle."[89] Paterson's commentaries on the life and society of both the settlers and the indigenous population are important historical sources, set out in unrhetorical language but imbued with an Enlightenment tolerance and reasonableness, noting among other things that the Khoikhoi who were retained in service proved more faithful than those brought up as slaves.

CHAPTER 5

Ennobling the Savage

MISSIONARY VIEWS

The idea that the Khoisan might represent an example of the "noble savage" was a very long time in coming, nor was it ever accepted widely among the European settler community at the Cape. As we have seen from the earliest times of the arrival of Europeans, the indigenous people were regarded as primitive savages, almost subhuman. The negative impressions had begun with the Portuguese, whose experiences at the Cape had not been happy ones; while the VOC promoted a policy of appeasement so that the necessary supplies for their passing ships would be forthcoming, it was always clear that this was a political gesture on the part of superiors to inferiors. Exceptional reports—such as the *Remonstrantie* (remonstrance) of 1649 that recommended the taking of the Cape by the VOC—argued for a conciliatory approach and the treatment of the Khoikhoi with decency and respect, but even that did not imply equality between the races. Rather, its progressive tone was aimed at bringing a backward, but not irredeemable, people into the colonial system so that they might contribute to it as well as benefitting themselves from the fruits of an advanced civilisation. Even when the idea of the noble savage did gain ground, no one imagined that there was any merit in living in the primitive conditions of the state of nature that characterized his existence.

Among the few Europeans who did not share an attitude of open disdain for the Khoikhoi were certain missionaries who have been described as "the main mediators of colonial politics among the Khoisan and amaXhosa."[1] The missionary societies developed from a renewed proselytizing Protestant ethic; having revived religious faith among the lower classes at home, their attention turned to the "savages" in the newly conquered colonial territories as the next target for conversion. This dissenting Puritan tradition became closely linked to the movement for the abolition of slavery. Antislavery sentiment grew among the Quakers, who in the early 1780s set up a committee to promote the cause of abolition. The London Missionary Society (LMS) was founded in 1795, representing dissenting opinion that, by this time, was also influenced by radical Enlightenment ideas. This connection to radical ideas in the period leading up to the French Revolution made the LMS highly suspect in the eyes of the Anglican establishment. Whether the missionaries' cultivation of the indigenous people was motivated by disinterested compassion or an urge to subjugate them to colonial domination remains debatable. A Xhosa oral tradition says "when the missionaries came, they carried a bible in front, but behind their backs a musket."[2]

Most prominent among the earlier eighteenth-century missionaries was the Moravian Georg Schmidt (1709–1785), who arrived in Cape Town in July 1737 at the age of twenty-six. Schmidt, whose own life had been difficult (he had been imprisoned and badly treated for his religious beliefs) entirely rejected the notion that the Khoikhoi were a lower species of men, almost on a level with animals without souls. Instead, he believed that with proper instruction and encouragement, they could be converted to leading an ordered, Christian life in a settled community. He set about showing how that could be done at Genadendal (formerly Baviaanskloof, the Vale of the Baboons), where he established a small settlement that still exists. The Khoikhoi who came there were given neat, modest houses, surrounded by fields in which they were taught to plant and sow crops. They were also taught to read and write so as to be able to take up the Christian mantle fully. By taking these steps, Schmidt earned himself the title of the "Apostle of the Hottentots."

Schmidt's efforts were at first ridiculed but soon began to be seen as subversive by the elders of the Dutch Reformed Church, firmly in control of the religious life of the Colony. Not only was his success undermining the social structure, based on a rigid inequality between the settlers and the Khoisan, but by baptizing his followers, he was raising the possibility of their gaining legal rights and usurping the place of the largely illiterate white farmers. Schmidt soldiered on for seven years against continuous opposition and troublemaking by the established Church leaders. Eventually they managed to defeat him, casting doubt on the validity of his baptisms by discovering that he himself was not ordained.

In 1744 Schmidt left for Holland to become ordained (a letter received in the Cape from Count Nicolaus Ludwig von Zinzendorf on behalf of the Moravian order confirming his ordination was not deemed sufficient), but he never returned to the Cape. The station at Genadendal was closed down. Nevertheless, Schmidt's legacy survived. Some fifty years later, when Moravian missionaries were again admitted to the Cape, they found Magdelena, a lady in her nineties who had been converted to Christianity by Schmidt and who proudly showed them a Dutch New Testament Bible he had given her.

A favourable account of the revived Moravian mission is given in the *Cape Journals* of Lady Anne Barnard, who clearly supports the missionaries in their efforts to make the Khoikhoi as independent of the settler community as possible. She says: "I then descended with him [the missionary] and hastily went thro' a dozen of the little gardens of the Hottentots, they were *not* very neat, but each one had *something* growing in it, the Huts were of clay thatch'd with rushes, some square as in Ireland others round in the original Hottentot fashion, and brought up to the top without rushes, a hole only, being left in the middle to serve as a vent, and another for the door."[3] Although she does not consider the gardens to be neat, they are nevertheless planted, and the Khoikhoi work in the fields growing a variety of vegetables—including beans, which she sees being dried in the sun. They also lay out hides of animals, specially treated, to form leather for a variety of uses. However, Lady Anne's most enthusiastic remarks are about the service she witnesses in the simple church that the missionaries had built with the help of the Khoikhoi. She admires the singing of the psalms by people who are "mild and tender by nature."[4] Her comments are a tribute to the work of the Moravian Brethren as well as being a clear indication of her own liberal attitude toward the locals.

The next significant missionary to preach a radical doctrine of racial equality was Johannes van der Kemp (1747–1811), who arrived in the Cape in 1798. Van der Kemp had a colourful background. A graduate of the famous medical school at Leiden, he also studied at Edinburgh University before taking up practice in his native Holland. He then served in the cavalry and is rumoured to have led a fairly dissolute life, not uncommon among the young officer classes of the time. While in Britain he discovered the London Missionary Society, which he joined. As a Dutchman who was also a graduate of a British university, van der Kemp was the ideal person to be sent to the Cape, which had just passed into British hands. Although his life has been described as a "bundle of contradictions,"[5] he was clearly motivated by a sense of the unjust treatment of the indigenous peoples of the colony. His religious leaning was millenarian, and "his belief in the imminent intervention of God on the side of the oppressed resonated closely with rebelliousness among the indigenous people."[6] It certainly did not resonate with the colonial establishment in Cape Town.

From his arrival at the Cape, van der Kemp expresses a horror that the Khoisan and the slaves are so badly treated "'by the wicked rulers of this country' and that slaves 'are sold off as beasts and separated from their children by monsters who call themselves Christians.'"[7]

His first contact with the local people was with the Xhosa of the Eastern Cape. It was the beginning of the period when the British were pushing the boundaries of the Colony eastward, establishing the new province of Albany—where settlers from Britain were given land on which they had to eke out a life based on subsistence farming, as we shall see in chapter 7. A provincial capital was established at Grahamstown, where a cathedral was built at the insistence of Lord Charles Somerset. The Xhosa were driven over the Kei River into an area designated as "Caffraria."

Despite managing to engage with the local king, van der Kemp did not have much success in his evangelical mission to convert the Xhosa to Christianity. After two years he turned his attention to the Khoisan and in 1803 founded a mission community at Bethelsdorp, on the Swartkops River, north of Port Elizabeth. The mission started as a refugee camp for those escaping from the turmoil of the frontier wars, and its inhabitants were at first women and children and older men. Over the decade its numbers swelled to 450 of a possible population of 12,000 Khoisan living in the Eastern Cape. The mission, which "stood for an egalitarian, non-racial Christianity as opposed to the exclusive version of the Boers, demarcating membership in the moral community and access to the law,"[8] was fiercely disliked by the settlers, who regarded it as a threat to the master-servant order. Attempts were made to close down the mission and even kill van der Kemp and James Read (1717–1752), who was assisting him. During the renewed Dutch occupation under the terms of the Treaty of Amiens (1802), teaching was stopped at the mission and van der Kemp and Read recalled to the Western Cape.

A graphic illustration of the eccentric missionary was given by Henry Lichtenstein, who met him at Bethelsdorp in 1803. Impressed by van der Kemp's learning (he was a particularly good linguist), Lichtenstein describes him as "dressed in threadbare black coat, waistcoat and breeches, without shirt or neckcloth or stockings and leather sandals on his feet, the same as are worn by the Hottentots."[9] He portrays a man of straightforward goodwill, who by this time had married a Khoikhoi woman—a highly unusual alliance in a society where cohabitation was not uncommon but seldom involved marriage.

With the return of British rule in 1806, van der Kemp and Read were allowed to return to Bethelsdorp, and a new period in the development of the missionary station began. There was once again an emphasis on literacy, and in addition to the Khoisan, links were established with the Xhosa. Van der Kemp, believing that the only way the Colony could survive was by fair treatment of the indigenous people, was also keen on proselytizing work being undertaken by Khoisan and Xhosa converts who had been trained at Bethelsdorp. The abolition of the slave trade in the British Empire in 1807 was a cause for celebration at the settlement, but conditions there were still far from satisfactory. Under various investigations, including one ordered by Governor Du Pré Alexander, Earl of Caledon, accusations of laziness and filth were reported among those sheltering at the mission. Van der Kemp was not to be stopped—he and Read put in numerous complaints about ill treatment of farm workers to the newly established circuit court, whose business was to ensure that the Boer farmers were complying with the new code of treatment. Nevertheless, despite the introduction of this more liberal regime, the British authorities allowed the apprenticeship of Khoisan children to the farmers, placing them in a condition hardly different from slavery. Van der Kemp's struggle to obtain justice for the local peoples continued until his death in 1811. His revolutionary work was carried on by Read and then Dr. John Philip, with a greater emphasis on the assimilation of the Khoisan (emerging as the "Coloureds") into the fabric of colonial society, as we shall consider in chapter 7.

French Philosophes

During the long eighteenth century, the notion of the noble savage, the indigene who led a simple but not immoral life, gained strength among French philosophers. The term *"le bon sauvage"* had long existed in French literature, indicating a wildness that did not necessarily suggest that savage man was amoral. If the *sauvage* was naïve and carefree in his way of living, he could also show great kindness and loyalty, even offering the hand of peace to strangers. Such representations of primitive people stood in stark contrast to Thomas Hobbes's depiction of North American Indians living in a state of nature to whom human qualities could hardly be ascribed, which corresponded to most of the descriptions of the Cape inhabitants we have already considered. The French ideal of *le bon sauvage* became linked to the Enlightenment belief that men were everywhere the same, even if cultural expression was entirely different from one society to another. That belief was shared by the Scottish philosophers, such as David Hume, who had close connections with the French intelligentsia. In time the doctrine evolved into one demanding equality for all men and in that form became the basis for the egalitarian ideals of the French Revolution. By that time, at the end of the eighteenth century, visitors to the Cape, imbued with this emerging radicalism, had applied the concept to the indigenous inhabitants, the Khoisan.

One of the most influential exponents of the myth of *le bon sauvage* at the end of the seventeenth century was the aristocratic François de Salignac de la Mothe-Fénelon (1651–1715), cleric, theologian, philosopher, and courtier. At one time well favoured by Louis XIV, Fénelon fell afoul of the king by his covert criticism of absolutist monarchy in his work *Les aventures de Télémaque* (The Adventures of Telemachus) (1699). Purporting to be a mythical story of the travels of Telemachus, the son of Ulysses, searching for his father long due home from Troy, it is a mixture of classical mythology, pagan fiction, and commentary on theological and political matters. At one point the adventurer encounters a society of primitive people living in a coastal region who were "a savage race who lived by hunting and by the fruits which the trees spontaneously produced."[10]

Fénelon's description could very well be applied to the "beachcombers" of the Cape at the time of the arrival of the first Europeans there. In *Telemachus,* Fénelon has the leader of the *sauvages* deliver a noble oration:

> We abandoned for you the pleasant sea coast, so we have nothing left
> but those inaccessible mountains, at least it is just that you leave us in
> peace and liberty. Go and never forget that you owe your lives to our

feeling of humanity. Never forget that it was from a people you called rude and savage that you receive this lesson in gentleness and generosity.... We abhor brutality, which under the gaudy name of ambition and glory ... sheds the blood of men who are all brothers.... We value health, frugality, liberty and vigour of body and mind: the love of virtue, the fear of the God, a natural goodness towards our neighbours, attachment to our friends, fidelity to all the world, moderation in prosperity, fortitude in adversity, courage always bold to speak the truth, and abhorrence of flattery.[11]

Fénelon's views, so apposite to the situation in the Cape, were influential throughout the eighteenth century, attracting widespread attention and appearing in numerous editions in various European languages. Nevertheless, it took some time before the notion of *le bon sauvage* was applied to the Khoisan. Most French commentators of the seventeenth century agreed with the opinion of Jean Baptiste Tavernier, who said that the inhabitants of the Cape "are but a sort of human beast."[12] Whatever admiration they occasionally expressed about their physical prowess, the moral character of the Khoisan was always regarded as dubious and characterised by the twin evils of idleness and deceitfulness. In that respect these French visitors (and those who merely echoed the opinion of others) agreed for the most part with other European descriptions of the Khoisan as a base and savage people.

Although describing the Xhosa rather than the Khoisan, the one exception to this largely negative view of the indigenous inhabitants of the greater Cape area was that given by Guillaume Chenu de Chalezac, "the French Boy." Chalezac was a Huguenot boy of fifteen years of age who found himself a castaway among the Xhosa of the Ciskei in 1687 following a shipwreck. He spent a year among the Xhosa, virtually adopted by their chief, and wrote up observations on their manner of living and their hunting prowess. His direct and unique experience led him to qualify various aspects of the orthodox and largely negative European view of native peoples. In a striking passage about what might be described as their "natural religion," he says:

> Although it is said of the Caffres that they live without religion, never-theless it seems they once had beliefs. I saw them make shrines and on certain days kill a beast, almost as if making a sacrifice, giving half to the dogs and burning the other half. Meanwhile the whole group would stand round the fire in deep silence, until their offering (if they give it such a name) was consumed. When I asked them the reason for doing what they did, they replied that they knew of none, but that they sim-ply did what their brothers had always done.[13]

Acknowledging that they are "brutal and rough," he also notes his sur-prise at their upholding of rules of "decency and decorum."[14] Had he not seen this behaviour with his own eyes, he would have found it hard to believe. His testimony is particularly significant for being based on first-hand experience rather than on opinions relayed by others, as was often the case with the commentaries.

Rousseau's *Discours* of 1755

By far the most influential work of the eighteenth century in the dialogue about primitive life was Jean-Jacques Rousseau's *Discours sur l'origine et les fondements de l'inégalité parmi les hommes* (A Discourse on the Ori-gin and Foundation of the Inequality of Mankind, 1755). While Rousseau (1712–1778) did not use the term *le bon sauvage* (rather keeping to the more neutral *l'homme sauvage*), his attack upon the corruption that he saw as a concomitant of advanced society was a strong plea for the moral value of primitive life, no matter how much it appeared as an uncomfortable and regressive state for modern Europeans. However, he was not suggesting, as certain critics falsely claimed, that there should be a return to life in a state of nature. The *Discours* is a polemical document aimed at exposing the corruption that Rousseau believed endemic to advanced societies. It

is a form of conjectural history, relying on deduction to reach "solid observations"[15] about what life would be like outside civil society in a state of
nature. By this method of analysis the psychological foundations of society would be explored, with the purpose of understanding the constraints
that civil society had put on men. While empirical evidence from primitive societies might be alluded to as examples of the kind of life that men
everywhere led in a state of nature, such examples were secondary to the
main intention of presenting an ideological reconstruction of social progress, which would free men from the bondage imposed by living in modern society.

Rousseau makes a number of references to the Hottentots, stressing
their physical prowess—including fine eyesight and ability to run fast—
which makes them superb hunters, entirely adapted to their physical environment. Their nomadic life, with periodic disasters from extreme climate
or lack of food and water, was extremely uncomfortable on modern
European standards. Nor was the condition of savage man, focused on
the struggle for daily survival, a sociable one. He was a creature who
wandered in the forest without a permanent home, with no industry
unconnected to his search for sustenance and little power of communication with his fellows. He was a self-sufficient creature, subject to few passions, with knowledge necessary only for tackling his immediate needs.
He was neither vain nor particularly rational, and chance discovery would
be lost as there was no art or written language as a tool for communicat-
ing knowledge from one generation to the next.

Nevertheless, there were compensations. The fact that his needs were
simple meant that they were easier to satisfy. Savage man did not have that
insatiable appetite of man in polite society to improve his condition, to
change his status in the complex social hierarchy of civil society in which
he lived. Without those pressures and the stress that came with them, savage man could well be judged a happier creature than later men, trapped
as they were by the demands of civilized living. Timid of contact with
other men and living mainly in isolation, there was little chance of conflict

with his fellows. Any dispute was settled on the spot, since there was no authority to which it had to be referred. There being no notion of property or private possession, the provisions of nature were open to anyone who came to take them. While Rousseau did not recognise morality as a feature of life in a state of nature, he was concerned to ameliorate the harshness of Hobbes's description of it as a war of all against all. Savage man was not faced with moral choices, but he was not bereft of a sense of pity for the suffering of others; on the basis of this natural benevolence, Rousseau believed that it would be possible to build the foundations of a truly moral civil society.

Rousseau's description of a state of nature accords in many ways with the descriptions given of Khoisan life, particularly by that minority of commentators whom we have seen to be sympathetic to the indigenous peoples. The life they described was of a carefree, nomadic existence in which small groups roamed over what was usually a hospitable environment in search of sustenance. Among them there was no sense of ownership; there was no political authority to which they owed allegiance. The only restraints upon them arose in times of shortages of food or water, when conditions became too harsh: their response was to move to new pastures.

Rousseau's Legacy

While Rousseau's political theory gradually altered the opinion of the earlier French visitors who had written about the Khoisan, it did so in a way that did not radically challenge the notion that progress was beneficial. Noble savages they may have been, but no European settler, in his relative comfort, could envy their life of insecure poverty, subject to the whims of nature. Nor was there any suggestion that the state of nature was a golden age worth returning to. Nevertheless, the new thinking did give rise to a different view of the part the Khoisan could play in colonial society.

One of the exponents of a more benign view of the indigenes was Jacques-Henri Bernardin de St. Pierre (1737–1814), who passed through the

Cape on his way to Mauritius in 1768 and made a number of further visits. Bernardin de St. Pierre, said to have read *Robinson Crusoe* at an early age, was an inveterate traveller who had visited parts of Europe and Russia before heading to the Cape. While in Paris he had become a friend and disciple of Rousseau, sharing with him a love of botany. He went on to write a utopian political tract (*L'Arcadie* [Arcadia], 1781) and an essay in the spirit of Rousseau deploring the corrupting effects of civilisation (*Etude de la Nature* [Study of nature], 1784). However, Bernardin de St. Pierre's celebrity had come about after the publication of his romance, *Paul et Virginie* (Paul and Virginia, 1787).

His early career was as an engineer in the army, and in that capacity he was sent to Mauritius. His account of his time there was the subject of his first work, *L'isle de France* (Isle of France, 1773). His view of the indigenous people is sympathetic, ascribing any faults they might have to the lack of the pillars of Enlightenment reasoning—good governance and good education. In *Paul et Virginie* he tells the story of two young lovers living in idyllic natural surroundings, which ends in tragedy as a result of the advent of civilisation. In his later work, *La chaumière indienne* (The Indian cottage, 1790) a traveller finds wisdom in the courage of an Indian outcast. In all these works, Bernardin de St. Pierre contributed to an ideology that sought to rebalance the relationship between colonists and indigenous peoples, emphasizing the commonality of human nature and advocating policies based on the just treatment of people who would then become useful citizens of the state rather than remaining in a condition of rebellious serfdom. The Cape looked like an ideal setting for the development of such a mix. After a hard climb up Table Mountain, he records that "never had a trip given me so much pleasure."[16] Another world traveller who visited the Cape at about the same time as Bernardin de St. Pierre was Pierre Pagès (d. 1793). He was a naval officer who had seen service in North America and had travelled to many other parts of the world. In developing the views of Rousseau and Bernardin de St. Pierre, Pagès emphasised the importance of a new system of governance that would be based on a more just and humane treatment of the indigenes, so that they could be integrated into the colonial structure. This accorded with something of the "civilising" intentions of the earlier missionaries we have seen and was generally the political bent of all those who espoused the notion of the noble savage.

François Le Vaillant at the Cape (1780–1784)

By far the most influential French writer of the eighteenth century who had firsthand knowledge of the Cape was François Le Vaillant (1753–1824). Born in the Dutch colony of Surinam in South America in 1753, he played a great deal on his colonial upbringing, claiming this gave him the status of a "savage" in France, which he continued to regard as the country of his adoption until late in adult life.

Le Vaillant's parents were French, and they left Surinam when he was ten years of age to return to France. Like many who had had a colonial upbringing, Le Vaillant bore the "torn identity of children of empire,"[17] retaining a deep loyalty to the country of his birth and early upbringing. His unhappy tone in describing his departure from the shores of South America for the cold north finds echoes in the experience of generations of colonial children. Moreover, his unusual background was later to prove particularly useful to him during the revolutionary period in France, when he came into his own as a celebrated writer and naturalist. Insisting all the time on his patriotism toward France, he declares that he was nevertheless "independent, born free, raised in the most southern climes, with a language and principles very different from our own."[18] The different official language of Surinam happened to be Dutch, another factor that was to prove of incalculable benefit for one visiting the Cape of Good Hope at the end of the eighteenth century, still run in the last period of its suzerainty by the VOC.

Le Vaillant's upbringing was hardly conventional. Although his father was the French consul in Surinam, Nicolas François Vaillant senior (the

"Le" was added by François) seems to have made his living by trading animal specimens and, to support his business, travelled extensively in what was a remote and wild country, with his wife and the young son in tow. This experience may have induced wanderlust in the young François; it also made him a pragmatic adapter to whatever environment he found himself in. Even more significantly, the travels with his parents instilled in him a lifelong passion for animal, bird, and plant life as well as a keen interest in observing the customs and manners of indigenous peoples. By contrast, it also turned him into an avid hunter, which did not, in his mind, appear to conflict with his love of the animal world. All these influences came to fruition during his adventurous travels in Southern Africa, where he became both a celebrated naturalist (with a particular interest in birds), an intrepid hunter, and also an important social commentator on the life and manners of the local inhabitants, the Khoisan.

Le Vaillant's early childhood experience had also accustomed him to being the solitary European or white person among a dependent group of natives—in the patriarchal role of commanding but also protecting those under his care, typical of both the worst and the best aspects of the imperial experience wherever it has been found. But whatever the moral implications of his position of privilege, there can be no doubt that the young François was an adapter who embraced rather than rejected different cultures and who was prepared to judge them on their own terms rather than impose European values on them. However much of a poseur Le Vaillant became, as a sophisticated man of letters and a man of the world working from a country retreat convenient enough for him to be able to make frequent trips to Paris to attend to his literary affairs, this empathy with other cultures was genuine and informed his entire experience in the Cape. At the same time, as his modern editors have observed, his description of how he grew up almost a savage allowed him to present himself as an outsider to French habits and French artifice, someone closer to Rousseau's idea in *Emile* and elsewhere of what an ideally educated citizen should be like.[19]

After being schooled in Metz (his father's hometown), where he concentrated on natural history, Le Vaillant enlisted in the military, failing
apparently to make the highly prized status of a cavalry officer but finding
himself with enough free time to pursue his interest in natural history. In
due course, through his parents' connections with the VOC, he made an
important contact in the person of Jacob Temminck (1748–1822), the
powerful secretary of the Company. Temminck seems to have adopted the
young Le Vaillant as a protégé, giving him introductions to the scientific
community at Leiden where, as we have seen, the university still basked
under the reflected glory of Herman Boerhaave, the great botanist and
physician. Even more significantly, whether acting directly for the VOC
or on his own behalf, Temminck secured sponsorship for Le Vaillant's
planned trips to the Cape of Good Hope. In 1780, still in his late twenties,
Le Vaillant sailed for Cape Town on one of the VOC's ships to begin what
was to become a highly publicized series of trips to the interior of the Cape
region.

After his arrival in Cape Town, Le Vaillant soon became well-known
on the social scene, although he expressed a preference for solitary excursions on his own—up Table Mountain or Signal Hill, then as now great
physical landmarks of the city. Soon he was making hunting trips into the
hinterland around the town, at that time still the home of wild animals.
No doubt his prowess as a marksman was good (and his military service
had provided an opportunity to perfect his knowledge of arms, already
incipient in Surinam), but these excursions provided opportunity for raising the exotic profile of his Cape sojourn as well as for bragging about
his own bravery in the face of threats from wild animals. One of the more
colourful of these accounts concerns the shooting of a panther, which
he reminds his reader is more feared than a lion, on an occasion when Le
Vaillant was only accompanied by one loyal Khoisan follower:

> The frightful Tiger [panther] let out terrifying screams. At each moment,
> I expect him to rush out. The dogs, no doubt responding to his slightest

movement, jumped back hastily and scampered away as fast as they could. A few rifle shots, aimed at random, made up his mind for him. Out he came. This sudden appearance was, for everybody, the signal to beat a hasty retreat. . . . There I stand alone with my Hottentot. The Tiger, to get to another bush, passes fifty paces from us, with all the dogs at his heels. As he goes past, we salute him by firing our three shots.[20]

Le Vaillant holds his ground, wounds the animal, and in due course moves in to administer the fatal shot.

The native servant who accompanied Le Vaillant was probably "Klaas," who became a great favourite of his, a man whom he proclaims "would have given up his life for me in any circumstances"[21] and whom he describes as a "young student of Nature, fine spirit that our brilliant institutions had not spoiled" (see figure 18).[22]

In that description Le Vaillant pays lip service to Rousseau's *Emile*, emphasizing the moral quality of a life of one brought up amid nature and contrasting it with the corrupt influences in civilized society. Klaas was later to take up the cause of his own people in an attempt to resist the VOC but was humiliated and subdued.[23]

After his initial trips around Cape Town and Saldanha Bay, Le Vaillant made two long treks to the interior—in 1781, he travelled to the Eastern Cape; whilst in 1783–1784, he went northward toward the Orange River. All were considerable journeys over difficult terrain, undertaken by oxen-drawn wagon and accompanied by a large retinue of camp followers. The wagons contained supplies (other than meat, which would be obtained by hunting), ammunition, and most importantly, space for carrying the specimens that he collected on the way. Among the supplies, tobacco and brandy were particularly important, since these were prized by the Khoisan and could be used to barter for food or to bribe one's way out of an awkward situation.

As Le Vaillant's predecessors had learnt, travelling in the Cape in this period was no easy matter. Gushing rivers, impenetrable forest, and

difficult mountain passes with vertiginous falls had to be negotiated by
teams of oxen dragging the wagons as well as by the camp followers who
might themselves be carrying heavy weapons or other equipment. Le
Vaillant describes the difficulties of setting up camp in the driving rain,
of panic around him when lions or elephants have been spotted or heard,
of the extremes of temperature (at one moment unbearable heat and at
another the surprising chill of dawn in Africa), and of difficult repair
jobs when the wheels of wagons got broken. By contrast there are many
mentions of the warm hospitality afforded by Cape colonists, no doubt
dazzled by the dress and manner of the dashing French explorer, accompanied by his pet monkey called Kees—only partly domesticated and a
compulsive thief, who nevertheless became a close and indispensable
companion to his master.

　　While Le Vaillant was driven by his overriding desire to gather a collection of animal and bird specimens the like of which would stun Europe
and make his fame and fortune, his political sensibility was soon aroused
by what he saw of the situation of the Khoisan tribes living in the Cape
area. Away from the comforts of Cape Town, he became increasingly hostile to the colonial regime, still administered by the VOC. Noting that the
slave population in the city itself was not badly treated on the standards
of the times, Le Vaillant comes to realize that the reasonably benevolent
governance system of the VOC holds little sway among the settlers in the
vast interior of the colony. With a jaundiced eye, he surveys the history of
the European occupation of the Cape in 1652. He says of Jan van Riebeeck
that his "policy [was] of [the] able peacemaker and he used all the devious
means necessary to attract the goodwill of the Hottentots, and covered the
lip of the poisoned cup with honey."[24] In the language of Rousseau and
Thomas Paine he goes onto say, "These masters [the Khoisan] of the whole
portion of Africa by imprescriptible rights, these savages, were won over
by these cruel lies and did not see how this culpable abasement was taking away their rights, their authority, their peace and their happiness."[25]
The natural law basis of Le Vaillant's political stance is therefore clear: the

Khoisan natives, as original inhabitants of the Cape, have an inalienable right to the land and its produce, and that right has been illegitimately taken from them by the European settlers. Even worse, the settlers, far from offering any reasonable compensation for their unlawful seizure of the land, have instituted a harsh regime against the Khoisan and have committed "shocking atrocities against savages who have no protection and no support."[26] If some semblance of justice is written into the colonial governance system, the settlers in their frontier outposts have paid no attention to it, instead remorselessly exploiting the locals as a source of cheap labour.

Until the arrival of the Europeans, the Khoisan were indeed noble savages with simple needs. Leading a nomadic life in a country naturally rich in resources (of water, fuel, and food) they also lived in a communal, egalitarian manner. However, they were vulnerable to the allure of alcohol and tobacco with which the Europeans bribed them. Their contact with the white settlers was the source of their corruption and led to a life of decadence unknown to their untainted predecessors, a gentle and happy people. Le Vaillant's sympathetic, if somewhat hyperbolic, description of these character traits—based, as he never tires of telling his reader, on direct observation—is an elaboration of Rousseau's more sombre portrait of savage man in the *Discours* of 1755. As Le Vaillant travels through rough countryside, dependent on his followers (as his parents had been on theirs during their Surinam expeditions), Le Vaillant's fondness for the Khoisan increases, though he recognizes shortcomings in their nature such as a natural indolence that puts them off physical work and a disinclination to plan for the future.

Although Le Vaillant still thinks about the Khoisan in terms of their contribution to the economy of the Cape as a source of labour, he, like Pierre Pagès, also considers how they might best be integrated into colonial life as citizens with rights like those of others. Some form of devolved rule (as Adam Smith advocated for colonies) would ensure greater success and the rightful enjoyment of it by the original inhabitants.

Overall, Le Vaillant's commentary is a highly critical and radical attack on European colonialism, remarkable in the history of the travel literature of the Cape. Moreover, while previous visitors such as Carl Thunberg had expressed some sympathy for the Khoisan, suggesting that the VOC treatment of them was both unjust and cruel as we have seen, they nevertheless continued to regard them as a rude and savage people. Although Le Vaillant shared Anders Sparrman's more sympathetic view of the locals, he nevertheless dismisses the Swede's account as being inauthentic.

Le Vaillant also rejects the widely held belief among European visitors that the Khoisan lacked moral character; indeed, he extends his radical defence of savage virtue to include the so-called Caffres or Xhosa (black) tribes of the Eastern Cape, who put up a stiff resistance to the settlers' advance into their traditional territories. These tribes, Le Vaillant tells his readers, have obviously taken up arms against the European invaders, but "they are not by nature cruel. Like all the savages in this part of Africa they live on the ample produce of their herds, feed on milk products, and cover themselves with animal skins. Like the others they are indolent by nature, then wage war when circumstances demand it. But they are not a hateful nation whose very name should inspire terror."[27]

The Genre of the Travels

As we have already seen, there was a considerable body of travel literature about the Cape by the time Le Vaillant came to write his own account. There was also a much wider tradition of exotic travel writing that, since the seventeenth century, had concentrated on the East. The landmark work for the eighteenth-century development of this literature was Antoine Galland's *The Arabian Nights Entertainment*, which came out in a series from 1704 onward. Often the purpose of such tales was to contrast Arab or Turkish society unfavourably with the benefits of life in European, polite societies. These *contes de fées* could be merely diverting or intentionally satirical—in Dr. Samuel Johnson's dictionary's definition, "a feigned story intended to enforce some moral precept,"[28] which applied to his own oriental tale, *Rasselas* (1755), where exotic wrappers enfold a story meant to challenge the prevailing optimism of his day.

But not all accounts were biased in that direction—Lady Mary Wortley Montagu, for example, writing in the early part of the eighteenth century, had many favourable things to say about Turkish life and was open-minded enough to say of the Koran that it is an example of the "purest morality delivered in the very best language."[29] William Beckford, writing during the same period as Le Vaillant, was in the camp of those who took Eastern culture seriously. His *Vathek* (1786) and its sequel of episodic tales show a considerable interest and respect for Oriental culture, as well as a vast erudition in the literature and lore of the East. Even more significantly for these citizens of the world, Sir William Jones's seminal work on languages would provide an intellectual framework for a radical reappraisal of the relative merits of European and Eastern cultures by putting Sanskrit on a higher level of sophistication than Latin or Greek.

Le Vaillant's book was, of course, undertaken to create his fame and fortune, and we have seen how political a tract it was in tone. His planning for it was part of an ambitious programme that involved selling his collection of animal and bird specimens to the nation. The literary work itself was announced as part of a larger project, with considerable emphasis on the fact that it was a firsthand account of territory virtually unknown to Europeans: "This is a pure, simple easy text written by the traveller himself in the most honoured, most universal language, it is a *compte rendu*, completely truthful, of the discoveries of the author in a part of the world very little visited, not to say unknown before him."[30]

Preoccupied with the negotiations in connection with placing his collection of specimens, Le Vaillant was first helped by his father before handing over the task of editing his *Travels* to Casimir Varon (1761–1796), an influential figure in the revolutionary movement. The work was first published in 1790, with a second part in 1796; thus, both were produced during the stormy revolutionary decade. Varon's involvement during such a period, especially given his own political views, inevitably raises the question of what degree of editing took place and whether his influence was greater than otherwise might have been the case. Augustus St. John, an early commentator on the *Travels*, dismisses out of hand any suggestion that Varon composed a text on the basis of mere notes made by Le Vaillant. Without stating clearly why he comes to that conclusion, he says that such a view is a mistake as "he [Varon] merely read the proof sheets for the purpose of correction. Le Vaillant was not sufficiently acquainted with the French language to enable him to confide in his own judgment."[31]

In the absence of a manuscript that we might be able to compare with the published work, the matter of the extent of Varon's editorship remains an open question, and even with the possibility of such a comparison, it is possible that Le Vaillant himself thought it wise to make his work more in tune with the times—since he, among many others, was arrested and then released during the revolutionary decade.

An easier point to deal with is on the exact veracity of descriptions in the text. J. M. Coetzee, the contemporary South African writer, has warned against the academic tendency to correct literature like a school teacher. While it is evident from some of the detailed descriptions in the *Travels* that they must have arisen from observation on the ground, there is a flourish and exuberance to some of Le Vaillant's utterances that must be ascribed to that very French pursuit of style, something that Buffon had famously said was the man himself.[32] Le Vaillant's descriptions of scenes, especially when danger is threatening, are graphic and deliberately heightened by the use of suspense and last-minute triumph. He knows he is writing to entertain the reader and more than once refers to the romance of his African adventure and the need to maintain its illusion.[33] Nevertheless, as St. John rightly says, Le Vaillant's style is "graceful, natural and full of vivacity."[34]

At least part of its charm lies in the directness of his manner of addressing the reader, something that is immediately reminiscent of Rousseau. It also adds a modern tone to his flowing and easygoing style, with its occasional conceits and surprises. The influence of the *Travels* is also not in doubt.

His modern editors have said that Le Vaillant's account was the first literary work about South Africa to reach a wide audience and to have had a profound effect that shaped European perceptions of that country.[35] That perception was of an exotic and wild frontier country, rich in unusual and diverse fauna and flora (which he portrays in vivid images; see figures 13, 14, 15, and 17). The effect of the colourful and fantastic was exactly the effect that Le Vaillant had intended. Critics have also noted that Le Vaillant's criticism of the VOC rule was very much accepted by the British authorities, who were shortly to take over at the Cape from the Company—but to do so, of course, would have been in their political interest.

Although Le Vaillant's writings on his travels in the Cape are highly significant documents, his reputation was built on his work as an ornithologist. Le Vaillant made a point of rejecting Linnaeus's systematic nomenclature (followed, as we have seen, by his Swedish disciples Sparrman and Thunberg), instead giving French names to the new species he discovered. In fact his references to Sparrman's comments on the Cape are not positive: "The example of Dr Sparrman was scarcely one I wanted to follow."[36]

A number of birds, including the cuckoo, were named after Le Vaillant, just as Thunberg had had many Cape flora named after him. Le Vaillant's vast output on the subject—six volumes between 1796 and 1808 on the birds of Africa—was a grand and costly project, finely illustrated with drawings by Jacques Barraband.[37] At the same time, the famous natural history museum at Leiden University became the repository for the vast number of bird skins Le Vaillant sent to Jacob Temminck and that were eventually put in order by Temminck's son, Coenraad Jacob Temminck.

However significant Le Vaillant's contribution to ornithology has been, his *Travels* is a work remarkable as a political critique and an important addition to our knowledge of the life of the early inhabitants of the Cape.

Whatever the authorial motive—and we know that it was to make his name and his fortune—the *Travels* is a biting criticism of European colonialism, clearly inspired by Rousseauist political theory with its egalitarian undertone but taking it further with a considerable emphasis on the humanity as well as the nobility of this "savage" race.

Le Vaillant insists that it is the rapaciousness of individual colonists that has led to the enslavement in all but name of the local inhabitants. While certain elements of justice were written into the governance arrangements, even the governor had little power in the face of the behaviour of the settlers, as Le Vaillant makes clear in this rhetorical passage: "But frankly, in colonies where the general good is subordinated to the private advantages of a few united entrepreneurs, interested in stifling any conception that might tend to diminish their profits, what is a Governor?"[38] Clearly the model of a monopoly company controlling the Cape was no longer acceptable: Le Vaillant's sympathy with the Khoisan pushed him in the direction of a new deal in which they, together with the settlers, would benefit.

Prior to the appearance of the *Travels*, various candidates had been identified as the noble savage—for example, the North American Indians or the indigenous peoples of South America—but Le Vaillant establishes the Khoisan of Southern Africa above all others as representatives of man in that happy condition before the arrival of the corrupting influence of civilization. The radical political philosophy of the *Travels* makes Le Vaillant's account one of the most significant statements about the European perception of the indigenous people made during the colonial period.

CHAPTER 6

Paradise Regained

THE EMERGING BRITISH COLONY

In September 1795 a British force took control of the castle of Good Hope, ending a period of almost 150 years of VOC rule. With a brief interruption from 1803 to 1806, when the Cape was returned to the Dutch, the British colony continued in existence until the formation of the Union of South Africa in 1910, when Louis Botha became the first prime minister. Over this period of more than a century, there was a considerable expansion of the Cape Colony eastward and northward and the transformation of what was a weak and financially draining outpost—which was nevertheless important to the British as a sea link to India, as it had been to the Dutch as a sea link to Batavia—into a commercially viable port and trading centre in its own right.

During the first British occupation, debate about the merits of retaining the colony was fuelled by considerable threats to its security and stability both from settler resistance on the one hand, and from indigenous uprisings of the Khoisan and Xhosa peoples on the other. Both these sources of instability were inherited from the VOC period. The Company had always struggled to control the settlers in the frontier communities outside Cape Town; periodic rebellions and consistent hostility from both the Khoisan and the Xhosa had also persisted throughout the Dutch

occupation. To these difficulties was added the financial dependence of
the Cape on whoever possessed it, something that had been a constant
source of concern during the long VOC period but that was accepted as
the price to be paid for maintaining the important fuelling station for the
Eastern trade. Those favouring abandonment of the British colony won
the day, albeit temporarily, when the Cape was handed back to the Dutch
(during the period of the Batavian Republic) under the terms of the
Treaty of Amiens (1802).

For a brief three years the new Dutch administration, under the leadership of J. A. de Mist, aimed at reforming both the cumbersome and ineffective system of governance and stimulating the flagging economy. There
was some attempt to create a more inclusive society in which local Cape
personnel could be given more prominent roles, loosening the tight grip
on expatriate officeholding that had existed under the VOC. De Mist's
proposals were radical. Accepting that there was some truth in the British accusation that the colonists were idle, he also recognised the difficulty
of their life in the face of continuous warfare with the indigenous population, especially the San raiders to the north and the Xhosa in the East. One
remedy he proposed was a reduction in the size of the colony—something
unlikely to be welcomed by the *trekboers*, but which he saw as providing
more living space for the Khoisan and Xhosa and thereby reducing their
aggression against the colonists. Another suggestion was to make the Cape
formally part of the Netherlands. By doing that, a coherent policy could
be implemented without the constant to-and-fro dialogue between the
authorities at home and in the Cape, which led to endless delays and sometimes the complete abandonment of policies already agreed on. One of
the most interesting reports of this brief Batavian period was made by
Lodewyk Alberti (published in 1810) on the Xhosa peoples of the Eastern
Cape. Described as the "first ethnographic monograph" in Dutch, it was
soon translated into French and German. In it Alberti adopts the system
described in Baron Joseph-Marie de Gèrando's questionnaire in a book
he published in 1800: "The considerations that needed to be taken into

account included the origins of the peoples being described, their physical attributes, their social arrangements and moral codes (for these did exist), their habits in warfare, and how they might be induced into life in a more advanced society than their own although the latter was recognised for its own ordered characteristics."[1] The structural problems of the Cape economy derived from a sparsely populated, undercapitalised enclave with a poor transport system linking it to the interior. What agricultural produce there was could not be competitive on international standards, debilitated by the high cost of imported materials and a rigid fiscal control of the currency.

These problems did not disappear when the Cape was forcibly taken for the British Crown in 1806. Indeed, a further difficulty was the hostility of the largely Dutch settler population, the main food producers in the colony upon whom both Cape Town itself and passing ships depended for provisions. Recognition of the need to keep the Boer settlers appeased—principally by turning a blind eye to slavery and other labour practices beginning to be opposed in Britain—was a major consideration in the making of British colonial policy. The focus of the new regime remained the provision of a reliable entrepôt for ships on the way to and back from the East. Nevertheless, despite these difficulties, the period up to 1815 was one of considerable expansion, partly brought about by ending monopolistic practices and promoting free trade. This took place under direct British administration rather than under the aegis of the English East India Company, despite the preference of Lord Macartney, the first British governor, that the Company should take control in the manner of the VOC.[2]

The free trade approach opened up Cape Town as a port; a large increase in British but also foreign shipping is recorded over the period. The stimulation of trade that this brought about led to higher levels of European immigration to the colony so that by 1815, the free population had almost doubled and with it the dependent slave population. The growth outside Cape Town itself was even more marked than in the town itself. The Cape was also brought into the system of British imperial preferences, making

its goods more competitive. This led to rapid expansion of certain indus-
tries, such as wine production, which now began to get a foothold in European markets on a scale not hitherto achieved. While the economic
development came gradually and unevenly in different sectors, over the
period the Cape was developing from a mere staging post to a colonial
export economy—despite the continuance of certain restrictive practices,
such as the loan farm system, which discouraged private enterprise.[3]

The social and racial mix on which this growth was based had a certain fluidity inherited from the VOC period. Intermarriage between the
races continued; certain prominent citizens of Cape Town came from
mixed ethnic backgrounds. At the top of the social pyramid was a group
of elite Cape families, the "Cape gentry,"[4] which had established themselves in the latter part of the eighteenth century. At the other end of the
social scale were decommissioned soldiers and sailors who typically married into the local coloured population. The most clear-cut social distinction was that between the free population and the majority of slaves and
servants subordinate to it. While in Britain slavery was increasingly
challenged (and the slave trade was abolished in 1807) the British authorities in the Cape tended to favour the maintenance of the status quo in a
colony where slaves were the principal labour force. In the outlying settler areas, opposition to British rule would most easily be fomented if
colonial policy became too radical on the issue of slavery. While the
administration introduced measures to mitigate the abuses of the system
by providing for slave complaints to be heard, there was no sustained
attempt to condemn what was increasingly seen in Britain as an economically outmoded and morally reprehensible state of subjugation.

The British authorities also made determined efforts to gain the loyalty of the Khoikhoi population. One measure they took to increase its
feeling of commitment was to revive and promote the Hottentot Corps (of
Khoikhoi volunteers) to act as a backup to the British garrison. Service in
the corps was not universally popular because it entailed separation from
family, but in a situation of unemployment among the free Khoikhoi

population, it at least provided a livelihood. At the same time attempts were made to improve the education system. The *Cape Gazette*, a government organ, was set up to distribute official propaganda. There was no free press.

Rigid subordination of labour remained colonial policy as it had been under the VOC, although it was challenged by individual British officials and visitors as well as by the growing missionary groups, especially the London Missionary Society under Johannes van der Kemp, which we have considered in the previous chapter. Enlightenment ideas—of a secular modern order based on just and effective administration, with greater technical efficiency—were checked in the Cape by the colonial system as well as by the fear among conservative politicians of the excesses of the French Revolution. The British administration was primarily concerned with maintaining public order, while turning the colony into a more effective economic part of the expanding British Empire. To consolidate British rule, local Dutch leaders like Willem van Rijneveld were kept on in prominent positions (he continued as fiscal until his death in 1812), and the professionalism of the administration was improved. Although the official structure was a unitary one under the control of the governor and his council, in practice power was dispersed, since the colonists could appeal directly to London about decisions with which they did not agree. Outside Cape Town the old Dutch system of the *landrosts*, supported by appointed farmers, continued to function.

Sir John Barrow at the Cape (1797–1798)

It is against this backcloth that a new generation of British travellers and officials arrived in the Cape, one of whom was John Barrow (later Sir John; 1764–1848). Barrow, though himself of a poor background, came as secretary to Lord Macartney, the first British governor. Barrow had already had considerable overseas experience before arriving at the Cape at the age of thirty-three. He had been a member of Macartney's unsuccessful expedition to China in 1793, where he was one of the few British officials to master Chinese. Although intending to settle in the Cape—he married Anna Maria Truter, a Capetown lady—his plans were changed when the Cape was handed back to the Dutch in 1803. He returned to England, where he was appointed secretary to the Admiralty, overseeing various exploratory voyages to the Arctic during a long tenure of office that lasted until 1845. However, Barrow maintained a close interest in Cape affairs, donating books to the first national library when it was founded in 1818 in Cape Town. In 1835 he was created a baronet, and he had been involved in the foundation of the Royal Geographical Society.

Barrow's *Travels into the Interior of Southern Africa*, published in 1801, covered his four journeys to the interior during the years 1797 and 1798. The book was dedicated to Henry Dundas, secretary of state for war and an advocate of establishing a permanent British colony at the Cape. As well as a survey of geographical and geological matters (including a map of Southern Africa later criticised for inaccuracies by William Burchell), Barrow's work is a wide-ranging commentary on the general conditions of Cape life, including radical remarks on the treatment of the Khoisan and Xhosa. It was well received in Britain. While Barrow emphasises that his work is based on direct observation, in the time-honoured manner of travellers intent on emphasising the authenticity of their accounts, he nevertheless shows familiarity with the works of previous travel writers of whom he is highly critical. Pieter Kolb, Anders Sparrman, Carl Thunberg, and William Paterson—whose account he describes condescendingly as a "mere journal of occurrences"[5]—all come in for a verbal lashing.

Barrow is impressed by the neat layout of Cape Town on its grid system, if not by the inhabitants of the town—whom he regards as spending far too much time eating and drinking and taking little exercise. The colonial life he describes, with its endless round of social engagements, was exactly what had amused other more relaxed visitors, like William Hickey. But for the serious-minded Barrow it was too frivolous an existence and sapped up energy better directed to productive ends.

Joining the debate on whether Britain should retain the colony or give it up, he extols its advantages, observing that "a temperate climate, a fertile soil, a mild and peaceful race of natives, were advantages that few infant colonies have possessed, and as they still exist may one day be turned to account."[6] Turning the Cape into a viable colony in its own right could take place under ordered British rule, with its "spirit of improvement,"[7] but a condition for its success would be the integration into the colonial fabric of the Khoikhoi, which would also obviate the need for slavery. In fact, as we have seen, Jan van Riebeeck had a similar ambition but was forced to look for labour elsewhere, as the Strandlopers were unwilling to be brought into his net. Whatever had happened in the past, Barrow condemns the contemporary treatment of the Khoisan roundly, saying: "These weak people, the most helpless and in their present condition perhaps the most wretched of the human race, duped out of their possessions, their country and finally of their liberty have entailed upon their miserable offspring a state of existence to which slavery might bear the comparison of happiness."[8] Although recognising a certain indolence among the locals, Barrow deplores what he calls the "prejudice of colour"[9] and is convinced that failing to make the indigenes feel that they have a stake in society is a counterproductive policy that will store up resentment and lead to future trouble.

He notes that the San—Chinese-looking men (something Thunberg had remarked upon, because of the Oriental shape of their eyes)—seem to be livelier than the Khoikhoi, keeping themselves busy and with energy enough to dance through the night when celebrations were at hand. While they are by nature mild and could be corralled into colonial society, they have also suffered discrimination: "They were driven out of their own country, their children seized and carried into slavery, by the people on whom they now commit their depredations, and on whom they naturally take every occasion of exercising their revenge."[10] Instead of being treated fairly and "moulded into any shape,"[11] the San too have been exploited. The land seized by the colonists for expanding their farms was the very source of subsistence for these hunter-gatherers. Their violent attacks on the European settler farms are a direct result of their displacement from the land. Barrow is also one of the earliest travellers to remark upon San rock art, noting the San cave drawings of zebras and gemsbok as well as of other invented creatures, such as the unicorn, in charcoal and using ochre. The sophistication of their art "could not be expected from savages."[12]

Barrow is equally progressive in his view of the Xhosa Negroes. Their manners and codes (including condemnation of murder and of theft) "have the appearance of civilisation,"[13] while his description of them and their life harks back to the image of the noble savage, a muscular and elegant figure, which we have considered in the previous chapter in the context of the French writers and, particularly, of François Le Vaillant. Barrow says of the Xhosa:

Their diet is simple; their existence of a salutary nature; their body is neither cramped nor encumbered by clothing; the air they breathe is pure; their rest is not disturbed by violent love, nor their minds ruffled by jealousy; they are free from those licentious appetites which proceed frequently more from a depraved imagination than a real want: their frame is neither shaken nor enervated by the use of intoxicating liquours, which they are not acquainted with; they eat when hungry, and sleep when nature demands it. With such a kind of life, languor and melancholy have little to do. The countenance of a Kaffer is always cheerful, and the whole of his demeanour bespeaks content and peace of mind.[14]

Barrow's Enlightenment scepticism about religion is clearly displayed when tackling the accusation that the Xhosa are without religion, for he says that they have not "bewildered their imaginations so far with metaphysical ideas of the immortality of the soul."[15] Further remarks suggest he does not consider it worth anyone worrying unduly about matters that are unfathomable to the human mind.

While Barrow's references to Thunberg are respectful of the professor's authority in matters of fauna and flora, he criticises his grasp of topography. He is even more scathing in dealing with Le Vaillant, whose somewhat brash showmanship he is determined to expose. Visiting a family with whom Le Vaillant stayed, Barrow tests out the Frenchman's aggrandising account of his hunting a tiger (as we have seen, actually a panther) by reading out a passage from his book to the local farmers. He records wryly: "They laughed very heartily, and assured me that although the story had some foundation in fact the animal had been shot through the body by stell-roar or trap-gun, set by a Hottentot, and was expiring under a bush by the time they found it, when the valiant Frenchman discharged the contents of his musquet into the tiger and despatched him."[16]

Barrow's contention is that Le Vaillant's first book contained "much correct information, accurate description, and a number of pointed and just observations" but was corrupted by insertion of fabricated material, including the panther hunt, so as to boost the sales of a second edition—the real author of which he claims was one Abbé Philippo.[17] We know that Le Vaillant sought editorial help from Casimir Varon,[18] so that there is some room for doubt about the authenticity of parts of the final version of his travels.

It may be that Barrow realised more than he was willing to admit on paper that he shared Le Vaillant's sympathy with the Khoisan and, together with his commitment to the study of birds and animals, the Frenchman deserved some credit. In fact, Barrow agrees with Le Vaillant's criticism of Cape Town society, which he finds isolated and distant from the frontier life of the settler communities. That, of course, was a problem throughout the VOC period, as we have seen: edicts from the castle were simply ignored by the farmers in outlying areas. If he is critical of Cape Town officials, Barrow's opinion of the Dutch settlers is not particularly flattering: they seem to be struck by the same indolence as the Khoikhoi, living in uncomfortable and sometimes squalid homes and unable to stir themselves into making the most of a promising environment. They are not the material on which a new order can be built.

Barrow considers that part of the misgovernance of the colony arises from sheer ignorance on the part of the administration about the geography and agriculture of the country they nominally controlled. Talking to local officials does not inspire him with any confidence in their abilities to govern a vast and growing territory. But beyond that limitation there was also the social gap between the free and the slave populations. It was a rigid distinction that could only occasionally be put aside when slaves were freed; by a statute dating from VOC times, the children of slaves were bound in the service of their parents' masters until the age of twenty-five. Although, like others, Barrow notes that slaves are not badly treated in Cape Town itself, they and the subservient Khoisan population do not share in the growing prosperity of the town.

The only Europeans who had successfully bridged the gap between the social groups were the missionaries whose communities were modelled on the idea of bringing everyone into the productive cycle. Like Lady Anne Barnard after him, Barrow admired the Moravian missionary station at Genadendal (then still known as Baviaanskloof), near Caledon, which he considers could be a model for the running of the whole colony. The missionaries, "by their mild and humane conduct, inspire them [the locals] with a degree of confidence in men of a different complexion to themselves."[19] Instead of learning from their mistakes, the British have acquiesced in the unfair and ultimately unproductive system inherited from the Dutch. In that way they have abdicated their responsibility to govern the colony justly, in the interests of all its inhabitants rather than just a few of them—a policy also flawed economically.

LADY ANNE BARNARD'S RESIDENCE (1797–1802)

In May 1797 Lady Anne Barnard (1750–1825) arrived in Table Bay on board the ship *Sir Edward Hughes*. She was one of the most observant and talented visitors to the Cape in the early British period. Although her stay lasted only five years, she left an extensive record in the form of a private journal, diaries, and voluminous correspondence and in pictorial form in a series of paintings and sketches illustrating every aspect of local life. In later years Lady Anne looked back on her Cape sojourn with some nostalgia, regarding it as the golden period in her life; it was certainly one that she enjoyed to the full and of which she left a powerful legacy (figures 22, 25, and 26).

Anne Lindsay was the eldest daughter of the Earl of Balcarres, scion of an aristocratic but impoverished Scottish family. Her own Scots credentials were proved in her youth when she composed the poignant lament "Auld Robin Gray," later set to music. Her family was well connected and moved in the highest Edinburgh circles—where, among others, she befriended Henry Dundas (then solicitor general for Scotland, who later, as secretary of state for war, was a strong advocate of British control of the Cape as a protection against French occupation and the potential blocking of the sea route to India). As a young woman she joined her sister, Margaret, in London in the latter's newly acquired Adam-style mansion in Berkeley Square. The sisters, though of slender means, made the most of their social connections, attending soirées in the best London houses and forming friendships with politicians and diplomats, as well as literati such as Horace Walpole. Lady Anne also formed a long and lasting friendship with George, Prince of Wales, who was still living out his bohemian life as the reckless heir to the throne. To everyone's surprise, at forty-three years of age, she married Andrew Barnard, a former serving officer whose ill health had landed him on half-pay at home.

Meanwhile Henry Dundas's star was rising. Brought into William Pitt's cabinet, he assumed responsibility for India; Lady Anne became a confidante and thereby an influential figure in national affairs. Dundas was convinced of the importance of British control of the Cape, and he cast about for someone of authority to take on the governorship at what he judged to be a critical moment. His choice was Lord Macartney, who had

had a distinguished diplomatic career in various posts abroad, including
at the Court of the Russian Empress Catherine. Knowing that Macartney's
wife was unlikely to accompany him to the Cape, Dundas also arranged
for the post of colonial secretary to be offered to Andrew Barnard at the
princely salary of £3,000 a year, with the understanding that Lady Anne
would accompany her husband and act as hostess at Government House.
Barnard accepted the offer, and the couple spent the months before their
departure preparing for the posting, pouring "over old maps, trying to
piece together the pattern of their future life,"[20] and collecting an array of
objects including glass, cutlery, and curtains that the fastidious Lady Anne
considered essential for setting up a comfortable home. Seventy-one days
after leaving Plymouth, the Barnards arrived in Table Bay on 4 May 1797.
Only a few days later Lady Anne was already informing Dundas in a letter that "we feel ourselves much disposed to this place—the air is exhila-
rating and the climate delightful."[21] She also applauds the secretary of
state's foresight in appointing Lord Macartney as governor, as his conciliatory manner is exactly what the hitherto "languishing"[22] colony needs.
Macartney plays his part in Dundas's strategy, suggesting that the Barnards take over Government House while he himself stays in more modest
bachelor apartments within the castle precincts. Nothing could make it
clearer to Cape Town society that Lady Anne was primus inter pares and
would act as hostess at all official functions.

Despite her position, with its opportunity to give an account of Cape
Town life from the very centre of the administration at the castle, in her
Journals Lady Anne makes out that she is writing for herself and for "dear
people at home,"[23] and not as a political reporter for a wider audience. In
fact, she claims that she has no intention of publishing her work. Moreover, her account will be based on things "seen with her own eyes"[24] and
as accurate and truthful as possible. Africa must be allowed to "speak for
itself,"[25] and all hyperbole of the sort employed by Le Vaillant to elaborate
his account, full of "tall stories,"[26] must be avoided. Instead, her account
will retain a somewhat artful simplicity and be free of all prejudice or

charges of plagiarism. Nevertheless, as her editors point out, she "has the writer's ability to amuse and entertain."[27] Her correspondence also shows an awareness of the person to whom she is writing, with appropriate changes of tone when addressing different correspondents.[28]

Like other visitors before her, Lady Anne finds Cape Town "a respectable town, clean, correct in its regularity."[29] Even so, she quickly comes to appreciate that the Dutch residents are not over-enthusiastic about the British takeover, despite the fact that they are able to make money out of the newcomers by selling agricultural produce at a higher price than what they paid the local farmers for it. Nevertheless, they prove to be pragmatic, and soon Dutch ladies are joining in the festivities at the castle—providing some relief for the young British officers, largely marooned without any female company. To ensure that the policy of appeasement works, Lady Anne sets about revamping the state rooms at the castle, although she is aware of not overdoing public expenditure in bringing it up to a decent standard. Within a fairly short period a series of balls and soirées are held there, so that the castle becomes the very centre and hub of social life in Cape Town. The hostess's hand was greatly strengthened in her approaches toward the Dutch community by the support of Governor Macartney.

Organising the social affairs of the colony does not distract Lady Anne from admiring the natural wonders around her, of which Table Mountain is the most striking. Surveying its immensity brings out the philosophical in her, for she says that it will long survive the wonder of St. Peter's in Rome or the ephemeral creations of humankind, such as the glorious kingdom of Prussia or the glittering ministry of Pitt. Undaunted by its scale, she organises an expedition to the summit of the mountain, leaving the castle at six in the morning with a retinue of servants and slaves, carrying mattresses, blankets, and cutlery as an overnight stay was planned. Barrow, whom she greatly admires for his sharp intellect, was part of the group that set off on horseback but had soon to dismount because of the steepness of the ascending path. The scenery is grand—sleek leaves of the silver tree and profuse yellow flowers of the Waboom envelope the rocky path along which the guide, Mentor (whom she later sketches), takes them. Dressed in clothes borrowed from her husband's wardrobe, Lady Anne stops every now and again to sketch what she sees before her, while Barnard searches for plants and fossils to take back to show the governor.

The fine morning gives way to a brisker temperature as they scramble further up the slopes. Lady Anne produces a supply of port, Madeira, and Cape wine from which each of the party imbibe as protection against the sudden coolness, recorded as a startling drop of fifteen degrees on the thermometer. When they finally reach the summit, she is able to look down on the town "with much conscious superiority,"[30] while Barrow, "a man of infinite charts and maps,"[31] explains the topography to her. She just has time to sketch the scene from the top at sunset. A toast, in loud enough chorus to echo around the mountain, is sung for the king before the group start to think of supper. Finding their own food contaminated, the Europeans share the native stew, which is highly spiced and containing the local fish, snoek. As night descends, the tents are erected, mattresses are laid out, and all is made comfortable for a night on the summit. The next morning the trek down the mountain begins in a pleasant coolness.

Descending from the heights of Table Mountain, Lady Anne may have seen the slaves who were sent up on their daily mission of retrieving wood to be used as fuel by the townsfolk. Her reaction is one of compassion for the men struggling along under the weight of the bundles of wood they were carrying on their bare backs. Like other visitors, she records that "slaves are but rarely ill-used at the Cape,"[32] but clearly she is disturbed by the existence of the institution of slavery itself. Among her own household slaves, she notices individual intellectual or artistic qualities to which she warms. One of these slaves, Urbain, was an accomplished flute player and, despite her earlier warnings against flowery language, she says that the sounds he makes on his reed are singular and sweet, worthy of Pan himself.[33] Among the slave community, the Malays were well known for their musical aptitude.[34]

Nevertheless, Lady Anne soon appreciates that the issue of slavery is a tricky one, as the colonists depend upon slave labour to run their farms. Any attempt to alter the status of the slaves and their children would be strongly resisted by the very people who Macartney had been sent to the Cape to appease and turn into loyal subjects of the British Crown. In those circumstances, whatever her personal opinion about slavery as an institution, she had to remain silent if official British policy was to be followed successfully. Not all the British at the Cape agreed with Macartney's conciliatory approach. General Francis Dundas (a nephew of the secretary of state) seemed to regard the Barnards as social climbers and Lady Anne to be far too influential in the running of the colony. The only way the British were going to succeed, according to the general (who had been in charge until the governor's arrival), was to impose an iron rule of law on settlers who, in the past, had undermined the VOC regime exactly because of its lack of such a policy. Nor, it seems, did the general have much time for the governor's attempt to influence the somewhat dissolute behaviour among the officers at the garrison by gentle example rather than by outright disciple.

While Lady Anne tried to keep some distance from local politics, it was difficult to do so, given her husband's official position. She recognised that her husband and Macartney were perfectly suited to each other and both determined to carry out a conciliatory policy toward the Dutch. Her own attitude toward the Dutch seemed to vary at different times. She shared something of Barrow's view that they were indolent and uncouth, remarking upon the fact that the settlers outside Cape Town came from the lowest and ill-educated class. They, in their turn, would certainly not have appreciated Lady Anne's relaxed aristocratic manner and her considerable erudition.[35] She finds the wives of the farmers unpolished and, in some cases, gross. Most of the women, once they have had children, become rotund and seem to have no idea of remaining attractive in the eyes of their husbands. On the other hand, she also acknowledges the well-known hospitality of the settlers, remarking upon the generous meals that are served whenever a visitor chances at the door, always accompanied by the highest quality of butter, which they have produced themselves.

Even some members of the Cape gentry do not escape her criticism of uncouthness. In one entry she describes a visit to Constantia, where Hendrik Cloete, the owner of the estate, passes summer months. Although he himself is an amiable host, showing them round the estate and serving excellent wines, made from the famous Constantia grapes, she finds part of his summer house squalid, with small, cramped rooms where old slaves live. Nevertheless, Lady Anne's political antennae do not desert her—she understands how threatened the Dutch settlers feel by the arrival of the British and diplomatically keeps certain opinions to herself.

From the very outset Lady Anne shows liberal and even radical views about the Khoisan and the Xhosa in her diaries. The artist in her is attracted to them as exotic models, but as well as an aesthetic interest, a note of genuine compassion is struck in her remarks on the general conditions of their life in the colony. Describing their dress of leather round the waist and sheepskin round their shoulders, she goes on to say, "I cannot say I think the Hottentots so uncommonly ugly or disgusting as they are reported to be—their features are small and not ill shaped, the expression of their eyes is sweet and inoffensive, their cheek bones are certainly immense and one misses the cheek altogether, but they are not uglier than the malay slaves, or those from Masambique who have uncouth features but fine persons."[36] She rather breezily passes over the habit of eating the entrails of animals with the remark that Europeans do not think anything of the production of classical music on instruments made of similar animal matter. And she roundly dismisses the accusation that the Khoikhoi are nasty and unclean: neither characteristic has she observed in her contact with them.

The closest chance to see how the Khoikhoi might be improved by better treatment came when Lady Anne visited the Moravian mission at Baviaanskloof (Genadendal), near Caledon, which impressed her as much as it had Barrow. On approaching the simple church building, she is struck by the sweet and melodious sound of the congregation singing the twenty-third psalm. But the most impressive aspect of the settlement was the emphasis that the Brethren put on teaching the Khoikhoi to be self-sufficient by learning how to cultivate crops and practising various arts and crafts to improve their environment. Passing gardens that were "not very neat,"[37] she enters one of the thatched *rondavels*, which remind her of peasant houses in Ireland. Here, she says, "furniture there was none, a few sticks were in the Centre to boil their kettle, and tied to the sticks of the roof were a few skins. Some calabashes . . . an iron pot . . . a couple of spoons made of bits of wood to the end of which a deep shell was spliced and tied on, some Calabash ladles and bowls. At the doors several of them were employed in drying hides in the Sun, and at the same time softening the leather by a preparation of their own."[38] Simple though these conditions were in her eyes, they represent a considerable improvement in the lot of the Khoikhoi, but the mission is deeply resented by the local settlers, who are threatened by the prospect of the labour force on which they depend no longer needing to rely on them for employment.

Lady Anne is equally enthusiastic about the Xhosa, although she would not have seen many of them in Cape Town itself. She quotes a resident of Graaff-Reinet, an informant of Barrow, that they are "extremely clever, political and fine in their dealings, but by no means so cruel as we have reason to believe by writers."[39] Like any other people in desperate straits, they will resort to extreme measures, but even when committing an act of robbery, if their victim willingly hands over whatever they are after, they will deal with them amiably, even hospitably. Some of their customs—such as polygamy—obviously conflict with European values, but a strict code of marital faithfulness applies to a man, however many wives he may have. Like others, she can also find no commitment to religious worship, but she notes that they do have a notion that the spirits of their ancestors may still influence their daily lives.

Physically and, as an artist, aesthetically, Lady Anne is attracted to these "tall and well made" men.[40] She records details of their appearance in shaving their heads and tattooing the sides of their faces. Although wandering about almost naked, they are in fact great lovers of clothes and ornaments, particularly shiny emblems and glass beads. As in many primitive societies, the burden of work falls upon the women, who act in labouring roles while the "men sit round the fire smoking"[41] in the midst of the kraal of round, mud huts that are their homes.

Some of the most important records left by Lady Anne are the numerous paintings and sketches that she made of the landscape, fauna and flora, and inhabitants of the Cape. She is fascinated by the racial mix of the colony's inhabitants, vowing in her *Journals*: "I must try to catch a face of every different caste or nation here, the Collection cannot be short of 20, if I have time I will attempt this, but when will that be?"[42] While her portraits of Europeans tended to be formal or mere sketches—she sometimes preferred painting the back views of the lady farmers so as not to offend them by presenting an unfortunate face—her studies of the indigenes attempt to capture their character in their facial expression and by suggestion of their body movements. One of the most remarkable is the sketch of a Hottentot whose expression is reserved but sharply intelligent, looking directly at the viewer without fear (figure 25).

There are also striking portraits of a Xhosa man and woman, which it has been suggested might have been sketched during a visit of a chieftain to the castle shortly after the arrival of the Barnards.[43] In two other striking watercolours, the figures, dressed for combat and posing on Table Mountain, are given a neoclassical touch. They strongly resemble Samuel Daniell's aquatint entitled "Bushmen Hottentots Armed for an Expedition" in his collection *African Scenery and Animals*, which was published in London in 1804–1805.

Daniell had arrived at the Cape in 1799 as part of the entourage of Sir George Yonge, the new governor who replaced the ailing Macartney. Macartney's departure and the temporary control of General Dundas marked the turning point in the Barnards' ascendency in the Cape. From that time on they were sidelined: the new governor arrived with a new hostess, a Mrs. Blake.[44] Daniell, who later became Barrow's secretary, was considerably influenced by his employer's views. He was one of the early independent traveller-artists who invested in his own expedition to benefit directly from it.[45] His representations of the Cape compare with the style of Oriental scenery gaining popularity in Britain. His style was a blend of topographical precision with Claudian composition and sensibility.[46] In respect of his figures of people, he follows Barrow in idealizing the Khoikhoi and Xhosa, often drawn in neoclassical mode, while depicting the Boers in less edifying sketches implying their peasant nature (figures 16 and 19).

At first Lady Anne seemed unimpressed by his drawings, but in due course befriended him as a fellow artist and allowed him to stay in the Barnards' home. It was not long before a rumour, perhaps circulated by Mrs. Dundas (the wife of the still hostile General Dundas), suggested that Lady Anne had in fact made copies of Daniell's drawings, especially of animals, with the intention of passing them off as her own. In correspondence with Macartney (now home in England), Lady Anne hotly denies that she had entered Daniell's bedchamber to make copies without his knowledge, although she admits to having copied one or two of his sketches of animals. Her account is contradicted by Barrow, who by this time had joined the Dundas faction. He claims that Daniell himself approached him, telling him that when he, Daniell, had confronted Lady Anne with the theft by copying, she was highly embarrassed and burnt all the copies she had made.[47] The two versions of what happened cannot be entirely reconciled, but what is apparent is that there are striking similarities in the portraits of the figures drawn by the two artists, as well as another scene showing the newly constructed theatre in Hottentot Square (figure 12).

Lady Anne's subject matter extended to landscapes, houses, and of course the fauna and flora of the Cape with which she was so taken, like others before her. There are Arcadian views of mountains and lakes made on her journey to the interior, and there are detailed studies of birds and insects. The houses she lived in—"Paradise" in Rondebosch (the idyllic rustic retreat of the Barnards) or Dutch colonial houses on the vineyard estates in the hinterland—take on a Romantic feel under her brush. But the undoubted masterpiece is her panorama of Cape Town as seen from the castle: beginning at Devil's Peak, it sweeps across Table Mountain and Lion's Head, with the neatly laid out town and harbour beyond the battlement wall. With the Union flag shown twice on the landscape, the sweeping panorama is nothing less than a celebration of British imperial order in a new and exotic setting. It is also a fine tribute to her talents as a painter and recorder of local scenes in the early days of the British colony, which match her talent as a diarist and journalist portraying every aspect of life and politics during her productive stay at the Cape.

The Batavian Restoration: Henry Lichtenstein (1803–1806)

British criticism of the old Dutch regime, particularly by Barrow, did not go unchallenged: in 1803 Martin Hinrich Karl Lichtenstein (1780–1857), usually called Henry, arrived in the service of General Jan Willem Janssens, the governor who succeeded de Mist during the brief period of the Batavian restoration. Attacking Barrow's account became something of an obsession with Lichtenstein, although he seems only too aware of the circle of criticism by one Cape traveller of another. In the long preface to his weighty *Travels*, he warns his reader: "Le Caille and Menzel are severe on Kolbe, Sparrman criticises La Caille and Menzel, and Le Vaillant comes under the censure of Mr Barrow."[48] He then adds somewhat sententiously: "For myself I must confess that the two descriptions of the two latter [i.e., Le Vaillant and Barrow], partly given without sufficient impartiality, partly too much loaded with ornament, have had considerable influence upon the form which I have given to my work, earnestly desirous as I am of avoiding former failures."[49] Barrow did not fail to return the compliment when he said later in his lengthy article in the *Quarterly Review*, "We apprehend that Doctor Lichtenstein was made 'Professor of Natural History in the University of Berlin' in consequence of a box of insects presented to that learned body: for we find nothing in his book which indicates the slightest knowledge of science."[50]

Admitting that every traveller will have a different view because of his "peculiar turn of thinking,"[51] Lichtenstein is nevertheless determined to defend the Dutch regime as well as the character of the settlers, whom he says have been falsely maligned by Barrow. He realises that he cannot entirely put aside the failings of the last VOC period: the colony, he admits, was in an "unusual state of anarchy and internal distraction"[52] when the British took over in 1795. However, during their eight-year tenure of control the British had done little to improve the situation and returned the Cape to Holland "in a wretched condition."[53] He also dismisses Barrow's criticism that the Dutch did not secure Saldanha Bay as an important protection of Cape Town itself, as well as a potential area for agricultural development. It simply would not have been possible to defend the straggling coastline, nor was the supply of water there as plentiful as Barrow had claimed.

Lichtenstein's strongest repudiation of Barrow is over the character and behaviour of the Dutch settlers. The "African" settlers, as he habitually calls them, are not slothful and violent. In fact, Dutch landowners are busily engaged in the running of their estates, some of which were very large. He gives various examples, including that of one Jacob Laubscher, whose farm holds hundreds of cattle, thousands of sheep, and other animals and in which about a hundred people are employed. Managing such a farm, with the vagaries of the Cape climate, is a challenging task that requires energetic commitment. Nor does Lichtenstein find the Afrikaners uncontrolled and violent: they are, in fact, restrained in manner and only resort to severe discipline where it is required, as it is when dealing with marauders and cattle thieves. Slaves on the whole are well treated: Lichtenstein cites the case of a slave who could have been a hundred and twenty years old who was looked after by his Dutch master long after he was capable of working. He denies that the settlers are uncouth and vulgar: they express themselves "by a concise, yet expressive African Dutch language."[54] Their hospitality is legendary, something that Barrow and almost every visitor to the Cape had in fact remarked upon.

Lichtenstein does not have much good to say about the Khoisan, especially the San. The latter are a race of ugly, ungovernable savages who are at the "very lowest step in the order of civilisation."[55] Although he acknowledges that their traditional hunting grounds have been invaded by Europeans, he points out that they were in fact incompetent hunters on account of their idleness and poor weapons. The areas in dispute were sufficiently rich in game to meet the needs of the San and the settlers, if only the former would realize that they could still subsist on the shared land.

His view of the Xhosa is much more positive and begins with a surprising tribute to Barrow for his accurate description of them. He explains rather fulsomely, "I consider myself bound to make this acknowledgment, since I have in many other instances combated the views he took of things."[56] The tribe Lichtenstein praises the most are the "Koosa," who he says inhabit the area of the coast stretching eastward from Cape Point toward the Kei River. Physically they are impressive: "They are much taller, stronger and their limbs are better proportioned than the Khoisan. They have high foreheads, the prominent nose of the Europeans, the thick lips of the negroes, and the high cheekbone of the Hottentots."[57]

Although he notes that polygamy is practised and that the Xhosa can be fierce in their treatment of the enemy, he echoes Barrow is saying that they incline to civilisation, teaching their children to behave respectfully. They also lead a frugal and temperate life, which contributes to their good health. He never notices any of them sneezing or coughing! Nevertheless, while there appears to be no outward performance of religious rites among them, "they believe in the existence of a great being who created the world, but in their own language, as Van der Kemp assured me, they have no name by which he is called: they have therefore adopted one from the Gonaaquas [the name of one of the Khoikhoi tribes] who called him Thiko."[58]

In one area—their belief in witchcraft—they display a deep superstition, believing that certain individuals have the power of enchantment and their instructions have to be followed to avoid evil. When crimes such as murder have been committed, people have to be "cleansed" by the witch doctor, who will also give them a new name.

Lichtenstein gives detailed accounts of the landscape and locations that he visits on his journeys, including a mention of any unusual plants or animals. He is much taken by the beauty of the coasts from Mossel Bay to Algoa Bay in the east, noting the gradual declivity of the land. He finds much evidence of destruction on the farms of settlers from the marauding San and Xhosa nomads but admires the farmers' toughness in refusing to be subdued or scared away. The rugged, mountainous countryside presents real challenges for the wagon traveller: Lichtenstein cites a number of very difficult moments, with the exhausted oxen dragging the carriages over precipitous passes. Nevertheless, Lichtenstein too displays tough qualities and a considerable ability to concentrate on what he sees and record it in fine detail.

WILLIAM JOHN BURCHELL: HUMANIST AND BOTANIST (1810–1815)

A few years after Lichtenstein's visit, William Burchell (1782–1863) made a great tour of the interior and left the most extensive record of fauna and flora of this period, well illustrated with his careful sketches. Burchell came from a botanical background: his father, Matthew Burchell, owned the Fulham nursery; William served as an apprentice at Kew but was already showing considerable talent as an artist in his teens. His first venture abroad was to St. Helena, where he set up in business as a trader with one William Balcombe. For various reasons, including temperamental differences, the partnership did not last. Burchell then joined the British East India Company in the dual capacity of teacher and botanist, glad to escape from the island society that he found suffocating and in which he never felt at home.[59]

After two weeks at sea, with his ship unable to dock due to stormy weather, Burchell finally arrived in Cape Town in 1810. He soon taught himself Dutch and started to prepare for his great trek into the interior, during which he gathered a vast amount of scientific material and a large collection of specimens. He covered something like 7,000 kilometres on the journey and collected over 60,000 specimens, which included animals, insects, and fish as well as plants.[60] Wherever possible on his travels, he tried to record place names according to their Hottentot appellation, adding English names in brackets where they applied. Well advised about the difficulty of travelling in the rugged terrain of the interior, he had special wagons designed to withstand the rough jolting that resulted from the uneven surfaces of the tracks. In addition to his supply of food and medicines, the enlightened polymath carried fifty or sixty volumes of books that he read or consulted on the way.[61]

Burchell was a man of deep religious conviction, and a natural good nature made him highly sympathetic toward the Khoisan. Recognising that their existence is pitifully near the edge of survival, he adds plaintively that after a day of difficulties they "return to their wretched huts to pass the painful night in hunger, and unsheltered from the storm."[62] This is a harsh existence, but the Khoisan have adapted to it to survive: "But to a European the case is widely different; and some powerful feelings of the mind are required for supporting the body through all the inconveniences and privations of savage life."[63] Burchell does recognise that the simplicity of the Khoisan life is suitable for survival in the environment of Southern Africa. When the San need a pot to melt down animal fat, they hollow a stone that is crude but serves the purpose. The Khoikhoi had developed an ingenious method for cooking ostrich eggs by piercing them delicately so that they could be held over an open fire and, in effect, made hardboiled. Neither the Khoi nor the San had any conception of private property; their nomadic lifestyle was increasingly threatened as European settlers made claims to land. Nevertheless, even in the primitive conditions of nomadic life, certain standards of behaviour were expected and serious crimes punished. The Khoikhoi took good care of their children, whom they expected to behave properly. Much of the degeneracy of the indigenous people had been caused by an addiction to alcohol and tobacco, both encouraged by the colonists as a way of keeping control of them.

His description of the San is one of the most detailed and sympathetic on record. He visited and stayed at a number of San kraals to observe "man in an uncivilised state"[64] at close quarters. Noting that for the "fidelity of [his] narration . . . [he must] relate the pleasing, as well as the unpleasing parts of this people's character,"[65] his account is nevertheless largely favourable. Burchell shares the Enlightenment belief that all men have the same feelings and emotions, however they are disguised by the particular cultural practices that they follow and whether they are deemed to be civilized or not on European standards. They must be treated with respect and with fairness. His manner evoked a positive response: the locals, while highly amused at his ability to repeat words they had taught him from script he had written down, were also enchanted by his flute playing.

The positive points of the San are their complete lack of avarice and their decent treatment of each other within their own communities. At one of the Bushmens' kraals, of about 120 inhabitants, which he visited on his own, Burchell is received in a friendly fashion "everywhere with smiling faces."[66] While no one seems curious about his own origins or country, they appreciate some of the things he is wearing (such as his leather belt), and they are pleased by his interest in their way of life. Their behaviour is exemplary as he goes from hut to hut to talk to the women, who are as bashful as women in "polite" society. Joining them in the evening around the fire, Burchell seems enthralled by their dancing and music. The dancer, totally self-absorbed, uses sticks and follows an intricate pattern with his feet, rattling beads on his ankles as he circles the audience.

Other characteristics of the San were less attractive. Curiosity was lacking as well as higher intellectual achievements; the San are also not clean in their own bodies and look weather-beaten and old before their time. Some of their habits—eating live worms or lizards—are unpleasant to watch. Their abodes are not inviting, and they sleep on the floor on a skin, huddled together if it is cold. Nevertheless, despite these limitations, there is something of the character of the noble savage in his description of them, leading a life of enviable freedom. In some respects their style of life differed little from the wild animals that surrounded them; their integration into the colonial community was probably unrealistic. This did not necessarily apply to everyone. Some individuals might differ in their ability to adapt: his own San guide shows gratitude and a certain ceremoniousness in presenting him with a skinned goat in thanks for the good treatment he has had en route.

Burchell enthuses about the scenery of the Cape, and it inspired his art. There is an appreciation of the sublime in his view of it. Stopping at a picturesque spot on the journey northward, he records: "Our station with all its living men and cattle, presented a scene so romantic, so curious and so fit for a picture, that I employed the remainder of the day making a drawing of it."[67] As well as being much taken by the variety of plant life, Burchell also enjoyed the animals and insects of the Cape. Many plants were named after him, but also animals such as zebra, gazelle, and white rhino, as well as certain insects.

One of his other legacies was more unexpected, arising from the evidence he gave to a House of Commons Select Committee on the Poor Laws in 1819. Questioning continued for three hours, but the witness enthused about the climate and benefits of the Zuurveld with such eloquence that the committee was persuaded by his vigorous advocacy. As a result, in the following year settlers, including Thomas Pringle, were sent to that part of the Eastern Cape then known as the province of Albany.

The antagonism between Barrow and Burchell continued long after both had left the Cape. Burchell not only criticized Barrow's map on grounds of inaccuracy (although it remained the standard for Cape cartographers who followed), he also cast doubts on Barrow's knowledge of animals in comparison to Sparrman's, whom he points out was an anatomist and zoologist of standing as well as a botanist.[68] The only common ground between them seems to have been on their sympathetic view of the Xhosa and, in particular, of the young king of the Rharhabe, Ngqika.[69]

John Campbell's Visits (1812–1814 and 1818)

The Reverend John Campbell (1766–1840) came to inspect the missionary stations in Southern Africa on behalf of the London Missionary Society in 1812. The full account of his journey into the interior, "among the Hottentots and other Tribes," was published in 1815, and in a fuller version in 1822[70] it included details from his visit to the interior with Dr. John Philip in 1818 to inspect the LMS stations. His work earned him a place in the annals of travel writing as the "African traveller."[71]

Various catastrophes visited Cape Town during his visit: a smallpox epidemic, which particularly affected the slaves, and several earthquakes might have been regarded by those of superstitious leanings as warnings from God—at any rate, they encouraged a greater attention to religion, something that Campbell, as a clergyman, naturally welcomed. What he was less enthusiastic about was that the new spirit of religiosity encouraged the growing Muslim community of clerics to preach conversion to Islam. They had considerable success among the slave population.

Like Barrow and Lady Anne, Campbell is duly disturbed by the institution of slavery. He finds the prohibition on slaves marrying to be "a heinous sin against God,"[72] although like others he notes the gentle treatment of slaves in Cape Town itself: "In general, the slaves are treated with tenderness in Cape Town. In the house where I lodged they were treated as if they were their own children and most of them would be sorry to leave the family."[73] Even more surprising, he records that the children of slaves, who of course become the chattels of the masters, are given schooling "and play about the room where the family sit at their meals; and receive as much attention as if they were their own children."[74] This upbringing encourages good behaviour: Campbell observes their disciplined demeanour at Mr. Bakker's free school.

So far as the Khoisan are concerned, he also makes the usual distinction between the Khoikhoi and the San. The former are docile and teachable; the latter, though they can be brought into the community if induced at an early age, are far more savage and independent. Nevertheless, despite the belief that the indigenes should be brought into society, there is a touch of nostalgia in his remarks on the freedom and simplicity of their erstwhile life, echoing the theme of the noble savage. Pondering on the reasons why insanity is rare in Africa, he opines: "Can this be ascribed to the climate, or to their exemption from the cares of life? For an African can sleep as soon and as sound when he has not a morsel to eat as when he has plenty. They calculate no time, consequently have no care respecting old age, till it comes, and they feel it. We might go to them, as well as to the fowls of the air, to guide against carking worldly cares and anxieties."[75] Campbell is impressed by the manner and appearance of the Khoikhoi at the Moravian mission at Bethelsdorp (in the Eastern Cape), founded in 1803 by James Read. There they are neat and clean and have been taught useful arts, such as agriculture and husbandry, so that they can sustain themselves. Their singing is harmonious, and their attachment to Christianity seems heartfelt and sincere.

The most outstanding of the converts, Cupido Kakkerlak, who was baptised by van der Kemp, rises to become an assistant missionary himself. Cupido was taught as a sawyer, but his ability to study and absorb theological texts, as well as to preach, singled him out for higher things. He rose to become a deacon and then an assistant missionary. Campbell was impressed by hearing him preach to a congregation of about sixty people of all races and colours. Clearly he was an unusual, charismatic character of considerable talent. Cupido's later lonely and unsuccessful mission to convert the nomadic Korana people is imaginatively recreated in André Brink's novel, *Praying Mantis*.

The most significant moment in Campbell's journey was his arrival at Klaarwater, far north, near the Orange River in what became Bechuanaland. The missionary settlement had been established a decade or so before Campbell's visit; its principal inhabitants were the Griqua people— descendants of the eighteenth-century Bastaards, or mixed-race people. Among them was a king, Mateebe (whom Campbell befriended after an initial stand-off), and various powerful local families (the Koks and the Barends, who provided several generations of leaders). Arriving in Lattakoo, Campbell observes that the whole place was deserted, as the locals thought that a punitive expedition had been sent out to revenge an earlier massacre of an expedition from the governor of the Cape, Lord Caledon (figure 20).

From the start Campbell set about educating the local people into a stricter, ordered life of worship, as well as paying attention to the development among them of skills in all the practical arts of survival. The town had 7,500 inhabitants and 1,500 houses, so the task was not a small one. Cultivation of crops—maize and wheat—was encouraged, but most significantly Campbell drew up a constitution, recognising Adam Kok and Berend Berends as chiefs who would also be responsible for ensuring the security of the mission. But more radically, certain popular elements were to be represented in the governance of the place by the creation of magistrates with punitive powers. Offences such as murder, theft, and robbery were to be treated as serious crimes and attract heavy punishments. The other innovation of his visit was to encourage native agents (or local converts, rather on the model of Cupido) to become deacons and assist in the running of the mission. Campbell's legacy was thus a considerable one, and it formed the basis of a quasi-independent and later assertive community, with a symbolic change in its name from Klaarwater to Griquatown.

JAMES EWART'S JOURNAL (1811–1814)

James Ewart (c. 1791–1823), another young Scots visitor, was a serving officer in the Ninety-third Regiment, which was stationed at the Cape from 1811 to 1814. The record he left in the form of his *Journal* remained unknown until 1969, when it was acquired by Peter Barlow; it was published in the following year.[76] It has a fresh and direct approach to his new environment, which makes it a positive and valuable account.

Ewart was at once captured by the majesty of Table Mountain, mentioning its "cloth" of hanging cloud and adding that the European visitor "will not be a little surprised on finding on the most distant extremity of Africa, a large and populous town, built with a degree of regularity and neatness not often seen, and notwithstanding the want of a good police kept extremely clean."[77]

The cosmopolitan mix of the town's inhabitants, including the "ingenious"[78] Malays, fascinates him. He notes, as others had done, that slaves were reasonably well treated in Cape Town itself, while the Khoikhoi, once the slaves became the principal source of labour in the colony, were increasingly badly treated. The result is that the condition of the Khoikhoi is little above "brute creation."[79] Like Barrow, he regards their exclusion as a foolish policy, which will only do long-term damage to the development of the whole community. If the Khoikhoi had been properly treated, "they might now have been a useful and industrious people."[80] Instead, they have no stake in colonial society and its progress. While he considers that they could be integrated into European society, he is less sure about the San, whose continued nomadic existence and deep hostility to the settlers' encroachment on their traditional hunting lands would be much harder to deal with.

Ewart's description of the Cape landscape—sublime and beautiful—brings us firmly into the Romantic view of a terrestrial paradise ready to be enjoyed and occupied. He enthuses on the bold and majestic scenery of the Cape Fold Mountains, sometimes echoing something of the sinister undertone of the Adamastor myth that we have considered in chapter 2. There is a threatening quality about their immensity and in the wildness of the weather, in which raging storms can be followed by severe drought. It is the vastness of the land of "South Africa"[81]—here an individual farmer can hold fifty square acres—that most appeals to him and excites his enthusiasm. Like Barrow, he champions the cause of taking it over, proclaiming, "There cannot exist a doubt in my opinion, that it [the colony] would not only maintain itself, but would in a short time be one of our most valuable possessions."[82]

Figure 14. *Le Vaillant and Giraffe,* by François Le Vaillant, 1811 (copyright Parliament of the Republic of South Africa).

Figure 15. *Camp Scene at Orange River,* by François Le Vaillant, 1811 (copyright Parliament of the Republic of South Africa).

Figure 16. *Kaffir on the March,* by Samuel Daniell, 1805 (copyright Parliament of the Republic of South Africa).

Passage dangereux de la Rivière des Éliphants.

Figure 17. *Crossing the River,* by François Le Vaillant, 1811 (copyright Parliament of the Republic of South Africa).

Figure 18. *The Worthy Hottentot, Klaas,* by François Le Vaillant, 1811 (copyright Parliament of the Republic of South Africa).

Figure 19. *Boors Returning from Hunting,* by Samuel Daniell, 1805 (copyright Parliament of the Republic of South Africa).

Figure 20. *View of Town of Lattakoo,* by Samuel Daniell, 1805 (copyright Parliament of the Republic of South Africa).

Figure 21. *View of Cape of Good Hope and Southern Whaler Medland,* by William Daniell, 1804 (copyright Parliament of the Republic of South Africa).

Figure 22. *The Lutheran Church, Strand,* by Lady Anne Barnard, 1797–1802 (copyright National Library of South Africa).

Figure 23. *Khoi Woman,* by William Daniell,
1801–1802 (copyright Parliament of the Republic
of South Africa).

Figure 24. *Khoi Man,* by William Daniell,
1801–1802 (copyright Parliament of the Republic
of South Africa).

7056

Figure 25. *A Hottentot Man in Conical Hat and Kaross,* by Lady Anne Barnard, 1797–1802 (copyright National Library of South Africa).

Figure 26. *The Native Policeman,* by Lady Anne Barnard, 1797–1802 (copyright National Library of South Africa).

CHAPTER 7

A Call for Freedom

)

A WAVE OF NEW OPINION: THE 1820S

In the 1820s a group of liberal and enlightened visitors, among whom were Dr. John Philip, Thomas Pringle, and John Fairbairn, arrived in the Cape and challenged the colonial regime on a number of fundamental policy matters, including slavery, a fairer system of treatment of the Khoisan, and press freedom. Although reforms had been attempted during the Dutch Batavian period, little progress had been made—so entrenched was the Cape class system, based on a distinction between freemen and slaves and the dependence of the economy on cheap labour. The newcomers shared the aspiration of radicals in Britain who were pressing for the abolition of slavery throughout the Empire and the amelioration of conditions of dependent peoples. There was also a strong missionary aspect to their activities, and in that way they were successors to James Read and John Campbell—whose work on behalf of the London Missionary Society was in the same liberalising direction. A considerable block on progress toward a more liberal regime during the second British period was the person of Lord Charles Somerset (1767–1831), who had become the governor in 1814.

Somerset was an aristocrat and a friend of the prince regent who had no interest in upsetting the oligarchic colonial system. He understood that the Cape elite were happy to acquiesce in the formality of the governor's absolute control of the colony's affairs, so long as he did not pursue policies that might threaten the fabric of colonial society. Somerset's own lifestyle—building extravagant residences at public expense and much centred on hunting—presented no affront to the ruling Cape Town families, who accepted it as the standard behaviour of a colonial governor. Somerset's extravagances also meant that it was difficult for him to criticise the behaviour of senior Dutch officials still in posts during the early British period. To consolidate his standing with them, Somerset appointed Colonel Christopher Bird, a conservative and a Dutch speaker, as the head of the civil service. The law (based on Roman-Dutch principles) continued to apply with some minor concessions to Anglicisation—for example, in the use of English as the official language.

Nevertheless, things were stirring at home in Britain, where the Colonial Office inaugurated a policy of sending immigrants out of what was considered an overpopulated country. So far as South Africa was concerned, a first settlement was planned for Albany in the Eastern Cape, following, as we have seen, recommendations from the House of Commons Select Committee on the Poor Laws, whose members had been persuaded by William Burchell's evidence. At first, the intention was to encourage small agriculturist entrepreneurs to migrate and set up a society of gentry that reflected the social structure in the English countryside and would no doubt have been quite acceptable to the aristocratic Somerset, who would be able to preside over them in a grand manner. In the event, recruitment took place through certain "joint stock parties," and the groups formed consisted as much of urban artisans and unskilled labourers as people with ties to the land. Such entrepreneurial flair as there was among these settlers tended to be as traders and merchants rather than as cultivators. On arrival they soon realised that a lucrative living could be made by supplying useful items such as cloth and iron utensils to the settlers (who mainly relied on bartering) and Xhosa in exchange for the more valuable items such as ivory and animal hides. Local centres, such as Graaff-Reinet, began to grow in wealth and importance as a result of this trade.

Before long it became apparent that the newly arrived settlers represented a new political factor in the colony. Committed to free trade and small business, the newcomers resented the attempt of the governor to impose an autocratic regime on them. The Cape Town administration was in any case torn by internal strife, as a struggle developed between Somerset and the deputy governor, Sir Rufane Donkin (1773–1841), who acted as governor in Somerset's absence from 1820 to 1821. Donkin attempted to establish himself in the post permanently and was generous in his patronage. The new settlers who arrived on his watch were largely appeased, but on the return of Somerset from Britain, tensions once more arose.

Certain scandals involving misuse of public funds and a questioning of the role of the fiscal and the application of the Roman-Dutch system of law had led to the setting up of a commission of inquiry into the affairs of the colony, as well as of Mauritius and Ceylon. In 1822 the commission made sweeping recommendations that, in effect, brought the old Dutch system to an end: a supreme court was established, a jury system was introduced, and the *landrost* structure of local government was swept away. Free trade and a lighter system of control, with a civil service based on merit, were set out as objectives of the reforms. Richard Bourke, a mere lieutenant governor but a man of reformist tendencies, was later appointed in place of Somerset to ensure that the reforms were carried through.

While Somerset resisted changes to the social order, he was enthusiastic about turning Cape Town itself into the hub of a British colonial town with communal projects and new public buildings. A commercial exchange had been established originally on temporary premises in Plein Street; it then moved to a coffeehouse in Berg Street. In 1819 Somerset laid the foundation stone of a fine, new building, on a day "gay with tents, bunting, music and festivity. Regimental bands were playing, a salute was fired from the Castle, and afterwards all the leading townsfolk sat down to 'tiffin' in a large tent erected close by as they always seem to have done on occasions of this kind."[1] Two years later the building was opened, with grand Corinthian pillars at its entrance. It became the centre of social life in Cape Town, housing the new South African Library, a philanthropic society that helped the rehabilitation of freed slaves, and an office of the Masonic Lodge. The library itself began with about 30,000 books and was uniquely funded by a wine tax on the booming Cape industry of the day.

Perhaps the most prestigious public building of all was the Royal Observatory. We have seen how Father Guy Tachard began serious astronomical work in the Cape in the late 1680s and how Abbé Nicolas Louis de La Caille had also worked as an astronomer in Cape Town in the mid-eighteenth century. No doubt as a result of discreet lobbying, the Board of Longitude in England decided to set up a base in Cape Town. A neo-Grecian Regency style building was designed by the architect Sir John Rennie and soon attracted high-calibre incumbents like the astronomer Sir Thomas Maclear.[2] However, not all of Cape Town was so elegant: the harbour area where both fish and animals were slaughtered was unhygienic and crammed full of the makeshift dwellings of workmen. The raging southeaster, known as "the Cape Doctor," blew away some of the rubbish accumulated in the poorer districts of the town. Attempts were made to improve the dwellings of the seamen and harbour workers, but ruthless landlords continued to divide and subdivide houses to maximise their profits. Life in those quarters was a far cry from the world of the castle and the comfortable houses of the merchant classes.

While these changes in Cape Town itself were taking place, expansion of the colony eastward led to a series of conflicts with the Xhosa, with Grahamstown as the centre of the British military operations. Somerset had approved the setting up of this settlers' capital, replete with a cathedral and a bishop to give it due status but also to strike a blow at Donkin's settlement at Fredericksburg in the so-called Ceded Territory, which was then abandoned. The settlers introduced woolled Merino sheep in place of the indigenous fat-tailed variety and set up their own paper, the

Graham's Town Journal. Soon the town began to show signs of its importance and prosperity: among the settlers' cottages, some grander houses were built, and a cluster of public buildings also appeared in the close behind the cathedral.

Resistance from the Xhosa was fierce: their expulsion after the "fourth" frontier war in 1811–1812 from the area of the Zuurveld had already deprived them of the important grain fields, and their cattle had been confiscated. In 1818 another war broke out. The British drove them further eastward, a new barrier being established at the Fish River in the Ceded Territory. Somerset was somewhat perfidious in his dealing with Ngqika (the Xhosa chief so admired by Barrow), depriving him of lands he thought had been guaranteed to him. This led to great bitterness among the Xhosa people and stiffened resistance. Four further wars took place during the nineteenth century, the last being in 1877–1879.

John Philip: Radical Reformer

The Reverend John Philip (1775–1851) was the greatest champion of the non-European population of the Cape and one of its most effective. Born in Kirkcaldy in Scotland, he was a humble linen draper before going to the Wesleyan theological college in Hoxton, where he was ordained. He came to the Cape in 1818 with the Reverend John Campbell, who had returned to investigate the threatened closure of the London Missionary Society's stations. Philip's first visit began a lifelong commitment to the betterment of the Khoisan and the Xhosa, as well as the emancipation of slaves. In 1828 his influential book *Researches in South Africa*,[3] in which he argued the radical case, was published in two volumes—by which time he had become the superintendent of the LMS missions in Southern Africa. Philip displayed character traits that mark him out as a politician as much as a missionary—the first was his indefatigable pursuit of the causes he espoused, and the second his understanding that the authorities in London and in Cape Town needed to be persuaded of their justness. He shared

the high Enlightenment ideals that men were born equal and that education should be universally available but nevertheless saw that progress in
all the colonies depended upon the order and system of Empire.[4]

Campbell's group went as far north as the border settlements near the
Orange River. From the start of his account of their travels, Philip delivers a strong attack on the conventional view of the San, very much siding
with Burchell's favourable opinion of them, which we have noted in the
previous chapter. The San are a pastoral people, but, he says, if they are
"deprived of their flocks and herds you scarcely leave them any alterna-
tive but to perish, or live by robbery. This was the case of the Hottentot
tribes in the seventeenth century. Driven to desperation by the loss of their
cattle, they were occasionally forced by hunger to seize a few sheep or cattle
belonging to the colonists."[5] The "very ignorant and degraded state"[6] in
which he finds them is entirely the result of colonial policies, which Philip
finds shocking and repulsive. Surveying the early history of the Cape, he
is aware that the directors of the VOC tried to protect the indigenous
people, but the colonists on the spot painted a picture of them in abject
tones and argued that severe coercion was the only way to maintain order
and produce the provisions needed for passing ships on their voyages to
and from the East. This argument was entirely disingenuous and put forward merely so that the colonists could confiscate the land on which the
San (and other Khoi) depended for survival. Their physical appearance is
not as repulsive as has been reported in Europe; part of the squalor of their
personal appearance is the result of being constantly on the run and living in the remotest parts of the wild to avoid capture.

While Philip's view can be seen as an Enlightenment expression of the
importance of education, he also understood the need for such instruction to be tailored to take account of the limitations of the locals. Thus,
he says "the first step towards the civilisation of a savage is to rouse the
thinking principle. This can only be done by proposing to his mind considerations of sufficient force to overcome his native indolence. These considerations must be addressed to his passions and suited to his capacity."[7]

Philip backs up his favourable opinion of the San by his own close observation of them. He is accompanied by San attendants who are perfectly at home in serving meals at his table in a civilised manner. One impressive piece of evidence from the local point of view is Philip's interview with Uithaalder, captain of the *Toverburg*. Philip calls the testimony of Uithaalder a "deposition" and takes some trouble checking the facts in it and having them verified by one or two local officials of an independent cast of mind. Uithaalder begins by saying "that many years ago, the father of Deponent and his people, whilst in perfect peace, and not having committed the smallest provocation, were suddenly attacked in the kraal by a party of boors from the colony. He and many hundreds of his people, men, women and children, were killed, and ten wagons, loaded with their children, were carried into the colony, and placed in perpetual servitude."[8] Whenever cattle or sheep are lost on European farms, the San are blamed, even though they may have been the result of wild animals of prey that have raided the pens in the night. Uithaalder himself was beaten up by settler farmers just for roving on their land in a desperate search for roots to eat. The commandos ignored the attempts of the missionaries to protect the local people who were being converted to Christianity. Uithaalder had appealed, in vain, to the settlers' own sense of Christian behaviour.

Philip also relies both on previous writers such as Anders Sparrman and on reports from British and Dutch individuals as to the character of the Khoisan. One of the colonists he quotes is Sir Jaheel Brenton, who praises the San for their sweet disposition. Although several officials, like Colonel Collins, argue for a more inclusive and liberal policy, as Barrow had done, Philip sees no improvement in the treatment of the aboriginals under the British. Indeed, their regime exceeds the Dutch in its passive toleration of cruelty and hardly puts them in a position to criticise other European countries on the issue of the slave trade.[9]

The specific matter that Philip and Campbell had come to investigate was the closing down of the missionary stations. This was done by the

colonial authorities on the pretext that the stations were breeding grounds
for the terrorist raids on their farms. Combined with the commando tac-
tics of armed attack upon the San, the policy is a "triumph of injustice and
oppression."[10]

Things are not a good deal better in Griqualand. The mulattos (those
of mixed ethnicity) have been treated as an "inferior race,"[11] although they
made good farmers once ownership of their own lands was clearly protected by law. When the missionaries first came in contact with them, they
were still living in a nomadic state. One of the principal aims of the LMS
was to show them—and the Khoisan—that living in settled communities
was beneficial and more conducive to practising their newly found Christianity. Their community began to develop; able leaders such as the de Kok
brothers set an example of what could be achieved by enterprise. Gradually they became more prosperous. One of the sticking points with the
Cape Town administration was their refusal to be drawn into the Hottentot Corps, but Philip says it would be a serious mistake if, on that account,
Somerset tried to impose his will over them with the threat of deporting
them to distant parts of the colony by dispersing them among the settlers'
farms. In any event, Somerset's threat proved too difficult a policy to implement and was abandoned.

At Lattakoo, as we have seen in Campbell's account, the missionaries
found the town deserted as the inhabitants had fled, fearing that the group
had come in retaliation against them for attacks on the settlers. Philip
observes the circular houses of the kraal, with a refinement in the addition of certain verandas to some of them so that guests could be received
and entertained in the shade. The party meet Mateebe, the chief, who is
"dressed in a pair of pantaloons, a shirt and waistcoat, with a cat-skin
kaross over his shoulder."[12] His wife, a lively creature, is dressed in an
English cotton gown. One of the courtiers is Teysho, a handsome man surrounded by good-looking women. When Philip remarks upon the enjoyment that Lattakoo women have for ornaments, Teysho counters wittily
that they do not covet them as much as Cape Town ladies.[13] After the visit

of Campbell and Philip, Robert Moffat (1795–1883), who had joined the LMS in 1816, settled at Lattakoo. In 1824 he moved to Griquatown. At a later stage Moffatt translated the New Testament into Sechuana and finally settled in Matabele country. His daughter married David Livingstone; his son, the Rev. John Smith Moffat, continued his father's missionary work in Bechuanaland. Moffat senior claimed to concentrate on spiritual rather than political matters and did not approve of Philip's radical approach and involvement in secular matters.

Philip's criticism of the treatment of the Khoisan under the British administration began with a close examination of the proclamations of 1809 and 1812. While the first of these ordinances was proclaimed as the "Magna Carta" of the Khoisan by Lord Caledon, Philip asserts that it was nothing of the sort, in fact introducing measures that made it impossible for the Khoisan to get out of the grip of their master-employers, the settlers. The right to complain of mistreatment often landed the complainant in prison, described by Captain Hope of Grahamstown as the "only school for Hottentots."[14] Once there, the word of a master that his employee was insolent or disobedient was sufficient for the *landrost* to order a punishment, which could be severe. The second proclamation allowed the children of Khoisan employees who had reached the age of eight to remain as "apprentices" with their parents' master for ten years, echoing the rather sinister regulation of 1775 in Stellenbosch, which bound over the child of Bastaards to be apprenticed until the age of twenty-five. Philip realised that by collecting firsthand evidence from locals about their treatment under these laws, he could present a stronger case for reform to the British government.

When he reached Bethelsdorp Philip was disappointed by the state of the settlement, which the missionaries had struggled to keep going in the face of considerable official pressure to close it down. Among measures taken against it was the levying of taxes that Philip regards as punitive. James Read's pleas with the administration, pointing out that the station supported many old and sick people, had no effect on the government, which brushed aside all calls for lenient treatment. Philip inspired a new spirit at the mission, reorganised some of the ways in which it was run, and was pleased to see a gradual improvement on his return several years later—when he found the Khoikhoi living in clean, respectable quarters, which he remarked compared favourably to some of the settler abodes.

The culmination of Philip's campaign for better treatment of the indigenous people came in 1828 when Ordinance 50 came into effect. Philip was not the sole supporter of the reform movement that led to this significant change, but he was an important player in its coming about, together with Sir Andries Stockenström and the governor, Sir Richard Bourke. In fact, when the ordinance was promulgated, Philip was in England, to which he had returned in 1826. In London he lobbied hard on behalf of the Khoisan, enlisting the support of William Huskisson (a Whig reformer) and even more significantly Thomas Buxton (the MP for Weymouth). Buxton used his position in the House of Commons to negotiate with the new colonial secretary, Sir John Murray, over the proceedings on a motion to guarantee equal rights to the indigenous subjects in the Cape. To avoid the publicity that would arise from a full debate, Murray agreed to back Buxton's motion and allow it to be agreed to on the nod.[15]

Philip had meanwhile published his voluminous *Researches*, based on material he had been gathering on his several trips to the interior. It ended with a vigorous plea to the British government to introduce a fairer regime in the colony for all people, of whatever race. Although the book may not have been read thoroughly, its very existence was a challenge to the British government to remedy the injustices of the existing system. Tim Keegan says "Philip's book was the first work of history, perhaps the first history of South Africa going back to the beginning of the European settlement. It was told in the main from the point of view of the colonised, rather than the colonisers, albeit with little of the anthropological sophistication we would expect today."[16] He adds that the book, though based on observation and analysis, was a work of propaganda, exposing the long processes

whereby local people lost their land and livelihood and came to be sub-
jected to an unjust system of governance.

Ordinance 50, which aimed at improving the condition of the Khoikhoi and "other people of colour," abolished the need for passes for the
Khoisan, gave them land rights, and ended the system of compulsory
apprenticeship of their children. Nor in future could they be conscripted
in any manner different from other British subjects, whether English or
Dutch, under the provisions of a motion agreed to in the British Parliament a few days later. The "free persons of colour" covered by the provisions
of the ordinance extended only to Khoisan within the colony, excluding
immigrants and slaves. Philip achieved a significant amendment that prevented the repeal of the ordinance without approval from the Crown.
There is no doubt that Ordinance 50 marked an important liberalisation
of the regime at the Cape; it was regarded by the Khoikhoi as being the
foundation of their liberty, although considerable economic differences
meant that their ability to actually get land under the property-owning
provision was extremely limited.

Although Ordinance 50 applied primarily to the Khoisan, it can be seen
in the context of a liberalising programme that affected the very structure
of slave society in the Cape. Among the specific measures that came into
effect at the same time was the creation of the Office of Protector of Slaves.
This was an official to whom slaves could complain of maltreatment,
although records show that the protector was as ready to take the side of
the slave owners as that of the slaves in considering complaints of mistreatment. Nevertheless, the very existence of the office symbolised the
development of a different attitude, which suggested that slaves had inherent rights to fair treatment and were no longer entirely at the mercy of
their owners. In Cape Town itself things progressed more rapidly than in
the communities outside; manumission increased the number of so-called
"free blacks," or emancipated slaves, who began working for themselves
as craftsmen. Some increase in the town's freed slave population also came

when slaves were seized on foreign ships by the Royal Navy once the trade was abolished in 1807. Some of the freed population were already Muslims from the East, but the Muslim community was augmented by conversion of freed slaves as religious centres in the town were more openly tolerated.[17]

While the immediate effects of the ordinance were not apparent, it led to the establishment of the Kat River Settlement, supported by Stockenström for the government and James Read for the missionaries. Read, whose reputation was high among the Khoisan and correspondingly low among the settlers, persuaded local families to move there. The governor, Sir Lowry Cole, prevented Read from being appointed pastor at the settlement, instead placing the Reverend W. R. Thomson, a more conservative and malleable character. At Kat River, Khoikhoi and Bastaards were able to own land in their own right[18] for the first time.

Philip continued his ceaseless campaign on behalf of the indigenous people for several decades after 1828. In 1834 after the Xhosa war, Philip returned to Britain, taking with him Andries Stoffels, a coloured man, and Dyani Tzatoe, a Xhosa, to show his fellow countrymen at first hand perfectly civilised people of "native" stock. For his campaigning and support of the local population he was reviled by the colonists, who saw the emancipation of the Khoisan as a threat to their very existence. The conservatives gained a partial reversal of the effect of Ordinance 50 by supporting new vagrancy laws, designed in effect to tie the indigenous people from free movement across the colony.[19] Philip returned to the Cape and died in Hankey in 1851.

THOMAS PRINGLE: SETTLER, POET, AND ANTISLAVERY CAMPAIGNER

Thomas Pringle (1789–1834) was the most prominent of the Albany settlers of 1820. His early life began on a farm in rural Roxburghshire amidst "pastoral and secluded scenery."[20] He himself described his family as "plain, respectable Scottish husbandmen."[21] Riding to school on horseback, it seems that he was already lame, as Josiah Condor, his first biographer, remarks in the preface to the 1834 edition: "It must have seemed very unlikely, at that time, that a young man suffering from incurable lameness, should become a traveller; but the congenial enthusiasm which the adventures of the African traveller [John Campbell] awakened in his mind, particularly assisted him in laying the foundations of a new colony in the wilds of Southern Africa."[22] After university at Edinburgh (where he met, among others, John Fairbairn [1794–1864]), Pringle entered the somewhat frenetic world of journalism, first with the *Edinburgh Monthly Magazine* (later called *Blackwoods*) and then the *Edinburgh Magazine*. The effect of the infighting among the literati through the various journals, he says, created "an aversion to literature"[23] in him, although it turned out to be a good apprenticeship for setting up the *South African Journal* in Cape Town with his friend Fairbairn. By the time the announcement was made about the proposed settlement in the Albany province, Pringle had made various South African contacts through Alexander Waugh, one of the founders of the London Missionary Society, and knew of their work, particularly that of Dr. John Philip. Pringle's financial situation, without a stable job, was precarious. The advertisement for the settlers' scheme, painting the Cape as a terrestrial paradise—no doubt influenced by Burchell's testimony to the House of Commons committee—was tempting. Pringle made what was probably the most significant decision of his life in deciding to join the settlers immigrating to South Africa.

Armed with a letter of introduction from Waugh, within days of his arrival at Cape Town Pringle met Dr. John Philip. The two began a friendship that was to prove decisive in influencing Pringle in his view of the colonial setup at the Cape. A week later he was on his way on board the *Brilliant* to Algoa Bay, disembarking in the bustling Port Elizabeth, just named in memory of Sir Rufane Donkin's deceased wife. As leader of the group of settlers, Pringle was able to disembark first. Even from the ship in the bay his first impression is enthusiastic, as it describes graphically: "an animated picture, as viewed from us from anchorage, was supplied by the heights over the Zwartkops River, covered with dense jungle, and by the picturesque peaks of the Winterhoek and the dark masses of the Zureberg ridge far to the northward, distinctly outlined in the clear blue sky."[24]

Not long afterward Pringle paid a visit to Bethelsdorp, a short distance away. His experience there—particularly finding the somewhat derelict nature of the location, not chosen by Johannes van der Kemp but forced on him by the authorities—began to shape his view of the treatment of the indigenous people by the colonial authorities. He witnessed the deportation of a Xhosa woman and her children to work for a distant colonist on the instruction of the local magistrates. Despite her pleading "in highly musical and sonorous language,"[25] she is ordered to be sent on, a decision the missionaries had no power to influence. Pringle opines that the incident made him begin "to suspect that [his] European countrymen, who thus made captives of harmless women and children, were in reality greater barbarians than the savage natives of Caffraria."[26] His view of the Khoikhoi was also beginning to form as a result of this visit. The congregation he saw was quiet and devout. Integration into the fabric of society is a possibility, for he says, "There was among the rudest of the people, an aspect of civility and decent respect, of quietude and sober-mindedness, which evinced they were under the control of far other principles than those which regulate the movements of mere savage men."[27]

The settlement they had come to found was further up-country at the Great Fish River, not far from Graaff-Reinet—where the magistrate, Stockenström, was a man of distinctly liberal convictions whom Pringle admired for his humane and yet efficient administration of the town. Pringle describes the journey through picturesque scenery, delighted at seeing for the first time a great salt pan. He collects what was probably a year's supply of salt for the group's culinary needs. The backdrop of the distant mountains, the abundant fauna and flora—all appeal to his sense of drama and difference. Quagga, antelope, and wild boar are among the more exotic creatures still inhabiting the region; suddenly the settlers realize that they are in the wilds of Africa. At Roodewal they are cordially greeted by the military authority. Pringle notes one of the officer's accents and says laconically that the "Scottish accent [is] seldom entirely lost even by the most polished of the middle ranks of our countrymen."[28]

However enthused Pringle was about the landscape, life was not easy at Glen Lynden, as the settlement was named. Pringle is soon petitioning to expand the territory they have been given so as to produce enough food to survive. The original location was not ideal; at a later date the settlement was moved slightly upriver. Insufficient funding added to their problems. Pringle writes to Henry Ellis, the deputy colonial secretary at the Cape, on December 1, 1820, telling of their difficulties in producing crops:

> As might be expected in our circumstances and from our ignorance of the country and climate we have made some mistakes in our cultivation and met with some disappointments. In the first place the frosts are more late and severe in this high situation than we had anticipated and have destroyed all the garden stuffs that we had sown in August and September . . . our wheat crops, which at first promised well, appear to have partially failed, partly it seems from a want of manure and in some places a scarcity of water.[29]

He finds himself having to be master of many arts and having to play many roles—civil and military leader, architect, gardener, religious guide. He has to turn his hand to any other job that arises. His own farm was named Eldon, which lay east of the settlement facing the Baviaans River Mountains, which he so admired. He seems to have established good relations with his Dutch settler neighbours, somewhat modifying his first description of them as rougher than Scots peasants and on about a par with English ones! He also comes to realize that the settlers have huge challenges in fending off attacks from marauding Xhosa and threats to their livestock and horses from wild animals, of which the lion was the fiercest. The settlement itself had a corps of armed soldiers to defend it, a safety net that scattered individual colonist farmers lacked.

From a nearby dispossessed farm, Pringle adopted a band of mulatto (ethnically mixed-race) men and women who had been employed by their German father on his farm. They are the brothers Christiaan and Karel Groepe, who prove to be good workers and begin the construction of a road leading to the settlement. Echoing the opinion of Philip, he says that despite the rough background from which they come, "our Mulatto auxiliaries were, as a body, on the whole extremely well behaved. Their marriage unions, recognised neither by the law nor the church were, with occasional exceptions, adhered to. Though too much addicted to hunting and other idle habits of semi-civilised men, they were not unwilling to labour, and to labour vigorously when an opportunity was afforded them of thereby improving their circumstances."[30]

Pringle's own servant was a young San boy, as no Khoikhoi could be found. Like Sparrman and Philip before him, he blames the savagery of the San on their exclusion from their traditional means of livelihood by encroachments by the settlers, so that a "mild, confiding race of shepherds" have become "suspicious and vindictive savages."[31] The Khoikhoi have equally been "debased by oppression and contumely,"[32] with lands taken away from them and rights ignored. Gradually Pringle's view becomes more and more antigovernment and, in particular, slanted against the policies of Somerset, whom he regards as having overturned Donkin's efforts to improve governance by providing a fairer system for the indigenous people. He later concludes that Somerset's regime is an "outrageous and obstinate misgovernment."[33]

Pringle seemed totally integrated into life in the wilds of the Albany province. His love of the landscape and its animals is given lyrical expression. In "Evening Rambles," Glen Lynden is painted in highly Romantic tones. The rough steep mountains, granite-like and dry, that rise above the settlement contrast with "Its sheltered nooks and sylvan bowers / Its meadows flushed with purple flowers."[34]

On his journeys in the countryside around Glen Lynden, he finds much to inspire him in the landscape of steep mountains and precipices and dark, impenetrable forests. Here and there the mood that we have seen in the Adamastor myth comes to the surface:

> O'er prospects wild, grotesque and strange,
>
> Sterile mountains, rough and steep,
>
> That bound abrupt the valley deep,
>
> Heaving to the clear blue sky
>
> Their ribs of granite, bare and dry
>
> And ridges, by the torrents worn
>
> Thinly streaked with scraggy thorn . . . [35]

In some of the verse he mingles the sadness of the dispossessed local peoples. The Bushman no longer inhabits his cave; the Xhosa no longer appears in the great valley, having been driven out by the "Oppressor's hand."[36] At other times the mood is lighter. Randolph Vigne calls "The Lion Hunt" a cheerful and lively jeu d'esprit in which the poet cries out: "Call our friends to the field for the lion is near."[37] Soon the whole party (including his manservant, Dugal) are marching forth, duly armed, to the hunt. These scenes, of course, appeal greatly to his British readership: lion hunts can be exceeded in excitement only by confronting elephants in the veld.

Despite all this soulful outpouring, it seemed that Pringle was concerned at not having a proper job. No doubt the financial insecurity of his life had left its mark. In 1821 an offer came from an unexpected quarter: Somerset proffered the post of sublibrarian of the newly established South African Public Library in Cape Town. The governor may not have had the highest opinion of the Albany settlers, but it may be, as Vigne suggests, that a letter of recommendation from Sir Walter Scott was too impressive to ignore.[38] Whatever the reasons, it was an opportunity that Pringle could not miss: he began his preparations to leave Glen Lynden.

En route to Cape Town, having installed his brother William at Eldon, Pringle sees more evidence of the mistreatment of local people, appalled at the conditions in which runaway slaves are kept in Beaufort prison while awaiting return to their owners. Although his published views were not yet available, it seems that his leanings were well-known to members of the administration, nor was his association with the troublesome Dr. Philip unnoticed. Once in Cape Town he hoped to be put in charge of the government press, but it seems that a chance remark of Captain Charles Fox, to the effect that Pringle was a Whig, immediately put the hackles of the high Tory Somerset up and put an end to Pringle's chance of getting any such preferment. Apparently undaunted, Pringle set about establishing an academy in the centre of town that the children of civil servants and military officers would attend, together with some local day pupils. He was joined in October 1823 by his Edinburgh friend Fairbairn, who became heavily involved with the academy.

Fairbairn's appearance in Cape Town undoubtedly encouraged Pringle to resume his life as a journalist. Soon, despite warnings from the fiscal, Daniel Dennyson, the two had drawn up a prospective for the founding of the *South African Journal*, which would be more lively and up-to-date on news from home than the *Government Gazette*. Another person involved with the two Edinburgh graduates was George Greig (1800–1863), a young entrepreneur recently arrived in Cape Town, who among other talents had those of a printer.

A struggle ensued with Somerset, who saw the trio as fomenters of dissent and disturbance. An attempt was made to dissuade Greig, but he would not desist from publishing his own paper, the *South African Commercial Advertiser*. Busy with his other business interests, he appointed Pringle and Fairbairn as editors. Somerset's room to manoeuvre was somewhat restricted by the arrival of the commissioners conducting the inquiry into the affairs of the colony, which we have seen was to be very wide-ranging in its recommendations. During Somerset's absence in England, Pringle had not hesitated to be critical of certain policies of the administration—for example, its handling of cattle thefts by the so-called local commando system. Even more provocatively he targeted the governor's son, Colonel Henry Somerset, who was stationed in the Cape. The scene was set for a full-scale battle: Somerset, back from leave, overturned the reforms of Donkin. He then turned his fire on Pringle. By early 1824 he had managed to terminate Pringle's librarianship and smash the *Journal*, forcing it to close. At the same time affairs in the academy took a turn for the worse, with pupils suddenly leaving.

Pringle also took up the cause of the abolition of slavery during his stay in Cape Town. In 1825, while in Graaff-Reinet, he had a meeting with Stockenström—for whom, as we have seen, he had considerable admiration as a fair and humane administrator. Stockenström had taken up the abolitionist cause, and no doubt that was one of the main subjects discussed by them on that occasion. Three weeks later Pringle informed Fairbairn that he was writing a pamphlet, which became "Letter from South Africa. Slavery," published in Thomas Campbell's *New Monthly Magazine* in October 1826 and in due course in the *Anti-Slavery Monthly Reporter*.[39] This publicity led to Pringle's appointment as secretary of the Anti-Slavery Society in London, when he left the Cape for good in July 1826, reduced to serious financial straits by Somerset's campaign against him. Before that he made a last visit to Glen Lynden, already established as the first poet who "had translated his romantic, Arcadian view of nature to the wilds of southern Africa."[40]

Fairbairn, on the other hand, survived Somerset's onslaught. After repeated censoring of the *South African Commercial Advertiser* by the government, he at last succeeded in getting the right to publish his paper without official supervision, a significant landmark in the development of press freedom in the colony. He continued to back a reformist programme, eventually becoming something of a national figure and getting elected to the newly established Legislative Council in 1854.

GEORGE THOMPSON'S *TRAVELS AND ADVENTURES* (1827)

In 1827 a book entitled *Travels and Adventures in Southern Africa* was published in London, written apparently by "George Thompson Esq." As we shall see, much of Thompson's book was in fact written by Pringle and reflected its ghost writer both in style and sentiment.

Thompson (b. 1796) himself had arrived in Table Bay aboard the brig *Garland* on 26 September 1818, at the age of twenty-two. His earlier career was as a clerk in various London firms, and he had travelled on business as far as Rio de Janeiro before coming to the Cape. Within weeks of his arrival he was writing to Somerset asking for permission to stay in Cape Town as a merchant, where he was to work for the firm Watson, Borraidale and Ravenhill. In 1821 on his way back to England, he attended Napoleon's funeral in St. Helena. In due course he rose to be a partner in the firm he had joined as a clerk; over the next fifty years he remained a prominent member of the merchant community, being a founding member of the influential Commercial Exchange in 1822. He left the Cape for good in 1859.

Thompson met Pringle soon after his arrival in Cape Town in 1821 and joined the campaign conducted by Pringle and Fairbairn for a free press, going to far as to sign a petition to the king in their support. In the preface to his book, Thompson modestly says that his education has been mercantile rather than literary or scientific, yet the book had the hallmarks of a fluent hand, well-versed in literary subjects. Whether from lack of confidence or lack of time, Thompson entrusted the writing up of his travels to Pringle—who, as we have seen, by 1825 was in fairly serious financial straits, having lost the battle with Somerset over the *South African Journal* and facing a collapse in the business of the academy.

Pringle's involvement in Thompson's project is confirmed in a letter that he wrote to Fairbairn on 14 October 1825, where he says that he means "to set tooth and nail to Thompson's book and get it off my hands."[41] It is possible that the two men met in London late in 1826 and discussed the book prior to its being sent to the printer. What emerges is that Pringle was later involved in correcting the proof. One part of the bargain between the two was that Pringle's poetry could be included in the book, giving it a distinctly literary flavour. That quality appealed to later writers like G. M. Theal, who regarded it as one of the best accounts written of South Africa at the time.

It is hardly surprising given the collaboration over the work that many of Pringle's sentiments can be found in the book, although one must presume that they were approved by Thompson himself. The tone toward the indigenous people, although qualified here and there, is still largely sympathetic: they are badly treated "under regulations and the illiberal prejudices of the colonists."[42] Some poignant lines of poetry on the "Hottentot" come from Pringle's pen:

> Mild, melancholy, and sedate he stands
> Tending another's flocks upon the fields—
> His father's once—where now the white-man builds
> His home and issues forth his proud commands:
> His dark eye flashes not; his listless hands
> Support the boor's huge firelock; but the shields
> And quivers of his race are gone: he yields,
> Submissively his freedom and his lands,
> Has he no courage?—Once he had—but, lo!
> The felon's chain has worn him to the bone.
> No enterprise?—Alas! the brand, the blow
> Have humbled him to dust—his HOPE is gone.
> "He's a base hearted hound—not worth his food"—
> His master cries;—"he has no gratitude!"[43]

So far as the San are concerned, while Thompson recognises that they are intent on destroying colonists' farms, he poses the rhetorical question: "Yet, on the other hand, have they not some cause to regard Boors and Griquas as intruders upon their ancient territories—as tyrannical usurpers who by seizing their finest fountains, and destroying the wild game on which they were wont to subsist; have scarcely left them even the desolate wilderness for an habitation?"[44]

Moreover, he denies that they are as ugly as they are portrayed: a Bushman woman he encounters is elegant and graceful. The plight they have been reduced to can be very severe: he comes upon one family who just survive by eating ants.

For the Griquas (mulattos) Thompson reserves some cautious praise. Klaarwater, renamed Griquatown in Campbell's time, has grown from a modest kraal of reed huts to a substantial town. This has been achieved by beneficent administration—the latest example being under a Mr. Melville, who has relied on a local person to run the affairs on behalf of his people. While the Griquas have their own sense of hierarchy like anyone else, there is more of a communal spirit among them that pulls the social fabric together. Signs of prosperity based on the adaption of European agricultural practices are to be found in the town. The Griquas are also sufficiently armed to fight off marauding attacks from the San.

In the third part of his work Thompson includes a detailed appendix on the history and culture of the amaXhosa.[45] Surveying something of their history, he does not find them of a "vindictive or bloodthirsty disposition"[46] and is much taken by their chief, Hinza, who is physically impressive and charismatic. Their knowledge of the medical uses of plants, their making of pots, and the various rituals they observe in life and especially in death show them to be a people of considerable social sophistication, well above the level of savages living in the wild.

While Thompson shares the awe of other travellers at the majesty of the scenery in South Africa, he also captures in a sensitive tone the frightening loneliness of its interior. One evening at the fireside he records that he has "sombre reflections upon my present predicament uncertain of our route, and surrounded by savage hordes, and ravenous beasts of prey. The flashing of our fires only added to the gloominess of the scene, making the heavens appear a vault of pitchy darkness nor was there any kind of moon to cheer our solitude."[47] One of the most interesting descriptions Thompson makes is of the Cango Caves, near Oudtshoorn. These had been discovered in the late eighteenth century, when an "irregular, dark looking gateway"[48] was found to lead down into a series of caverns. By descending a precipitous ledge, the first of these caves was reached, a long hall of six hundred feet in length: "The hall was adorned with the most splendid stalactites, some in the shape of columns, rising to the height of forty feet, and one majestic one not less than sixty, others assuming the fantastic forms of cauliflowers, festoons, and a variety of grotesque figures. Many of these were quite transparent, and reflected the glare of the torches with a very brilliant and enchanting effect."[49] Beyond the hall, named after the discoverer, Van-Zyl, the party proceeds into chamber after chamber until the stifling, fetid air forces them to beat a retreat. Their presence disturbs a large colony of bats that almost extinguish their torches by the flapping of their wings. With some relief Thompson emerges from the murky caverns to continue his journey above ground.

LADY HERSCHEL'S *LETTERS FROM THE CAPE 1834–38*

One of the most readable and charming recollections of the Cape of the period is to be found in the letters of Lady Margaret Herschel (1810–1884), who accompanied her husband, Sir John Herschel (1792–1871), during his period of astronomical researches in the Cape. Her letters are written to a circle of family and friends, prominent among whom is her mother, but their style is fluent and pleasing in a way that suggests she may have had publication in mind.

Sir John was the son of Sir William Herschel, the highly distinguished astronomer who, among other discoveries, identified Uranus as a planet. John himself went to Cambridge and, after some equivocation, also turned his attention full time to astronomy. He came to the Cape to study and map the southern skies in 1834, setting up his observatory at Feldhausen in Wynberg. He made a series of important discoveries during his four-year stay, including the identification of thousands of nebulae and clusters, and made progress in finding a means of measuring the radiation of the sun. He also saw Halley's Comet pass through the sky. In a curious twist to his later career, having turned down the presidency of the Royal Society, he became master of the Royal Mint, not entirely with success, never having had experience in business.

Margaret Brodie Herschel, whom he married in 1829, was the daughter of a Scottish Presbyterian minister, which may explain her belief in keeping herself busy, independently of her husband. While constantly mindful of her husband's important work, which involved a nightly surveillance of the skies, Lady Herschel developed her own interests in botany and gardening as well as in recording, with some acuity, the characteristics of both colonial and indigenous society. Neither she nor Sir John were particularly interested in the social rounds at the Cape, which they found trivial and uninteresting. They were fully occupied with their own interests and with raising their family. She pitches the contrast between the country and its inhabitants in a laconic aside: "the country is most romantic, and more than makes up for the disagreeable and pettifogging people. Nature is luxuriant in every possible way."[50] What did not endear the Herschels to the colonial hierarchy was their growing friendship with Dr. Philip—regarded, as we have seen, as a dangerous radical and disturber of the established order, based on the twin pillars of slavery and servitude by the indigenous people. However, Sir John's eminence as a scientist of distinction from a highly respected family prevented anyone from criticising them too openly.

The Herschels had arrived at the very time when the abolition of slavery in the British Empire was being implemented in the Cape Colony. However, despite its abolition late in 1834, the arrangement was that slaves remained indentured for four further years. Moreover, the cultural atmosphere would not change quickly. André Brink graphically re-creates the atmosphere:

> For years it had been hovering like a smell in the sky, a heavy smell that
> could make you drunk and light headed. A smell like young wine or
> must in a farmyard. But even when hope turned into knowledge, it was

not yet ready to be believed and accepted. For too long it has soaked into one's flesh and blood and sinews and deep into the marrow of one's bones. Now suddenly, it is there and, God knows, true. Monday, the first of December, in the year of our Lord, 1834. The slaves are free.[51]

Early on in her diary, Lady Herschel shows a lack of colour prejudice. She tells of her pleasing and helpful maid who attends upon the family, a nice person to be treated with respect. When the Herschels travel away from Cape Town, their staff are left to be supervised by a neighbour, but Lady Herschel adds: "I only hope she will treat my black women with kindness, for I still like them very much, and they are so happy and so good."[52] She develops the highest regard for Dr. Philip, who encourages her interest in the welfare of the Khoikhoi: "It is impossible not to feel interested in the affairs of the native Hottentots and slaves, while the good man Dr. Philip (I can tell you we love and admire him) takes their part so warmly."[53]

She holds up Philip's school as an inspiring example of what could be done to integrate the locals into useful service, as both the children of slaves and servants are admitted to it.

The Herschels soon became disenchanted with the treatment of the locals by the colonial regime. During their time the sixth war against the Xhosa took place on the eastern frontier of the colony. Lady Herschel does not accept that these "wise and skilful savages"[54] bear all the blame for the conflict. Much of the tension has arisen because the colonists have invaded the traditional Xhosa territory and stolen their cattle, pretending that the cattle had been stolen from them by the Xhosa on previous raids. The banning of the Xhosa from their traditional lands to an area further east is, in her opinion, too extreme a measure and one that she would wish to blot out from her recollection of their time in the Cape. Instead of showing some sign of Christian goodwill, the administration tries to blame the only people—Dr. Philip and other missionaries—who advocate more just policies. The colonial system is nothing short of tyranny:

"This same Cape of Good Hope is soiled and blackened by human nature in its worst shapes—one of which is tyranny over the black population."[55]

While these public events are disturbing, Lady Herschel happily builds up their family home in her own Eden at the "Grove." She is enchanted by the backdrop of the mountains—everything at home in England will seem diminutive after them—and delighted by the variety of the local flora. It is a perfect place to raise their children, and she writes home enthusiastically: "We are all continuing well and happy as usual—with a lovely earth and a lovely sky round us, and gardening and star gazing dividing the time."[56]

The areas around Cape Town—Hout Bay and Constantia—each have their own attractions: the first its beautiful bay; the second with its well-established vine land. And always Table Mountain looms majestically over the town. Even winters in the Cape are cool and refreshing and compare with summers in Britain.

One of the highlights of her journeys inland was when she and Sir John visited Genadendal. The journey, as usual, is an arduous track on the wagons, but they arrive at a site that she calculates is about eighty acres, with well laid out gardens and neat cottages that gladden the heart. Whilst at the mission station, they have the occasion to attend a service when one of the Khoikhoi plays the organ skillfully, while the congregation sings in harmonious unison. The "black faces" she sees are "as merry and eager as possible."[57]

Her impression of the Dutch settlers seems to vary. While she acknowledges that the Cape gentry live in some style in their comfortable houses, the farm settlers subsist in conditions of extreme dinginess and seem to be struck by apathy. Like others before her, she does acknowledge the well-known hospitality with which they treat visitors but comments unfavourably on their demeanour and boorish behaviour. The community at Franschoek, influenced by French manners, seems to her to be more refined.

One of the notable events during the Herschels' stay was the arrival, on 31 May 1836, of the *Beagle* in Cape Town, with Charles Darwin on board.

Herschel is of course a natural contact for the scientific Darwin to make. Darwin finds Herschel himself quiet and withdrawn, difficult to get on with, but is charmed by his lively and attractive wife. He is persuaded by the Herschels to speak up in favour of the indigenous people.

During the Herschels' period in Cape Town, the public amenities of the town were improving. Better housing and public buildings were replacing some of the earlier makeshift structures. Herschel was appointed to investigate and improve the school system. Whatever their reservations about the colonial regime, the couple made a very public-spirited contribution to Cape Town society as a whole. Representatives of a more enlightened spirit, the Herschels would have found the more strident, imperial atmosphere developing in the 1840s much less to their liking than the short-lived window of a freer society of which they had been committed members.

Afterword

The period covered by visitors to the Cape from Bartolomeu Dias to Lady Margaret Herschel is 350 years. From the vast, historical canvas of that long period it has been the intention in this book to select travellers who, in one way or another, left a mark and who recorded (among other subjects they were interested in) their impressions of the two principal indigenous peoples, the Khoi and the San, who inhabited the area of what is now the Western Cape. Most early visitors—whether they were Portuguese, Dutch, British, French, German, or Scandinavian—sought sanctuary in the Cape on their way eastward or on their return from the East to Europe. Cape Town was a staging post for refreshing supplies long before it became established as the centre of an expanding colony. In due course other Europeans came to settle in and around the town; scientists were attracted to the region on account of the variety of its fauna and flora or to study the southern skies.

The two themes of this study have been the encounter of the Europeans with the local Khoisan peoples and the accounts the travellers gave of the natural phenomena of the Cape area. The first of these subjects is about the perception that people from one culture had of another. To the first Europeans, the Khoisan appeared as an exotic but primitive people whose nomadic existence was totally different from that of the organised and settled societies from which they themselves had come. While, as we have seen, there was some admiration for the physical attributes of these Cape dwellers, there was also contempt for a species of man who, without what could be described as religion in any formal sense, were almost thought to be subhuman. The encounters of the Portuguese who first navigated the Cape began a perception of the Khoisan as a savage people who, unwilling to engage with the newcomers beyond limited bargaining, were unlikely to make much progress in the widely held stadial view of society from hunter-gatherer origins to the pinnacle of commercial society. Dias's ships had to leave the southern coast in a hurry; Vasco da Gama was injured in a skirmish with the locals in the same area. Later the death in Table Bay of the viceroy of India sealed the reputation of the Cape as being a hostile place as well as one of great danger from the physical element of wild and unpredictable storms.

The negative impression of the locals formed by the Portuguese was confirmed by other European travellers who called in to the Cape in the long period that elapsed before Jan van Riebeeck declared possession of the land for the Dutch East India Company in 1652. As we have seen, there were exceptions—several early commentators ascribed the behaviour of the indigenous people to the bad treatment they had received at the hands of the Europeans, whose Christian faith did not seem to extend to treating them decently or fairly. But these enlightened commenters were in a minority, and as Europeans settled in the Cape, their greed for land made it convenient to hold onto the claim of superiority over the indigenous inhabitants.

The descriptions of the Khoi and San are also to be found in the writing of visitors whose prime interest was scientific. There were two broad strands to the concerns of these early scientists. One was an interest in the fauna and flora of the Cape, soon discovered to be immensely varied and rich. Another was to study the southern skies and thereby advance knowledge of the heavens. Men of considerable distinction—Carl Thunberg and Anders Sparrman—made important contributions to botany; while François Le Vaillant was a celebrated ornithologist. The two Swedes, as disciples of Linnaeus, were engaged in the major scientific project of the times; Le Vaillant brought back hitherto unseen specimens to Europe on a grand scale. In the second area of scientific interest, Pieter Kolb and Sir John Herschel stand out as significant contributors to the science of astronomy, made possible by their opportunity to study and chart the southern skies from their Cape Town observatories. The records of these travellers form an important part of scientific advance as well as, in almost all cases, detailed observation of the social patterns of the indigenous as well as the colonial structure of Cape society. The most significant single factor in the development of that society was the importation of slaves from the early period of the VOC administration. References in van Riebeeck's diaries show his frustration at his failure to persuade the Khoisan to provide labour for the early development of Cape Town. Their involvement was limited to acting as barterers for the copper they so highly prized. Faced with the need to supply ships of the line on their way to Batavia in conditions of a severe labour shortage, van Riebeeck made what can be seen as the momentous decision to import slaves from Angola and East Africa and, later, Batavia. The arrival of slaves in large numbers over the decades entirely changed the character of Cape society, vitally affecting its ethnic balance so that for much of the period up to the British occupation of 1795, slaves outnumbered Europeans. It also made the Cape economy dependent on a continuous source of imported cheap labour. The social structure of society was for most of this period determined by the difference between freemen and slaves, a barrier that could be crossed only individually or by miscegenation, as in the case of the Griqua or Bastaards.

Two highly significant events took place in the 1830s that, in a sense, mark the end of the first extended period of Cape colonial history and the beginning of a new phase in the emergence of South Africa. The first of these markers was the abolition of slavery in the British Empire in 1833; the second was the Great Trek of Afrikaner settlers northward from 1835. The emigration of up to 15,000 Afrikaners was not unconnected to the liberalising policies that were being pursued by the British administration:

the settlers felt threatened by the end of the old order on which colonial society had been based and sought new territory to re-establish what they saw as a viable economic and social order. At the same time the expansion of the Cape Colony eastward meant the continuation of wars against both the Xhosa and Zulu peoples who inhabited those areas, with the resulting turbulence known as Mfecane.

These events are outside the scope of this book, but they are better understood against the background of the travel literature described here. New European mythologies of both a sinister (Adamastor) and an Edenic nature (the noble savage) were superimposed on already existing indigenous beliefs in a society that had become increasingly economically dependent on slave labour. At the same time a new and exotic image of Africa emerged through these writings, and scientific evidence of fauna and flora, as well as of astronomy, was transmitted to Europe. The mix of these beliefs and findings, recorded in highly readable and entertaining accounts, are important testimony to how Cape society had developed up to the crucial decade of the 1830s.

Notes

CHAPTER 1 — ANCIENT AND MYTHICAL PLACE

1. R. W. Johnson, *South Africa: The First Man, the Last Nation* (London: Weidenfeld and Nicolson, 2004), 3. A lively account of Raymond Dart and his work is given in Phillip Tobias, *Into the Past: A Memoir* (Johannesburg: Picador Africa, 2005), 214–220.

2. The Early Stone Age has been defined as 2.5 million years ago; the Middle Stone Age from 250,000 to 30,000 years ago; and the Late Stone Age from 22,000 years ago. See Alan Mountain, *The First People of the Cape: A Look at Their History and the Impact of Colonialism on the Cape's Indigenous People* (Cape Town: David Philip, 2003), 11. Tobias claims that Dart first came up with the name "habilis" (*Into the Past*, 218).

3. Tobias, *Into the Past*, 4.

4. For an account of the period of coexistence or conflict between the various human species, see Yuval Noah Harari, *Sapiens: A Brief History of Humankind* (London: Vintage, 2015), 3–22. The recent hominid discovery in Europe has been called *Graecopithicus* and is dated from a substantially earlier period than the migration from Africa (Sarah Knapton, "Europe Was the Birthplace of Mankind, Not Africa, Scientists Find," *Telegraph*, 22 May 2017, accessed 17 April 2018, http://www.telegraph.co.uk/science/2017/05/22/europe-birthplace-mankind-not-africa-scientists-find/). Ancient remains of *Homo sapiens* from a very early period have also been found recently in Morocco (Tom Whipple, "Moroccan Skeleton Find Rewrites Human History," *Times*, 8 June 2017, accessed 17 April 2018, https://www.thetimes.co.uk/article/moroccan-skeleton-find-rewrites-human-history-vnknpg92m).

5. R. R. Inskeep, *The Peopling of Southern Africa* (New York: Barnes and Noble, 1979), 62.

6. Quoted in Melanie Gosling, "Eureka Moment," *Cape Times*, 19 August 2009.

7. The etymology of these names is complex. "Khoikhoi" (or "Khoekhoen") means "man of man" in Khoikhoi, while "San" (or "Sanqua") was the Khoikhoi word for the Bushmen. "Hottentot" is said to derive from a Dutch word for a stammerer on account of the curious effect in European ears of the click sounds of the local language. It has been suggested recently that "Bushman" may come from the Nama name (*buchu*) for the aromatic plant *Pteronia onobromoides*, and not because the San were supposed to have lived in the bush, as implied in the Dutch word *bosjeman* (Heather Dugmore and Ben-Erik van Wyk, *Muthi and Myths from the African Bush* [London: Global, 2009], 84. "Khoesan" or "Khoisan" dates from 1928, when it was coined by the German anthropologist Leonard Schultze.

8. A. J. H. Goodwin, "Archaeology of Southern Africa," in *Encyclopaedia of South Africa*, ed. Eric Rosenthal (London: Frederick Warne, 1961), 21.

9. Rowland Raven-Hart, *Before Van Riebeeck* (Cape Town: C. Stuick, 1967), 28.

10. For an account of visitors impelled to climb Table Mountain, including those who felt inclined to stay overnight, such as Nicolaas de Graaff in 1679, and others, like François Valentijn in 1685, who preferred to rely on the accounts of others climbing up and remain firmly below, see Joan Kruger, *On Top of Table Mountain: Remarkable Visitors Over 500 Years* (Paternoster, South Africa: Paternoster Books, 2016), 88–94 and 95–101.

11. Carl Peter Thunberg, *Travels at the Cape of Good Hope, 1772–1775*, ed. Vernon S. Forbes, trans. and rev. J. Rudner and I. Rudner, 2nd ser. 17 (Cape Town: Van Riebeeck Society, 1986), 142.

12. Kruger, *On Top of Table Mountain*, 18.

13. William Hickey, *Memoirs of William Hickey*, ed. Peter Quennell (London: Hutchinson, 1960), 224.

14. Quoted in "A Russian Novelist at the Cape," in *An Entirely Different World: Russian Visitors to the Cape*, ed. Boris Gorelik (Cape Town: Van Riebeeck Society, 2015), 56.

15. For a detailed description of the geology of Table Mountain, see Carl A. Lückhoff, *Table Mountain: Our National Heritage after Three Hundred Years* (Cape Town: A. A. Balkema, 1951), 27ff.

16. Nicolaas Vergunst, *Hoerikwaggo: Images of Table Mountain, November 2000–April 2001* (Cape Town: South African National Gallery, 2001), 53.

17. Dante Alighieri, *The Divine Comedy*, trans. H. Cary (London: J. M. Dent, 1961), 112.

18. Malvern van Wyk Smith, *Shades of Adamastor: An Anthology of Poetry* (Grahamstown, South Africa: National English Literary Museum, 1988), 8.

19. Vergunst, *Hoerikwaggo*, 55.

20. Robert Ross, *A Concise History of South Africa* (Cambridge: Cambridge University Press, 1999), 6.

21. Inskeep, *The Peopling of Southern Africa*, 121.

22. Ibid.

23. Mountain, *The First People of the Cape*, 26.

24. Isaac Schapera, *The Khoisan People of South Africa: Bushmen and Hottentots* (London: Routledge and Kegan Paul, 1963), 95. Although Schapera's work was done over half a century ago, it remains a seminal source for the subject of the Khoisan and has been relied upon for material in this chapter.

25. James Ewart, *James Ewart's Journal Covering His Stay at the Cape of Good Hope (1811–1814)*, intro. A. Gordon-Brown (Cape Town: C. Struick Publishers, 1970), 47.

26. Sir John Barrow, *An Account of Travels into the Interior of Southern Africa in the Years 1797 and 1798* (London, 1801; repr., Cambridge: Cambridge University Press, 2011), 1:277.

27. For an extensive anthropological account of the San in the Kalahari, see James Suzman, *Affluence without Abundance; The Disappearing World of the Bushmen* (London: Bloomsbury, 2017).

28. William Paterson, *Paterson's Cape Travels, 1777–1779*, ed. Vernon S. Forbes and John Rourke (Johannesburg: Brenthurst Press 1980), 48 and 51.

29. Paterson refers to them as "shore Bushmen" (ibid., 156).

30. Schapera, *The Khoisan People of South Africa*, 419.

31. Ibid.

32. Barrow, *An Account of Travels*, 290.

33. Noel Mostert, *Frontiers: The Epic of South Africa's Creation and the Tragedy of the Xhosa People* (London: Jonathan Cape, 1992), 35.

34. Inskeep, *The Peopling of Southern Africa*, 152.

35. Schapera, *The Khoisan People of South Africa*, 292.

36. Dorothea Fairbridge, *A History of South Africa* (Oxford: Oxford University Press, 1954), 11–12.

37. André Brink, *Praying Mantis* (London: Secker and Warburg, 2005), 8.

38. Ibid. The mantis remains a powerful image in modern South African literature, for example making an appearance in K. Sello Duiker's novel, *Thirteen Cents* (Cape Town: Kwela Books, 2013), 151ff; and in Don Pinnock's *Rainmaker* (Auckland, South Africa: Jacana, 2010), 45.

39. Brink, *Praying Mantis*, 8.

40. André Brink, *The First Life of Adamastor* (London: Vintage, 2000), 89.

41. Schapera, *The Khoisan People of South Africa*, 384.

42. J. D. Lewis-Williams, ed., *Stories That Float from Afar: Ancestral Folklore of the San of South Africa*, (College Station: Texas A&M University Press, 2000), 53.

43. Ibid., 174.

44. Schapera, *The Khoisan People of South Africa*, 172.

45. Pinnock, *Rainmaker*, 23–24.

46. Peter Slingsby, *Sevilla Rock Art Trail* (Muisenberg, South Africa: Baardskeerder, 2006), 1:5. For a finely illustrated work on San art, see Pippa Skotnes, *Unconquerable Spirit: George Stow's History Paintings of the San* (Athens: Ohio University Press, 2008).

47. Ross, *Concise History*, 8. Elsewhere Ross adds that the cave paintings also record conflicts with the newcomers. See Robert Ross, "The World the Dutch Invaded: Pre-Colonial South Africa," *Good Hope, South Africa and the Netherlands from 1600*, ed. Martine Gosselink, Maria Holtrop, and Robert Ross (Amsterdam: Rijksmuseum, 2017), 25.

48. Peter Slingsby, *Cederberg Rock Art* (Muisenberg, South Africa: Baardskeerder, 2006), 3:4–5.

49. Dorothea Fairbridge speculates on the similarities between San rock art and that painted on the walls of caverns in Cogul in Spain (*A History of South Africa*, 8).

50. Slingsby, *Sevilla Rock Art Trail*, 1:38.

51. Peter Slingsby, *Bushmans Kloof* (Muisenberg, South Africa: Baardskeerder, 2009), 2:24.

52. Gavin Anderson, *Bushman Art of the Drakensberg*, photo. John Hone (Durban: Art Publishers, 2008), 10 and 42.

53. Barrow, *An Account of Travels*, 239.

54. Slingsby, *Sevilla Rock Art Trail*, 1:6.

55. Schapera, *The Khoisan People of South Africa*, 25.

56. John Cope, *King of the Hottentots* (Cape Town: Howard Timms, 1966), 30.

57. Ibid., 31.

CHAPTER 2 — ADAMASTOR'S REIGN

1. The Castilian explorer António de Saldanha eventually made contact with the Ethiopian court in 1519.

2. See Roger Crowley, *Conquerors: How Portugal Forged the First Global Empire* (London: Faber, 2015), 5.

3. Noel Mostert, *Frontiers: The Epic of South Africa's Creation and the Tragedy of the Xhosa People* (London: Jonathan Cape, 1992), 10.

4. See Gavin Menzies, *1421: The Year the Chinese Discovered the World* (New York: Harper Collins, 2003).

5. Eric Axelson, *Vasco da Gama: The Diary of His Travel through African Waters, 1487-1499* (Somerset West, South Africa: Stephan Phillips, 1998), 3.

6. For accounts of this and subsequent Portuguese voyages, see Kingsley Garland Jayne, *Vasco da Gama and His Successors, 1460-1580* (New York: Methuen Library Reprints, 1970). Jayne's thoroughly researched book was first published in 1910.

7. Quoted in Crowley, *Conquerors*, 32.

8. André Brink, *The First Life of Adamastor* (London: Vintage, 2000), 12-13.

9. Crowley, *Conquerors*, 50.

10. The best edition in English of the *roteiro* remains the highly illustrated version produced and edited by E. G. Ravenstein, *A Journal of the First Voyage of Vasco da Gama, 1497-1499* (London: Hakluyt Society, 1898).

11. Axelson, *Vasco da Gama*, 18.

12. A beachcomber, see chapter 1 of this volume, note 29.

13. For a discussion of the use of the names Table Mountain and Table Bay, see chapter 1, this volume.

14. Alexandre Lobato, *António de Saldanha: His Time and His Achievements* (Lisbon: Centro de Estudos Históricos Ultramarinos, 1962), 12.

15. Jayne, *Vasco da Gama and His Successors*, 72.

16. Lobato, *António de Saldanha*, 12.

17. Luís Vaz de Camões, *The Lusíads*, trans. Landeg White (Oxford: Oxford University Press, 1999), xxvi. White's is by far the most readable modern translation in English.

18. Ibid., 103.

19. Ibid., 105.

20. Ibid., 106.

21. Ibid.

22. Ibid., 108.

23. Ibid., 109.

24. Landeg White, *Translating Camões: A Personal Record* (Lisbon: Universidade Católica Editora, 2012), 26.

25. Camões, *The Lusíads*, 21.

26. George Marshall, "Description of a Voyage to and from the East Indies" (1812), in *Shades of Adamastor: An Anthology of Poetry*, ed. Malvern van Wyk Smith (Grahamstown, South Africa: National English Literary Museum, 1988), 20-21.

27. Ibid.

28. Randolph Vigne, *Thomas Pringle: South African Pioneer, Poet and Abolitionist* (Woodbridge, UK: James Currey, 2012), 71.

29. William Roger Thompson, "Cape of Good Hope" (1868), in van Wyk Smith, *Shades of Adamastor*, 78.

30. D. C. F. Moodie, "Adamastor or the Titan Shape of the Mighty Cape" (1887), in van Wyk Smith, *Shades of Adamastor*, 81.

31. W. C. Scully, "Table Bay" (1892), in van Wyk Smith, *Shades of Adamastor*, 83.

32. Ibid.

33. Lance Fallaw, "Land's End of Africa" (1909), in van Wyk Smith, *Shades of Adamastor*, 98.

34. Roy Campbell, "Adamastor" (1930), in van Wyk Smith, *Shades of Adamastor*, 111.

35. Ibid.

36. Peter Alexander, *Roy Campbell: A Critical Biography* (Oxford: Oxford University Press, 1982), 116–117.

37. Ibid.

38. Roy Campbell, "Luis de Camões" (1946), in van Wyk Smith, *Shades of Adamastor*, 112.

39. Fernando Pessoa, "O Mensagem," trans. F. E. G. Quintanilha, in van Wyk Smith, *Shades of Adamastor*, 65.

40. Guy Butler, "Elegy," in van Wyk Smith, *Shades of Adamastor*, 23.

41. Roy Macnab, "Entering Table Bay" (1960), in van Wyk Smith, *Shades of Adamastor*, 129.

42. Stephen Gray, "The Beast's History" (1974), in van Wyk Smith, *Shades of Adamastor*, 189.

43. Mostert, *Frontiers*, xvi.

CHAPTER 3 — PARADISE LOST

1. Rowland Raven-Hart, *Before Van Riebeeck* (Cape Town: G. Stuick, 1967), 14.

2. Ibid. For an account of the abduction of the Khoikhoi called Corey to England in 1613, see Neil Parsons "The Story of Corey and !Korana Origins at the Cape," *Bulletin of the National Library of South Africa* 71, no. 1 (2017): 3–16.

3. Raven-Hart, *Before Van Riebeeck*, 152.

4. Ibid.

5. Ibid., 18.

6. Ibid., 45.

7. Ibid., 38.

8. Ibid., 38–39.

9. Ibid., 39.

10. See chapter 1, this volume.

11. See chapter 1, this volume.

12. Raven-Hart, *Before Van Riebeeck*, 128.

13. Olfert Dapper, Willem ten Rhyne, and Johannes Gulielmus de Greven-broek, *The Early Cape Hottentots*, ed. and trans. Isaac Schapera (Cape Town: Van Riebeeck Society, 1933; repr. 2012), 123.

14. Raven-Hart, *Before Van Riebeeck*, 111–112.

15. Ibid., 112.

16. Ibid., 114.

17. Ibid., 177–178.

18. Dapper, ten Rhyne, and de Grevenbroek, *Early Cape Hottentots*, 47 and 65.

19. Ibid., 55.

20. Ten Rhyne, for example, talks of "native barbarism and idle desert life" being typical features of their existence (ibid.,, 123).

21. Raven-Hart, *Before Van Riebeeck*, 177. The report is called the "Remonstrantie."

22. Ibid., 178.

23. Dan Sleigh, *Jan Compagnie: The World of the Dutch East India Company* (Cape Town: Tafelberg, 1980), 23.

24. Johan Anthoniszoon van Riebeeck, *The Journal of Jan Van Riebeeck* (Amsterdam: A. A. Balkema, 1952), 1:115.

25. Victor de Kock, *Those in Bondage* (Pretoria: Union Publishers, 1963), 13–14.

26. For a full account of the slave trade in the time of the VOC, see Karel Schoeman, *Early Slavery at the Cape of Good Hope, 1652–1717* (Pretoria: Protea Book House, 2007).

27. Van Riebeeck, *Journal*, 2:258–259.

28. Schoeman, *Early Slavery at the Cape of Good Hope*, 266.

29. Van Riebeeck, *Journal*, 1:65. Noel Mostert says Harry was "the first native South African to collaborate freely and willingly with the European visitors" (*Frontiers: The Epic of South Africa's Creation and the Tragedy of the Xhosa People* [London: Jonathan Cape, 1992], 120).

30. Mostert, *Frontiers*, 120.

31. François Le Vaillant, *Travels into the Interior Parts of Africa via the Cape of Good Hope*, trans. and ed. Ian Glenn, with Catherine Lauga du Plessis and Ian Farlam, 2nd ser. 38 (Cape Town: Van Riebeeck Society, 2007), 1:121.

32. Van Riebeeck, *Journal*, 1:228.

33. Ibid., 1:118.

34. Ibid., 1:119.

35. Ibid., 1:330.

36. See Hatherley James Grace, "Studies of Intersexuality in South Africa" (PhD diss., University of Natal, 1977).

37. Karel Schoeman, *Cape Lives of the Eighteenth Century* (Pretoria: Protea Book House, 2011), 295-325.

38. Ibid., 326.

39. Van Riebeeck, *Journal*, 2:5.

40. Rowland Raven-Hart, *Cape of Good Hope, 1652-1702: The First Years of Dutch Colonisation as Seen by Callers* (Cape Town: A. A. Balkema, 1970), 1:64.

41. George McCall Theal, *History of South Africa under the Administration of the East India Company, 1652 to 1795* (Memphis, TN: General Books, 2012), 1:64.

42. Karel Schoeman, *Seven Khoi Lives: Cape Biographies of the Seventeenth Century* (Pretoria: Protea Book House, 2009), 11-42.

43. Ibid., 44.

44. Richard Elphick and Hermann Giliomee, eds. *The Shaping of South African Society*, 2nd ed. (Middletown, CT: Wesleyan University Press, 1988), 12. On the occasion of the erection of a statue to Doman in the castle, see Michael Morris, "Doman, Notable for Defying Our Rapine Past" (*Star*, 11 November 2016, accessed 19 April 2018, http://www.pressreader.com/south-africa/the-star-early-edition/20161111/281698319321528). For Khoisan raids, also see Nigel Worden, *The Making of South Africa: Conquest, Segregation, and Apartheid* (Oxford: Blackwell, 1994), 9-10.

45. Charles R. Boxer, *The Dutch Seaborne Empire, 1600-1800* (London: Hutchinson, 1965), 245.

46. Sir William Temple, *Upon the Gardens of Epicurus* (London: Pallas Editions, 2004), 54.

47. Ibid.

48. Raven-Hart, *Cape of Good Hope*, 1:275. The original comment was made in Tachard's *Voyage to Siam* (1686).

49. Raven-Hart, *Cape of Good Hope*, 1:282.

50. Ibid., 1:292.

51. Ibid.

52. See Annette Keaney, *The French Huguenots of South Africa* (Cape Town: n.p., 2010) for an account of the arrival and eventual assimilation of the Huguenots by the mid-eighteenth century.

53. Elphick and Giliomee, eds., *Shaping of South African Society*, 28.

54. Ibid., 26.

55. The figures in 1806 are estimated to be 26,768 white free burghers, 1,200 free blacks, 29,861 slaves, and 20,426 Khoisan (Martin Legassick and Robert Ross, "From Slave Economy to Settler Capitalism: Cape Colony and Its Extension,

1800–1854," in *Cambridge History of South Africa*, ed. Caroline Hamilton, Bernard K. Mbenga, and Robert Ross [Cambridge: Cambridge University Press, 2010], 1:257).

56. Elphick and Giliomee, eds., *Shaping of South African Society*, 109.

57. For an account of the growth and culture of the Muslim community in the Cape, see I. D. du Plessis, *The Cape Malays*, 2nd ed. (Cape Town: Maskew Miller, 1947). See also Muhammed Haron, "The Early Muslim Community in the Cape," in *Good Hope, South Africa and the Netherlands from 1600*, ed. Martine Gosselink, Maria Holtrop, and Robert Ross (Amsterdam: Rijksmuseum, 2017), 137–146.

58. G. E. Pearse, *The Cape of Good Hope, 1652–1833: An Account of Its Buildings and the Life of Its People* (Pretoria: J. L. Van Shaik, 1956), 39.

59. The Lutheran Church remains a principal landmark in Cape Town. A history of its foundation and development is described in an anonymous and undated pamphlet titled *The Evangelical Lutheran Church Strand Street: Cape Town, 1780–1980* (Cape Town: Marantha Press, n.d.).

60. Nigel Penn, *Rogues, Rebels, and Runaways: Eighteenth-Century Cape Characters* (Cape Town: David Philip, 2003), 22.

61. Ibid.

62. The fullest (and well-illustrated) biography of Gordon is Patrick Cullinan, *Robert Jacob Gordon, 1743–1795: The Man and His Travels at the Cape* (Cape Town: Struick Publishing Group, 1993). Also see Schoeman, *Cape Lives of the Eighteenth Century*, 557–623. The suggestion of collusion with the British and other shadier aspects of Gordon's character are explored by Dan Sleigh, "Gordon and the End of Company Rule," in *Good Hope, South Africa and the Netherlands from 1600*, ed. Martine Gosselink, Maria Holtrop, and Robert Ross (Amsterdam: Rijksmuseum, 2017), 171–176. This controversy is investigated by Ian Glenn in "Robert Jacob Gordon's Memoir of the Cape of Good Hope," *Bulletin of the National Library of South Africa* 71, no. 1 (2017): 17–26, to which is appended Gordon's memoir. The matter remains open to different interpretations. Also see chapter 4, this volume, for further details on Gordon.

CHAPTER 4 — ENLIGHTENMENT VISITORS

1. Siegfried Huigen, *Knowledge and Colonialism: Eighteenth-Century Travellers in South Africa* (Leiden: Brill, 2009).

2. Ibid., 78.

3. For a full account of mapping history, see Andrew Duminy, *Mapping South Africa: A Historical Survey of South African Maps and Charts* (Auckland Park, South Africa: Jacana, 2011). Longitude is discussed on page 79.

4. Ibid., 22.

5. Quoted in Patrick Moore and Pete Collins, *The Astronomy of South Africa* (Cape Town: Howard Timmins, 1977), 28.

6. Theophilus Hahn, *Tsuni-IIGoam: The Supreme Being of the Khoi-Khoi* (London: Trübner, 1881), 40. I am grateful to Peter Knox-Shaw for drawing my attention to Hahn's comments on Kolb.

7. Huigen, *Knowledge and Colonialism*, 49.

8. Ibid.

9. Ibid.

10. Ibid., 41.

11. Ibid.

12. See David Johnson, *Imagining the Cape Colony: History, Literature and the South African Nation* (Edinburgh: Edinburgh University Press, 2012), 51.

13. Huigen, *Knowledge and Colonialism*, 34.

14. Ibid., 42.

15. Pieter Kolb, *Present State of the Cape of Good Hope: Or, a Particular Account of Several Nations of the Hottentots: Their Religion, Government, Laws, Customs, Ceremonies and Opinions; Their Art of War. Professions, Language, Genius etc. Together with a Short Account of the Dutch Settlement at the Cape*, trans. W. Innys (London, 1731), 1:4–5. There is some suggestion that this shortened version of the original contains inaccuracies.

16. For an account of the knecht system, see Charles Boxer, *The Dutch Seaborne Empire, 1600–1800* (London: Hutchinson, 1965), 258–259.

17. Joan Kruger, *On Top of Table Mountain: Remarkable Visitors Over 500 Years* (Paternoster, South Africa: Paternoster Books, 2016), 105.

18. O. F. Mentzel, *Life at the Cape in the Mid-Eighteenth Century: Being a Biography of Siegfried Alleman, Captain of the Military Forces at the Cape of Good Hope*, trans. Margaret Greenlees, 1st ser. 2 (Cape Town: Van Riebeeck Society, 1919).

19. O. F. Mentzel, *A Geographical and Topographical Description of the Cape of Good Hope*, trans. G. V. Marais and J. Hoge, ed. H. J. Mandelbrote, 1st ser. 4 (Cape Town: Van Riebeeck Society, 1944) (University of Toronto digital version), 1: frontispiece.

20. Ibid., 11.

21. Ibid., 17.

22. Ibid., 2.

23. Ibid., 7.

24. Ibid., 260.

25. Ibid., 261.

26. Ibid., 264.

27. Ibid., 265.

28. Ibid., 282.

29. Ibid., 4.

30. Ibid., 8.

31. Moore and Collins, *The Astronomy of South Africa*, 33.

32. As its name implies, Strand Street (first named Zeestraat) was then on the seafront.

33. Kruger, *On Top of Table Mountain*, 30.

34. Moore and Collins, *The Astronomy of South Africa*, 29.

35. Abbé de La Caille, *Journal historique de voyage de Bonne Espérance* (*Journal of an Historical Voyage to the Cape of Good Hope*) (Paris: Guillyn, 1763), 170. La Caille's scientific papers are to be found in historical papers at the library of the University of Witwatersrand.

36. Ibid., 157.

37. Ibid., 331.

38. Anders Sparrman, *A Voyage to the Cape of Good Hope Towards the Antarctic Polar Circle Round the World to the Country of the Hottentots and the Caffres from the Year 1772 to 1776*, ed. Vernon S. Forbes, trans. and rev. J. Rudner and I. Rudner, 2nd ser. 6 and 7 (Cape Town: Van Riebeeck Society, 1975–1977), 1:3.

39. Ibid., 1:53.

40. Ibid., 1:234.

41. Ibid., 1:255.

42. Ibid., 2:91.

43. Ibid., 1:200.

44. Per Wästberg, *The Journey of Anders Sparrman*, trans. Tom Geddes (London: Granta, 2010), 196.

45. Quoted in ibid., 160.

46. Sparrman, *Voyage*, 2:61.

47. Ibid., 2:245.

48. Ibid., v1:211.

49. Ibid., 2:60.

50. Ibid., 1:52.

51. Ibid., 2:130.

52. Wästberg, *Journey*, 209.

53. Carl Peter Thunberg, *Flora Japonica* (*Japanese Flora*) (Leipzig: Mulleriano, 1784).

54. Carl Peter Thunberg, *Travels at the Cape of Good Hope, 1772–1775*, ed. Vernon S. Forbes, trans. and rev. J. Rudner and I. Rudner, 2nd ser. 17 (Cape Town: Van Riebeeck Society, 1986), 25.

55. Ibid.

56. Ibid., 155.

57. Ibid., 77.

58. Ibid., 209–210. The editors point out that as Thunberg could not speak any local language, this information must have been gleaned from talking to the settlers (ibid., 10n229).

59. Ibid., 210.

60. Ibid., 231.

61. Ibid., 319.

62. Ibid., xxxvii.

63. William Hickey, *Memoirs of William Hickey*, ed. Peter Quennell (London: Hutchinson, 1960), 225.

64. Patrick Cullinan says his main quest is to find Gordon the man (*Robert Jacob Gordon, 1743–1795: The Man and His Travels at the Cape* [Cape Town: Struick Publishing Group, 1993], 9).

65. Ibid., 25. Also see Dan Sleigh, *Jan Compagnie: The World of the Dutch East India Company* (Cape Town: Tafelberg, 1980), 171.

66. Duncan Bull, "Robert Jacob Gordon. A 'Philosophe' on the Veld," in *Good Hope, South Africa and the Netherlands from 1600*, ed. Martine Gosselink, Maria Holtrop, and Robert Ross (Amsterdam: Rijksmuseum, 2017), 162.

67. Ibid., 179.

68. Cullinan, *Robert Jacob Gordon*, 81.

69. Bull, "Philosophe," 177.

70. Cullinan, *Robert Jacob Gordon*, 33.

71. Francis Masson, *Francis Masson's Account of Three Journeys at the Cape of Good Hope, 1772–1775*, intro. Frank R. Bradlow (Cape Town: Tablecloth Press, 1994), 13.

72. Ibid., 106.

73. Ibid. The "quadrum" is granite.

74. Hickey, *Memoirs of William Hickey*, 225.

75. D. Johnson, *Imagining the Cape Colony*, 66.

76. William Paterson, *A Narrative of Four Journeys into the Country of the Hottentots and Caffraria in 1777, 1778 and 1779* (London, 1789; facsimile ed., Cambridge: Cambridge University Press, 2013), 4. For the history of the discovery of the manuscript of Paterson's journeys and illustrations of his work, see William Paterson, *Paterson's Cape Travels, 1777–1779*, ed. Vernon S. Forbes and John Rourke (Johannesburg: Brenthurst Press, 1980), 11ff.

77. Paterson, *Narrative*, v.

78. Ibid.

79. Ibid., 1.

80. Ibid., 77.

81. At a later date the importance of oxen is recorded by Thomas Philipps, who describes them as "noble" and says that ten to fourteen are needed to draw a wagon or to plough (*Phillips, 1820 Settler*, ed. Arthur Keppel-Jones and E. K. Heathcote [Pietermaritzburg, South Africa: Shuter and Shooter, 1960], 73–74). Philipps was another of the Albany settlers who lived in Bathurst, near the coast of what is now the Eastern Cape.

82. Ibid., 84.

83. William Hickey, *Memoirs of William Hickey (1808–1810)* (Google eBooks, 2012), 222.

84. Paterson, *Narrative*, 115.

85. Ibid., 71.

86. Ibid., 77.

87. Ibid., 93.

88. Paterson, *Paterson's Cape Travels*, 21.

89. Paterson, *Narrative*, 85.

CHAPTER 5 — ENNOBLING THE SAVAGE

1. Marin Legassick and Robert Ross, "From Slave Economy to Settler Capitalism: Cape Colony and Its Extension, 1800–1854," in *Cambridge History of South Africa*, ed. Caroline Hamilton, Bernard K. Mbenga, and Robert Ross (Cambridge: Cambridge University Press, 2010), 1:259.

2. Ibid.

3. Lady Anne Barnard, *The Cape Journals of Lady Anne Barnard, 1797–1798*, ed. A. M. Lewin Robinson, with Margaret Lenta and Dorothy Driver. 2nd ser. 24 (Cape Town: Van Riebeeck Society, 1994), 336.

4. Ibid., 330.

5. Basil Holt, *They Came Our Way* (Cape Town: Howard Timmins, 1974), 43.

6. Legassick and Ross, "From Slave Economy to Settler Capitalism," 1:260.

7. Holt, *They Came Our Way*, 53.

8. Legassick and Ross, "From Slave Economy to Settler Capitalism," 1:260–261.

9. Henry Lichtenstein, *Travels in Southern Africa in the Years 1803, 1804, 1805 and 1806*, trans. Anne Plumptre (London, 1812; reprint, 1st ser. 10–11, Cape Town: Van Riebeeck Society, 1928), 237.

10. François de Salignac de la Mothe Fénelon, *Telemachus, The Son of Ulysses*, ed. and trans. Patrick Riley (Cambridge: Cambridge University Press, 1994), 130. In his *Essay on the Cannibals* (1571), Michel de Montaigne had suggested that without all the advantages of civilized life, primitive man in Brazil also lacks

vices and lives in a paradise with a temperate climate. While not ennobling the savage, he cautions against applying European standards to primitive societies. See Michel de Montaigne, *Four Essays*, trans. M. A. Screech (London: Penguin, 1995), 10–11.

11. Fénelon, *Telemachus*, 130–131.

12. David Johnson, *Imagining the Cape Colony: History, Literature and the South African Nation* (Edinburgh: Edinburgh University Press, 2012), 38. Johnson provides a good summary of these views on pages 37–42.

13. Guillaume Chenu de Chalezac, *Guillaume Chenu de Chalezac: The "French Boy,"* ed. Randolph Vigne, 2nd ser. 22 (Cape Town: Van Riebeeck Society, 1993), 39.

14. Ibid., 41.

15. Jean-Jacques Rousseau, *Oeuvres complètes*, ed. Michel Launay (Paris: Editions du Seuil, 1971), 2:209.

16. Joan Kruger, *On Top of Table Mountain: Remarkable Visitors Over 500 Years* (Paternoster, South Africa: Paternoster Books, 2016), 126.

17. François Le Vaillant, *Travels into the Interior Parts of Africa via the Cape of Good Hope*, trans. Ian Glenn, with Catherine Lauga du Plessis and Ian Farlam, (Cape Town: Van Riebeeck Society, 2007), 11:xii (hereafter cited as "VRS ed.," with volume and page numbers).

18. VRS ed., 1:xxxvii.

19. Rousseau, *Oeuvres complètes*, 3:15–325.

20. VRS ed., 1:35–36.

21. Ibid., 1:125.

22. Ibid., 1:103.

23. D. Johnson, *Imagining the Cape Colony*, 37.

24. VRS ed., 1:121.

25. Ibid.

26. Ibid., 1:141.

27. Ibid., 1:135.

28. Samuel Johnson, *A Dictionary of the English Language*, ed. A. McDermot, 1st and 4th eds. (Cambridge: Cambridge University Press, 1996), CD-ROM.

29. Lady Mary Wortley Montagu, *Turkish Embassy Letters*, ed. Malcolm Jack (London: William Pickering, 1993), 62–63.

30. VRS ed., 1:xxxvii.

31. James Augustus St. John, *The Lives of Celebrated Travellers* (New York: J. and J. Harper, 1832), 3:332.

32. Georges-Louis Leclerc, comte de Buffon, *Discours sur le style* (Discourse on Style) (Paris, 1753).

33. VRS ed., 1:70.

34. St. John, *Lives*, 3:272.

35. VRS ed., 1:xlix.

36. Ibid., 1:70.

37. François Le Vaillant, *Histoire naturelle des oiseaux d'Afrique*, 6 vols. (Paris, 1796–1806).

38. VRS ed., 1:97.

CHAPTER 6 — PARADISE REGAINED

1. See Siegfried Huigen, *Knowledge and Colonialism: Eighteenth-Century Travellers in South Africa* (Leiden: Brill, 2009), 191–208, for a detailed analysis of Lodewyk Alberti's work *De Kaffers aan de Zuidkust van Afrika* (The Caffres of the South Coast of Africa; Amsterdam, 1810) and his dependence on Joseph-Marie Degèrando's *Considerations sur les diverses méthodes à suivre dans l'observation des peuples sauvages* (Thoughts on the Different Methods to Be Followed in Studying Savage Peoples; Paris, 1800).

2. For an account of the impact of free trade, see Marcus Arkin, *Storm in a Teacup: The Later Years of John Company in the Cape, 1815–36* (Cape Town: C. Struik, 1973).

3. I am indebted for information on and analysis of this period to William M. Freund, "The Cape under the Transitional Governments 1795–1814," in *The Shaping of South African Society, 1652–1840*, ed. Richard Elphick and Hermann Giliomee, 2nd ed. (Middletown, CT: Wesleyan University Press, 1988), 324–357.

4. Ibid., 334. The author ascribes the phrase to the historian Robert Ross.

5. This is referred to in the excellent article by Randolph Vigne, "Mapping and Promoting South Africa: Barrow and Burchell's Rivalry," *Historia* 58, no. 1 (2013): 18–32. Vigne also reminds us that later writings of Barrow, including an autobiographical memoir of 1847, contain much material about the Cape and provide Barrow with the opportunity to comment on those, like Burchell, whose accounts of the Cape followed his own.

6. Sir John Barrow, *An Account of Travels into the Interior of Southern Africa in the Years 1797 and 1798* (London, 1801; repr., Cambridge: Cambridge University Press, 2011), 1:46. Although "Southern Africa" appears in the title of the work, Barrow also uses the term "South Africa" (see, for example, 1:212, 238, and 245), which appears to be one of its earliest usages in English. See this chapter's note 81 for James Ewart's use of the name "South Africa."

7. Ibid., 1:17.

8. Ibid., 1:144.

9. Ibid., 1:198.

10. Ibid., 1:285.

11. Ibid.

12. Ibid., 1:239.

13. Ibid., 1:208.

14. Ibid., 1:205.

15. Ibid., 1:215.

16. Ibid., 1:360. François Le Vaillant's account is given in chapter 5 of this volume.

17. Ibid.

18. See Malcolm Jack, "The Torn Identity of a Child of Empire," *Bulletin of the National Library of South Africa* 66, no. 3 (2012): 35–38.

19. Barrow, *Travels*, 1:399.

20. Madeleine Masson, *Lady Anne Barnard: The Court and Colonial Service under George III and the Regency* (London: George Allen and Unwin, 1948), 153. I have used Masson's excellent book for biographical material about Lady Anne. The latest full biography is Stephen Taylor, *Defiance: The Life and Choices of Lady Anne Barnard* (London: Faber, 2016).

21. Lady Anne Barnard, *The Letters of Lady Anne Barnard Written to Henry Dundas from the Cape of Good Hope, 1793–1803*, ed. A. M. Lewin Robinson (Cape Town: A. A. Balkema, 1973), 31.

22. Ibid.

23. Lady Anne Barnard, *The Cape Journals of Lady Anne Barnard, 1797–1798*, ed. A. M. Lewin Robinson, with Margaret Lenta and Dorothy Driver, 2nd ser. 24 (Cape Town: Van Riebeeck Society, 1994), dedication and 147.

24. Ibid., 21.

25. Ibid., 145.

26. Ibid., 21n6.

27. Ibid., 3.

28. Taylor, *Defiance*, 226.

29. Quoted in Taylor, *Defiance*, 154.

30. Barnard, *The Letters of Lady Anne Barnard*, 49.

31. Barnard, *The Cape Journals of Lady Anne Barnard*, 221.

32. Ibid., 215.

33. Ibid., 214.

34. Charles R. Boxer, *The Dutch Seaborne Empire, 1600–1800* (London: Hutchinson, 1965), 260.

35. In Barnard's *The Cape Journals of Lady Anne Barnard* there are references to Jean-Jacques Rousseau on page 195 and to Lord Monboddo on page 250.

36. Ibid., 196.

37. Ibid., 336.

38. Ibid.

39. Ibid., 362.

40. Ibid., 417.

41. Ibid., 418.

42. Ibid., 196.

43. Lady Anne Barnard, *Lady Anne Barnard's Watercolours and Sketches: Glimpses of the Cape of Good Hope*, intro. Nicolas Barker (Simon's Town, South Africa: Fernwood Press, 2009), 51.

44. See Taylor, *Defiance*, 251ff, for an account of this latter period, during which Lady Anne was still successful in getting Governor Yonge recalled.

45. A detailed account of Samuel Daniell's art in a historical context is given in an excellent paper by Michael Godby ("'To Do the Cape': Samuel Daniell's Representation of African People During the First British Occupation of the Cape," *Journal of Historical Geography* 43 [January 2014]: 28–38).

46. Ibid., 29.

47. Ibid., 32.

48. Henry Lichtenstein, *Travels in Southern Africa in the Years 1803, 1804, 1805 and 1806*, trans. Anne Plumptre (London, 1812; reprint, 1st ser. 10–11, Cape Town: Van Riebeeck Society, 1928), iv.

49. Ibid.

50. Sir John Barrow, "Travels in Southern Africa . . . by Henry Lichtenstein," *Quarterly Review* 16 (December 1812): 365–377.

51. Lichtenstein, *Travels*, iv.

52. Ibid., 4.

53. Ibid., 40.

54. Ibid., 93.

55. Lichtenstein, *Travels*, 116.

56. Ibid., 250. His favourable opinion of the Xhosa was shared by Thomas Philipps, the Albany settler who records a "high approval of them" (*Philipps, 1820 Settler*, ed. Arthur Keppel-Jones and E. K. Heathcote [Pietermaritzburg, South Africa: Shuter and Schooter, 1960], 190.

57. Lichtenstein, *Travels*, 243.

58. Ibid., 252.

59. For a comprehensive account of Burchell, see Susan Buchanan, *Burchell's Travels: The Life, Art and Journeys of William John Burchell, 1781–1863* (London: Penguin Books, 2015).

60. See Vigne, "Mapping and Promoting South Africa."

61. Buchanan, *Burchell's Travels*, 66.

62. William Burchell, *Travels in the Interior of Southern Africa*, 2 vols. (London, 1824), 2:37.

63. Ibid., 2:24.

64. Ibid., 2:54.

65. Ibid., 2:69.

66. Ibid., 2:53.

67. Ibid., 2:16.

68. Vigne, "Mapping and Promoting South Africa."

69. Ibid.

70. John Campbell, *Journal of Travels in South Africa among the Hottentots and Other Tribes, in the Years 1812, 1813 and 1814* (Memphis, TN: General Books, 2012).

71. C. Hulbert, *African Traveller: Select Lives, Voyages and Travel* (London, 1817).

72. Campbell, *Travels*, 2n3.

73. Ibid., 2n2.

74. Ibid.

75. Ibid., 38n2.

76. James Ewart, *James Ewart's Journal Covering His Stay at the Cape of Good Hope (1811–1814)*, intro. A. Gordon-Brown (Cape Town: C. Struik Publishers, 1970), v.

77. Ibid., 21 and 18.

78. Ibid., 27.

79. Ibid., 44.

80. Ibid.

81. Ewart uses, as Barrow did, the name "South Africa" instead of the more usual "Southern Africa" at this period (*Journal*, 86). See this chapter's note 6 for Barrow's usage.

82. Ibid., 43.

CHAPTER 7 — A CALL FOR FREEDOM

1. Cornelis Pama, *Regency Cape Town* (Cape Town: Tafelberg, 1971), 11–12.

2. Ibid., 70.

3. John Philip, *Researches in South Africa Illustrating the Civil, Moral and Religious Condition of the Native Tribes: Journal of the Author's Travels in the Interior* (London, 1828), 2 vols.

4. For a full biography, see Tim Keegan, *Dr Philip's Empire: One Man's Struggle for Justice in Nineteenth-Century South Africa* (Cape Town: Zebra Press, 2016). Also see Malcolm Jack's review, "Tim Keegan Dr Philip's Empire: One Man's

Struggle for Justice in Nineteenth-Century South Africa," *Bulletin of the National Library of South Africa* 70, no. 2 (2016): 225–228.

5. Philip, *Researches*, 2:2.

6. Ibid., 2:8.

7. Ibid., 2:356.

8. Ibid., 2:50.

9. Ibid., 2:38.

10. Ibid., 2:25.

11. Ibid., 2:55.

12. Ibid., 2:126.

13. Ibid., 2:130.

14. Ibid., 2:174.

15. Keegan, *Dr Philip's Empire*, 107–121.

16. Ibid., 114.

17. Martin Legassick and Robert Ross, "From Slave Economy to Settler Capitalism: Cape Colony and Its Extension, 1800–1854," in *Cambridge History of South Africa*, ed. Caroline Hamilton, Bernard K. Mbenga, and Robert Ross (Cambridge: Cambridge University Press, 2010), 1:273.

18. For a full account of the history of the Kat River Settlement, see Robert Ross, *The Borders of Race in Colonial South Africa: The Kat River Settlement, 1829–1856* (Cambridge: Cambridge University Press, 2017).

19. Ibid., 80.

20. Thomas Pringle, *Narrative of a Residence in South Africa, to Which Is Prefixed a Biographical Sketch of the Author by Josiah Condor*, new ed. (London: Edward Moxon, 1840), ii.

21. Ibid., ix.

22. Ibid., 353.

23. Ibid., xi.

24. Ibid., 8.

25. Ibid., 15.

26. Ibid.

27. Ibid.

28. Ibid., 28.

29. Thomas Pringle, *The South African Letters of Thomas Pringle*, ed. and intro. Randolph Vigne, 2nd ser. 42 (Cape Town: Van Riebeeck Society, 2011), 40. I am much indebted to Randolph Vigne as a guide to Pringle through these letters, as well as through his authoritative biography of Pringle, *Thomas Pringle: South African Pioneer, Poet and Abolitionist* (Woodbrige, UK: James Currey, 2012). A similar account of the hardships of the Albany settlement was given in the

voluminous correspondence of Thomas Philipps, another settler (*Philipps, 1820 Settler*, ed. Arthur Keppel-Jones and E. K. Heathcote [Pietermaritzburg, South Africa: Shuter and Schooter, 1960]).

30. Pringle, *Narrative*, 115.

31. Ibid., 284.

32. Ibid., 327.

33. Ibid., 268.

34. Quoted in Vigne, *Thomas Pringle*, 88.

35. Ibid., 105. The lines are from "Evening Rambles" (1722).

36. Ibid., 88.

37. Ibid., 88–89.

38. Ibid., 89.

39. Vigne, *Thomas Pringle*, 154–155.

40. Ibid., 93.

41. Pringle, *The South African Letters of Thomas Pringle*, 261.

42. George Thompson, *Travels and Adventures in Southern Africa*, ed. Vernon S. Forbes, 1st ser. 48 and 49 (Cape Town: Van Riebeeck Society, 1967), 1:29.

43. Ibid., 1:30.

44. Ibid., 1:78.

45. Ibid., 2:191–219.

46. Ibid., 2:201.

47. Ibid., 1:65.

48. Ibid., 1:135.

49. Ibid.

50. Lady Margaret Herschel, *Letters from the Cape 1834–38*, ed. Brian Warner (Cape Town: Friends of South African Library, 1991), 31.

51. André Brink, *Philida* (London: Vintage, 2013), 270.

52. Herschel, *Letters*, 42.

53. Ibid.

54. Ibid., 137.

55. Ibid., 88.

56. Ibid., 66.

57. Ibid., 128.

Bibliography

ARCHIVES

Albany Museum, Grahamstown, South Africa.
British Library, London.
National Archives of South Africa, Cape Town.
National Library of South Africa, Cape Town.
Parliament of the Republic of South Africa, Cape Town.

PRIMARY SOURCES: TRAVELLERS' ACCOUNTS AND RECORDS

Barnard, Lady Anne. *The Cape Diaries of Lady Anne Barnard 1799–1800*. Edited by Margaret Lenta and Basil Le Cordeur. 2 vols. 2nd ser. 29 and 30. Cape Town: Van Riebeeck Society, 1994.

———. *The Cape Journals of Lady Anne Barnard, 1797–1798*. Edited by A. M. Lewin Robinson, with Margaret Lenta and Dorothy Driver. 2nd ser. 24. Cape Town: Van Riebeeck Society, 1994.

———. *Lady Anne Barnard's Watercolours and Sketches: Glimpses of the Cape of Good Hope*. Introduction by Nicolas Barker. Simon's Town, South Africa: Fernwood Press, 2009.

———. *The Letters of Lady Anne Barnard Written to Henry Dundas from the Cape of Good Hope, 1793–1803*. Edited by A. M. Lewin Robinson. Cape Town: A. A. Balkema, 1973.

Barrow, John Sir. *An Account of Travels into the Interior of Southern Africa in the Years 1797 and 1798*. London, 1801. Reprint. 2 vols. Cambridge: Cambridge University Press, 2011.

———. "Travels in Southern Africa . . . by Henry Lichtenstein." *Quarterly Review* 16 (December 1812): 365–377.

Bernardin de Saint-Pierre, Jacques-Henri. *Paul et Virginie*. Paris, 1787.

———. *L'isle de France*. Paris, 1773.

Buffon, Georges-Louis Leclerc, comte de. *Discours sur le style*. Paris, 1753.

Burchell, William Travels in the Interior of southern Africa. 2 vols. London, 1824.

Caille, Abbé de la. *Journal historique de voyage de Bonne Espérance*. Paris: Guillyn, 1763.

Camões, Luís Vaz de. *The Lusiads*. Translated by Landeg White. Oxford: Oxford University Press, 1999.

Chenu de Chalezac, Guillaume. *Guillaume Chenu de Chalezac: The "French Boy."* Edited by Randolph Vigne. 2nd ser. 22. Cape Town: Van Riebeeck Society, 1993.

Dante Alighieri. *The Divine Comedy*. Translated by H. Cary. London: J. M. Dent, 1961.

Dapper, Olfert, Willem ten Rhyne, and Johannes Gulielmus de Grevenbroek. *The Early Cape Hottentots*. Edited and translated by Isaac Schapera. 1st ser. 14. Cape Town: Van Riebeeck Society, 1933. Reprint. 2012.

Ewart, James. *James Ewart's Journal Covering His Stay at the Cape of Good Hope (1811–1814)*. Introduction by A. Gordon-Brown. Cape Town: C. Struik Publishers, 1970.

Fénelon, François de Salignac de la Mothe. *Telemachus, Son of Ulysses*. Edited and translated by Patrick Riley. Cambridge: Cambridge University Press, 1994.

Gorelick, Boris, ed. *An Entirely Different World: Russian Visitors to the Cape*. 2nd ser. 46. Cape Town: Van Riebeeck Society, 2015.

Herschel, Lady Margaret. *Letters from the Cape 1834–38*. Edited by Brian Warner. Cape Town: Friends of South African Library, 1991.

Hickey, William. *Memoirs of William Hickey*. Edited by Peter Quennell. London: Hutchinson, 1960.

———. *Memoirs of William Hickey (1808–1810)*. Google eBooks, 2012.

Hulbert, C. *African Traveller: Select Lives, Voyages and Travel*. London, 1817.

Johnson, Samuel. *A Dictionary of the English Language*. Edited by Anne McDermott. 1st and 4th eds. Cambridge: Cambridge University Press, 1996. CD-ROM.

A Journal of the Firsi. London: Hakluyt Society, 1898.

Kolb, Pieter. *Present State of the Cape of Good Hope: Or, a Particular Account of Several Nations of the Hottentots: Their Religion, Government, Laws, Customs, Ceremonies and Opinions; Their Art of War, Professions, Language, Genius etc. Together with a Short Account of the Dutch Settlement at the Cape*. Translated by W. Innys. 2 vols. London, 1731.

Le Vaillant, François. *Histoire naturelle des oiseaux d'Afrique*. 6 vols. Paris, 1796–1806.

———. *Travels into the Interior Parts of Africa via the Cape of Good Hope.* Translated and edited by Ian Glenn, with Catherine Lauga du Plessis and Ian Farlam. 2 vols. 2nd ser. 38. Cape Town: Van Riebeeck Society, 2007.

Lichtenstein, Henry. *Travels in Southern Africa in the Years 1803, 1804, 1805 and 1806.* Translated by Anne Plumptre. London, 1812. Reprint, 1st ser. 10–11, Cape Town: Van Riebeeck Society, 1928.

Lückhoff, Carl A. *Table Mountain.* Cape Town: A. A. Balkema, 1951.

Masson, Francis. *Francis Masson's Account of Three Journeys at the Cape of Good Hope, 1772–1775.* Introduction and annotation by Frank R. Bradlow. Cape Town: Tablecloth Press, 1994.

Mentzel, O. F. [Otto Fredrik]. *A Geographical and Topographical Description of the Cape of Good Hope.* Translated by G. V. Marais and J. Hoge. Edited, with introduction and notes, by H. J. Mandelbrote. 3 vols. 1st ser. 4, 6, and 25. University of Toronto digital version. Cape Town: Van Riebeeck Society, 1944.

———. *Life at the Cape in the Mid-Eighteenth Century: Being a Biography of Siegfried Alleman, Captain of the Military Forces at the Cape of Good Hope.* Translated by Margaret Greenlees. 1st ser. 2. Cape Town: Van Riebeeck Society, 1919.

Montagu, Lady Mary Wortley. *Turkish Embassy Letters.* Edited by Malcolm Jack. London: William Pickering, 1993.

Montaigne, Michel de. *Four Essays.* Translated by M. A. Screech. London: Penguin Books, 1995.

Moodie, Donald, ed. *The Record; Or, A Series of Official Papers Relative to the Condition and Treatment of the Native Tribes of South Africa.* Cambridge: Cambridge University Press, 2011.

Paterson, William. *A Narrative of Four Journeys into the Country of the Hottentots and Caffraria in the Years 1777, 1778 and 1779.* London, 1789.

———. *Paterson's Cape Travels, 1777–1779.* Edited by Vernon S. Forbes and John Rourke. Johannesburg: Brenthurst Press, 1980.

Philip, John. *Researches in South Africa Illustrating the Civil, Moral and Religious Condition of the Native Tribes: Journal of the Author's Travels in the Interior.* 2 vols. London, 1828.

Philipps, Thomas. *Philipps, 1820 Settler.* Edited by Arthur Keppel-Jones and E. K. Heathcote. Pietermaritzburg, South Africa: Shuter and Schooter, 1960.

Pringle, Thomas. *Narrative of a Residence in South Africa, to Which Is Prefixed a Biographical Sketch of the Author by Josiah Condor.* New ed. London: Edward Moxon, 1840.

———. *The South African Letters of Thomas Pringle.* Edited and with an introduction by Randolph Vigne. 2nd ser. 42. Cape Town: Van Riebeeck Society, 2011.

Raven-Hart, Rowland. *Before Van Riebeeck.* Cape Town: G. Stuick, 1967.

———. *Cape of Good Hope, 1652–1702: The First Years of Dutch Colonisation as Seen by Callers.* Cape Town: A. A. Balkema, 1971.

Ravenstein, E. G. *A Journal of the First Voyage of Vasco da Gama, 1497–1499.* London: Hakluyt Society, 1898.

Rousseau, Jean-Jacques. *Oeuvres complètes.* Edited by Michel Launay. 3 vols. Paris: Éditions du Seuil, 1971.

Sparrman, Anders. *A Voyage to the Cape of Good Hope Towards the Antarctic Polar Circle Round the World to the Country of the Hottentots and the Caffres from the Year 1772 to 1776.* Edited by Vernon S. Forbes. Translated and revised by J. Rudner and I. Rudner. 2 vols. 2nd sers. 6 and 7. Cape Town: Van Riebeeck Society, 1975–1977

Temple, Sir William. *Upon the Gardens of Epicurus.* London: Pallas Editions, 2004.

Thompson, George. *Travels and Adventures in Southern Africa.* Edited by Vernon S. Forbes. 2 vols. 1st ser. 48 and 49. Cape Town: Van Riebeeck Society, 1967.

Thunberg, Carl Peter. *Flora Japonica.* Leipzig: Mulleriano, 1784.

———. *Travels at the Cape of Good Hope, 1772–1775.* Edited by Vernon S. Forbes. Translated and revised by J. Rudner and I. Rudner. 2nd ser. 17. Cape Town: Van Riebeeck Society, 1986.

Valentijn, François. *Description of the Cape of Good Hope with Matters Concerning It.* Edited by E. H. Raidt. Translated by R. Raven-Hart. 2nd ser. 4. Cape Town: Van Riebeeck Society, 1973.

Van Riebeeck, Johan Anthoniszoon. *The Journal of Jan Van Riebeeck.* 3 vols. Amsterdam: A. A. Balkema, 1952.

Van Wyk Smith, Malvern. *Shades of Adamastor: An Anthology of Poetry.* Grahamstown, South Africa: National English Literary Museum, 1988.

SECONDARY SOURCES

Alexander, Peter. *Roy Campbell: A Critical Biography.* Oxford: Oxford University Press, 1982.

Anderson, Gavin. *Bushman Art of the Drakensberg.* Photography by John Hone. Durban: Art Publishers, 2008.

Arkin, Marcus. *Storm in a Teacup: The Later Years of John Company at the Cape, 1815–36.* Cape Town: C. Struick, 1973.

Axelson, Eric. *Vasco da Gama: The Diary of His Travel through African Waters, 1487–1499.* Somerset West, South Africa: Stephan Phillips, 1998.

Boxer, Charles R. *The Dutch Seaborne Empire, 1600–1800.* London: Hutchinson, 1965.

Brink, André. *The First Life of Adamastor.* London: Vintage, 2000.

———. *Philida*. London: Vintage, 2013.

———. *Praying Mantis*. London: Secker and Warburg, 2005.

Buchanan, Susan. *Burchell's Travels: The Life, Art and Journeys of William John Burchell, 1781–1863*. Cape Town: Penguin Books, 2015.

Bull, Duncan. "Robert Jacob Gordon. A 'Philosophe' on the Veld." In *Good Hope, South Africa and the Netherlands from 1600*, edited by Martine Gosselink, Maria Holtrop, and Robert Ross, 159–170. Amsterdam: Rijksmuseum, 2017.

Campbell, John. *Journal of Travels in South Africa among the Hottentots and Other Tribes, in the Years 1812, 1813 and 1814*. Memphis, TN: General Books, 2012.

Cope, John. *King of the Hottentots*. Cape Town: Howard Timms, 1966.

Crowley, Roger. *Conquerors: How Portugal Forged the First Global Empire*. London: Faber, 2015.

Cullinan, Patrick. *Robert Jacob Gordon, 1743–1795: The Man and His Travels at the Cape*. Cape Town: Struick Publishing Group, 1993.

Dugmore, Heather, and Ben-Erik van Wyk. *Muthi and Myths from the African Bush*. London: Global, 2009.

Duiker, K. Sello. *Thirteen Cents*. Cape Town: Kwela Books, 2013.

Duminy, Andrew. *Mapping South Africa: A Historical Survey of South African Maps and Charts*. Auckland Park, South Africa: Jacana, 2011.

Elphick, Richard, and Hermann Giliomee, eds. *The Shaping of South African Society, 1652–1840*. 2nd ed. Middletown, CT: Wesleyan University Press, 1988.

The Evangelical Lutheran Church Strand Street: Cape Town, 1780–1980. Cape Town: Maranatha Press, n.d.

Fairbridge, Dorothea. *A History of South Africa*. Oxford: Oxford University Press, 1954.

Freund, William M. "The Cape under the Transitional Governments, 1795–1814." In *The Shaping of South African Society, 1652–1840*, edited by Richard Elphick and Hermann Giliomee, 324–357. 2nd ed. Middletown, CT: Wesleyan University Press, 1988.

Giliomee, Hermann. *The Afrikaners*. London: Hurst, 2011.

Glenn, Ian. "Robert Jacob Gordon's Memoir of the Cape of Good Hope." *Bulletin of the National Library of South Africa* 71, no. 1 (2017): 17–26.

Godby, Michael. "'To Do the Cape': Samuel Daniell's Representation of African People During the First British Occupation of the Cape." *Journal of Historical Geography* 43 (January 2014): 28–38.

Goodwin, A. J. H. "Archaeology of Southern Africa." In *Encyclopaedia of South Africa*, edited by Eric Rosenthal, 21. London: Frederick Warne, 1961.

Gosling, Melanie. "Cape Town." *Cape Times*, 14 August 2009.

———. "Eureka Moment." *Cape Times*, 19 August 2009.

Gosselink, Martine, Maria Holtrop, and Robert Ross, eds. *Good Hope, South Africa and the Netherlands from 1600.* Amsterdam: Rijksmuseum, 2017.

Grace, Hatherley James. "Studies of Intersexuality in South Africa." PhD diss., University of Natal, 1977.

Hahn, Theophilus. *Tsuni-IIGoam: The Supreme Being of the Khoi-Khoi.* London: Trübner, 1881.

Harari, Yuval Noah. *Sapiens: A Brief History of Humankind.* London: Vintage, 2015.

Haron, Muhammed. "The Early Muslim Community in the Cape." In *Good Hope, South Africa and the Netherlands from 1600,* edited by Martine Gosselink, Maria Holtrop, and Robert Ross, 137–46. Amsterdam: Rijksmuseum, 2017.

Holt, Basil. *They Came Our Way.* Cape Town: Howard Timmins, 1974.

Huigen, Siegfried. *Knowledge and Colonialism: Eighteenth-Century Travellers in South Africa.* Leiden: Brill, 2009.

Inskeep, R. R. *The Peopling of Southern Africa.* New York: Barnes and Noble, 1979.

Jack, Malcolm. "Tim Keegan Dr Philip's Empire: One Man's Struggle for Justice in Nineteenth-Century South Africa." *Bulletin of the National Library of South Africa* 70, no. 2 (2016): 225–228.

———. "The Torn Identity of a Child of Empire." *Bulletin of the National Library of South Africa* 66, no. 3 (2012): 35–38.

Jayne, Kingsley Garland. *Vasco da Gama and His Successors, 1460–1580.* New York: Methuen Library Reprints, 1970.

Johnson, David. *Imagining the Cape Colony: History, Literature and the South African Nation.* Edinburgh: Edinburgh University Press, 2012.

Johnson, R. W. *South Africa: The First Man, the Last Nation.* London: Weidenfeld and Nicolson, 2004.

Juta, Réné. *The Cape Peninsula.* London: Bodley Head, 1927.

Keaney, Annette. *The French Huguenots of South Africa.* Cape Town: n.p., 2010.

Keegan, Tim. *Colonial South Africa and the Origins of Racial Order.* Cape Town: David Philip, 1996.

———. *Dr Philip's Empire: One Man's Struggle for Justice in Nineteenth-Century South Africa.* Cape Town: Zebra Press, 2016.

Knapton, Sarah. "Europe Was the Birthplace of Mankind, Not Africa, Scientists Find." *Telegraph,* 22 May 2017. Accessed 17 April 2018. http://www.telegraph.co.uk/science/2017/05/22/europe-birthplace-mankind-not-africa-scientists-find/.

Kock, Victor de. *Those in Bondage.* Pretoria: Union Publishers, 1963.

Kruger, Joan. *On Top of Table Mountain: Remarkable Visitors Over 500 Years.* Paternoster, South Africa: Paternoster Books, 2016.

Legassick, Martin, and Robert Ross. "From Slave Economy to Settler Capitalism: Cape Colony and Its Extension, 1800–1854." In *Cambridge History of South*

Africa, edited by Caroline Hamilton, Bernard K. Mbenga, and Robert Ross, 1:253–318. Cambridge: Cambridge University Press, 2010.

Lewis-Williams, J. D., ed. *Stories That Float from Afar: Ancestral Folklore of the San of South Africa*. College Station: Texas A&M University Press, 2000.

Lobato, Alexandre. *António de Saldanha: His Time and His Achievements*. Lisbon: Centro de Estudos Históricos Ultramarinos, 1962.

Lückhoff, Carl A. *Table Mountain: Our National Heritage after Three Hundred Years*. Cape Town: A. A. Balkema, 1951.

Masson, Madeleine. *Lady Anne Barnard: The Court and Colonial Service under George III and the Regency*. London: George Allen and Unwin, 1948.

Menzies, Gavin. *1421: The Year the Chinese Discovered the World*. New York: Harper Collins, 2003.

Moore, Patrick, and Pete Collins. *The Astronomy of South Africa*. Cape Town: Howard Timmins, 1977.

Morris, Michael. "Doman, Notable for Defying Our Rapine Past." *Star*, 11 November 2016. Accessed 19 April 2018. http://www.pressreader.com/south-africa/the -star-early-edition/20161111/281698319321528.

Mostert, Noel. *Frontiers: The Epic of South Africa's Creation and the Tragedy of the Xhosa People*. London: Jonathan Cape, 1992.

Mountain, Alan. *The First People of the Cape: A Look at Their History and the Impact of Colonialism on the Cape's Indigenous People*. Cape Town: David Philip, 2003.

Pama, Cornelis. *Regency Cape Town*. Cape Town: Tafelberg, 1971.

Parsons, Neil. "The Story of Corey and !Korana Origins at the Cape." *Bulletin of the National Library of South Africa* 71, no. 1 (2017): 3–16.

Pearse, G. E. *The Cape of Good Hope, 1652–1833: An Account of Its Buildings and the Life of Its People*. Pretoria: J. L. Van Shaik, 1956.

Penn, Nigel. *Rogues, Rebels, and Runaways: Eighteenth-Century Cape Characters*. Cape Town: David Philip, 2003.

Philip, Peter. *British Residents at the Cape, 1795–1819*. Cape Town: David Philip, 1981.

Pinnock, Don. *Rainmaker*. Auckland, South Africa: Jacana, 2010.

Plessis, I. D. du, *The Cape Malays*. 2nd ed. Cape Town: Maskew Miller, 1947.

Ross, Robert. *The Borders of Race in Colonial South Africa: The Kat River Settlement, 1829–1856*. Cambridge: Cambridge University Press, 2017.

———. *A Concise History of South Africa*. Cambridge: Cambridge University Press, 1999.

Rust, Renée, and Jan Van der Poll. *Water, Stone and Legend: Rock Art of the Klein Karoo*. Cape Town: Struik Travel and Heritage, 2011.

Schapera, Isaac. *The Khoisan People of South Africa: Bushmen and Hottentots.* London: Routledge and Kegan Paul, 1963.

Schoeman, Karel. *Cape Lives of the Eighteenth Century.* Pretoria: Protea Book House, 2011.

———. *Early Slavery at the Cape of Good Hope, 1652–1717.* Pretoria: Protea Book House, 2007.

———. *Seven Khoi Lives: Cape Biographies of the Seventeenth Century.* Pretoria: Protea Book House, 2009.

Skotnes, Pippa. *Unconquerable Spirit: George Stow's History Paintings of the San.* Athens: Ohio University Press, 2008.

Skuncke, Marie-Christine. *Carl Peter Thunberg, Botanist and Physician.* Uppsala: Swedish Academy of Advanced Studies, 2014.

Sleigh, Dan. "Gordon and the End of Company Rule." In *Good Hope, South Africa and the Netherlands from 1600,* edited by Martine Gosselink, Maria Holtrop, and Robert Ross, 171–176. Amsterdam: Rijksmuseum, 2017.

———. *Jan Compagnie: The World of the Dutch East India Company.* Cape Town: Tafelberg, 1980.

Slingsby, Peter. *Bushmans Kloof.* Book 2. Muisenberg, South Africa: Baardskeerder, 2009.

———. *Cederberg Rock Art.* Book 3. Muisenberg, South Africa: Baardskeerder, 2006.

———. *Sevilla Rock Art Trail.* Book 1. Muisenberg, SA: Baardskeerder, 2006.

St. John, James Augustus. *The Lives of Celebrated Travellers.* 3 vols. New York: J. and J. Harper, 1832.

Suzman, James. *Affluence without Abundance: The Disappearing World of the Bushmen.* London: Bloomsbury, 2017.

Tait, Barbara Campbell. *Cape Cameos.* Cape Town: Stewart Printing, 1948.

Taylor, Stephen. *Defiance: The Life and Choices of Lady Anne Barnard.* London: Faber, 2016.

Theal, George McCall. *History of South Africa under the Administration of the East India Company, 1652 to 1795.* 2 vols. Memphis, TN: General Books, 2012.

Tobias, Phillip. *Into the Past: A Memoir.* Johannesburg: Picador Africa, 2005.

Vergunst, Nicolaas. *Hoerikwaggo: Images of Table Mountain, November 2000–April 2001.* Cape Town: South African National Gallery, 2001.

Vigne, Randolph. "Mapping and Promoting South Africa: Barrow and Burchell's Rivalry." *Historia* 58, no. 1 (2013): 18–32.

———. *Thomas Pringle: South African Pioneer, Poet and Abolitionist.* Woodbridge, UK: James Currey, 2012.

Wästberg, Per. *The Journey of Anders Sparrman.* Translated by Tom Geddes. London: Granta, 2010.

Whipple, Tom. "Moroccan Skeleton Find Rewrites Human History." *Times*, 8 June 2017. Accessed 17 April 2018. https://www.thetimes.co.uk/article/moroccan -skeleton-find-rewrites-human-history-vnknpg92m.

White, Landeg. *Translating Camões: A Personal Record.* Lisbon: Universidade Católica Editora, 2012.

Worden, Nigel. *The Making of South Africa: Conquest, Segregation, and Apartheid.* Oxford: Blackwell, 1994.

Index

About the Author

Malcolm Jack is an author, critic, and university lecturer. Brought up in Hong Kong, he had a career in the British Parliament, gaining prominence as an authority on constitutional matters. From his first visit to South Africa, he felt a strong affinity with the diversity of Cape society and an enthusiasm for its cosmopolitan, travellers' history. He is a member of PEN South Africa, and a regular contributor to the *Bulletin of the National Library of South Africa*. His books include *Corruption & Progress: The Eighteenth-Century Debate* (1989); *William Beckford: An English Fidalgo* (1996); *Sintra: A Glorious Eden* (2002); and *Lisbon: City of the Sea* (2007). He was appointed KCB in 2011 and FSA in 2012.